VARIATIONS ON
THE THEME
GALINA
USTVOLSKAYA

"He who is having ears to hear - let him hear"
Matthew 13:9-16

VARIATIONS ON THE THEME
GALINA USTVOLSKAYA

The Last Composer Of The Passing Era
(Third Edition)

Translated by
Irina Behrendt and Simon Bokman
With editorial assistance of Jonathan Weiner

SEMYON Y. BOKMAN

ARPress
ILLUMINATING IDEAS
EMPOWERING VOICES

ARPress
45 Dan Road Suite 5
Canton MA 02021

Hotline:	1(888) 821-0229
Fax:	1(508) 545-7580

Ordering Information:

Quantity sales. Special discounts are available on quantity purchases by corporations, associations, and others. For details, contact the publisher at the address above.

Printed in the United States of America.

ISBN-13:	Softcover	979-8-89330-507-4
	eBook	979-8-89330-508-1

Library of Congress Control Number: 2024901005

CONTENTS

ACKNOWLEDGEMENTS

I wholeheartedly thank everyone who helped me author this book:

Solomon Volkov for convincing me to write this book and for generously sharing his professional and creative experience with me;

David Fanning, a musicologist whose great article about First edition of this book encouraged me a lot;

My daughter (and the translator) Irina Behrendt for her selfless help - moral and technical; She has her notes in this book which are mentioned as (note by transl.)

My special thanks to Jonathan Weiner, language editor of the book for his immeasurable work;

My wife Olga - for profound and interesting ideas and comments about culture and spirituality. She created the expression "musical icon painting" regarding Ustvolskaya's symphonies and produced a hypothesis about J.S. Bach's self-renunciation.

Mikhail Kazinik, who convinced me to publish it in Russian;

My friends Sergei and Rita Moiseev - for informative conversations about Spirit and spirituality, and for pointing out valuable sources;

My friend Helena Pletneva for her support and inspiration. My dear grandson Daniel Behrendt for technical support.

THIS BOOK HAS A HISTORY

The first, still incomplete, edition was published in English in January 2007 in Berlin. This edition is now unavailable as the publishing house has closed. Nevertheless, the book has received some interesting reviews (I know of three). This, the First Edition, is in over 60 libraries worldwide. This edition has also been translated into German.

I was inspired to author this book by Solomon Volkov. He said: "Senya! Write a book about Ustvolskaya. You knew her well. You learned from her." He just said, "Write it." As if all I ever did was write the books, and I just did not guess to write this one. But I am a gambling man. I like to discover new things about myself. And who is kidding? If I do not succeed, nothing will happen. That is all there is to it.

I have chosen the form of Variations for this opus. It is not because of being me so original, and it is not because of being me pretentious. If you read the book, you will understand why it was the only possible idea for me. Being around Galina Ivanovna for more than ten years (10) in the form of a student, and then in the form of - it is difficult to define exactly - a friend or a good acquaintance or a former student, I knew truly little about her, but I felt a lot and probably lived out and experienced something with her. Creating my narrative in the form of Variations, I wrote them like a composer. (This one is a scherzo variation. Here is a lyrical one. Let us try to deepen the theme. And here is a possible digression. And so on.) I did not have a plan. The idea was to make a logical complete form, to build it up. I was curious to see what I could do. And unexpectedly for me, this "essay" became research. The conclusions I draw when I talk about Ustvolskaya, about her music, about my relationship with her are not accidental. They are deeply meaningful and thoughtful. I have listened to her music dozens of times in performances by different musicians. I read everything that was written about her (not much) at the time. I listened to Shostakovich, Stravinsky, Mahler, Beethoven, even Tishchenko, and the music of many other composers. I needed to form my own idea and opinion about these composers, since Galina Ivanovna was in a relationship and opinion with them.

The idea of spirituality is paramount to understanding both Ustvolskaya's personality and her works. What is spirituality? What is a spiritual or spiritless person, how important is spirituality in life and in creativity? I became convinced that in most cases this quality is either not understood, or misunderstood, or not considered at all in art. And this is also quite significant for our time!

It would be unfair not to mention the esteemed Mikhail Kazinik, who, after reading fragments of the book on FB - I published them - became an admirer of it. He strongly advised me to publish it in Russian. And when I did, he wrote his Foreword to it. A warm thank you and hats off to you, Mr. Kazinik! I have translated it and placed it in this, third edition.

Thanks to all interested readers!

Belmont, 10/20/2023

FOREWORD BY MIKHAIL KAZINIK TO RUSSIAN EDITION*

This book needs to be read. It should be Reread! It was written by a man who is an Initiated one. After the first reading, you will know that there is a remarkable man living in the world. A personality, a thinker. He is an incredibly talented Composer. A Poet, also a talented one. And this man will come into your life. Because this book is infinitely warm. Ustvolskaya's personality is unique! And you will realize it very quickly.

Simon Bokman's book is not a monograph about Ustvolskaya's work. It is about a whole era. And about her last composer. This book is about Spirituality, about moral choices. It is a real book about music. And about life.

It, this book, is alive. It develops and grows like a plant. It grows from a seed into a branching tree. It has a macrocosm and a microcosm. If the same thing happens to you that happened to me, then we are on the same wave. I, having finished reading, felt the need to RE-read. Simon Bokman's book is quite small. But in it, as in a black hole, there is an incredible density of matter. Regardless of your attitude toward the personality and work of one of the most important composers of the 20th century, Galina Ustvolskaya, you will realize a great deal, for the book is written by an intelligent, lively, bright man. It is about World, about a vast and spiritually rich World, because its author is a true Renaissance person, and (going back to the beginning of my preface) he is an I N I T I A T E D M A N.

-- With respect, Mikhail Kazinik

---

*   Michail Kazinik is a world renown musicologist, lector and violinist, writer, philosopher, stage director..

Michail Kazinik and me before the premiere of my Sonata for Violin and Piano in San Francisco on May 20st in 2018. You may listen to it on YouTube.

Why did I decide on the third edition?

Enough time has elapsed since the previous two editions were published for some of the tendencies reported in them to emerge, and, I have decided to proclaim firmly and openly the ideas in which I believe and follow to, in the present, third edition.

There is another reason, which I do not intend to hide. This is the deception of the publishing house Xlibris, and the dishonesty of this publishing house, where the second edition of this book was published. I do not want to reconcile myself with such an attitude! Therefore, I accepted the Author Reputation Press's offer to try my luck and be published for the third time!

In this regard, I cannot fail to mention the Russian Publishing house "Moya Stroka" ("My Line"), which also lives by deceptions. All these and similar doers should be known, as it is the claim of the coming New Era!

Galina Ustvolskaya is the last composer of the passing Era, the Era of evil, iniquity, betrayals, deceptions, terrorism and cruelties of every kind! It is this Era that is ending! I believe and know that it is being replaced by the Epoch of Harmony, Goodness and Light! Good triumphs over evil! Light dispels darkness! Sounds idealistic, but it is true! This is why so many cruelties and injustices are happening on our planet right now: darkness is fighting for its survival! But the darkness is doomed. And not only those who live in evil, but their followers also, and those who hesitate and doubt in resisting evil will be not preserved too!

This book is my MANIFEST by which I declare about how culture and art should change or substitute the gone Era, of which Ustvolskaya is the most precise representative. Here is the statement.

Romanticism is the driving force behind Universal, cosmic creativity

NOT BY ME, BUT THROUGH ME.

This is the principle that guided Johann Sebastian Bach and the Viennese classics: Haydn, Mozart, Beethoven. The idea of Spiritual Guidance is very important for the coming New Age. I believe that the dominant direction in art should be IDEAL-ROMANTICISM, in which, unlike 19th century Romanticism, art becomes a practical basis. We should proceed from the fact that thoughts and creative images are a material force that, depending on their orientation, can affect nature and the world around us both positively or negatively depending on how they are directed. Everything new is the well-forgotten old. Therefore, the ancient philosopher Plato's statement in this regard is appropriate.

Plato said: "From beautiful images we shall pass to beautiful thoughts, from beautiful thoughts to beautiful life, and from beautiful life to absolute Beauty."

I am not a theoretician! I am practical composer, member of National Association of Composers of United States of America – NACUSA! My music you can listen on You Tube. Unfortunately, my most significant works are not performed yet, but this is the deal of the future.

With warm regards,
Semyon (Simon) Bokman
Belmont, October 10, 2023

We parted ways, but I would keep
your portrait close, upon my breast,
a pallid ghost of years that leap
into my soul, remembered best.

In love with others, did I feel
that I forgot you? I could not.
Forsaken shrines are worshipped still,
an idol fallen - still a god!

M. Y. Lermontov, translator unknown

ANNOTATION

There is neither in the history of music, nor in the history of art such a closed and contradictory composer and creator, as is Galina Ustvolskaya. The music of Galina Ustvolskaya (excepting commissioned works written not for internal reasons, but for necessity) is a kind of mysterious ritual. What is her music about? What are its dominating ideas? Ustvolskaya's music art is not so large in volume, but with a huge degree of tension. It concentrated on the main ideological problems and contradictions of our time. What is the Culture? What is Spirituality? What is the role of art in our lives? Do we need them? Is it possible to exclude these phenomena and concepts from our Being? And why is our Era passing away? The book is full of allusions, which the author uses to explain the talented composer, who, as a drop of water in an ocean, reflects the leading trends and tendencies of twentieth century and contemporary art.

PREFACE

"The baby's first step is the first step to his death" – Kozma Prutkov*.

The music of Galina Ustvolskaya is played more often in the West than in Russia. Not only in Europe, but here in the United States as well. In mentioning her name to professional musicians, I have never heard the question: who is she? Therefore, it is quite natural that the first edition of the book was published in English. This is not a musicology book, and it is difficult to define its genre. Galina Ustvolskaya is a phenomenon beyond definitions which is difficult to understand and, moreover, to write about it. "If I put all my strength into my compositions, then they have to listen to me in a new way, also putting their strength into listening!" She was charming, excitingly interesting, and influenced me by herself more than by her music. My interest was almost reciprocated, but Ustvolskaya was not genuinely interested in other people. She was extremely focused, really focused on herself. Her sympathies and dislikes were akin to royal favoritism. It seems that her love for herself - one of the necessary vehicles for survival for any person - helped her to pull through a difficult battle with life.

Just like a mother would sacrifice herself to save her child, Ustvolskaya sacrificed herself in the name of her creativity.

She had a delightful sense of humor, but her music does not reflect this quality of her character. She is controversial and withdrawn. Even though Galina Ustvolskaya is a 20th century composer who completed her life's journey in the 21st century, she is less known than

---

*   Kozma Prutkov is a collective pen name of Alexei Konstantinovich Tolstoy and his cousins, the Zhemchuzhnikov brothers: Alexei, Vladimir, and Alexander. Their fables, aphorisms, and plays published in Russian newspapers and magazines of the mid-19th century.

Bach. Bach's biography lacks details because he lived a long time ago. Ustvolskaya, however, is a famous composer and our contemporary! How fascinating! I started thinking. And what I discovered stunned me. To understand what I found, travel this path with me - read the book...

From the Middle Ages until the beginning of the XIX century, the time of Romanticism, composers were servants. They served by their arts to churches, rich nobles, kings, emperors. It is no accident that Leopold Mozart, the father of the great Wolfgang Amadeus, at the dawn of his career served as both the Kapellmeister and the valet for one of these nobles, which was common at that time.* And even his son, the first free artist in the history of music, who did not serve anyone, wrote music only on demand - there was only commissioned music then. Composers did not create music for the future. They were performing the will of their masters. The requirements for the church and secular music were strict. And, judging on the kind of music that was created, the customers were very demanding people.

In the 17th and 18th centuries music was the most essential element of the secular life of noble and rich people in Europe. It has been played both on solemn occasions and in everyday life: during friendly meals, meetings, and social gatherings. In W.A. Mozart's youth Salzburg musical academies took place every day and lasted for 5-6 hours. The noble people who ordered the music also played various instruments and were virtuosos often. Newness and immediacy were valuable. Therefore, composers had to compose not only brightly and talentedly,

---

*   Hermann Abert in his book about Mozart presents a characteristic episode. In 1771, the young W.A. Mozart received an order from Milan to compose a serenade on the occasion of the marriage of Archduke Ferdinand and Princess Maria Richard de Modena. The serenade was a triumph for the 15-year-old composer. Archduke Ferdinand wished to take Wolfgang into his service and sought permission from his mother, Empress Maria Theresa, who admired the young talent and generously rewarded him. She answered.

"You ask me for permission to hire a young Salzburger. I don't know, I don't think you need a composer or any useless people. However, if you enjoy it, I do not want to prevent you from doing so. If I am talking about it, it is only so that you do not burden yourself with useless people and never cherish people of this kind in your service. It is humiliating for someone who has these people to serve when they wander the world like beggars; besides, he has a large family. (Herman Abert. MOZART. Part one. The first book. Moscow. "Music "1987, p. 223) (Russian edition).

but quickly and plentifully. And even the great Joseph Haydn in 1765 got a rebuke from his patron Prince Nikolaus Esterhazy* that he should be more diligently occupied with composition.

Joseph Haydn

And it is Haydn! The official reprimand of 1765 included wording insisting that Haydn compose more works for the Prince's favorite instrument, the baryton. Haydn responded immediately, and in the period starting at this time and continuing into the mid-1770s wrote 126 baryton trios, as well as other works for the instrument. The baryton being quite obscure today, this music is not often played at present.

But both Mozart and Haydn, whom we admire for their creative fecundity, were by all means not the most productive composers.

---

*   Nikolaus did not hire Haydn, but rather "inherited" him from his brother, who had hired him as Vice Kapellmeister in 1761. He was responsible for the promotion of Haydn to full Kapellmeister on the death of the old Kapellmeister, Gregor Werner, in 1766. It is evident that, following a brief initial rough period (Haydn was reprimanded for negligence in 1765), the prince ultimately came to treasure Haydn. For instance, he frequently presented Haydn with gold ducats in praise of individual compositions, twice rebuilt Haydn's house when it burnt down (1768, 1776), and reversed a decision (1780) to dismiss the mediocre soprano Luigia Polzelli from the payroll when it became evident that Polzelli had become Haydn's mistress. Haydn was also allowed (1766) to retain another mediocre singer on the payroll, his younger brother Johann. (Internet)https://en.wikipedia.org/wiki/Nikolaus_I,_Prince_Esterházy

Prince Nikolaus Esterházy I

Carl Ditters von Dittersdorf

For example, the composer Ditters von Dittersdorf* composed choral and solo cantatas, three symphonies and a violin concerto for Bishop of Grosvardein's birthday! It was a delightful time for composers! Surprisingly! The elites of the then European communities and states controlled - consciously or unconsciously - the order and harmony of life and art.† What is more striking, that the persons to whom this amount of music was addressed were consuming it, listened to it, or even played something from it!

Atheism did not have a decisive influence on the minds of men during the Pre-Romantic Era, and almost everybody was a believer. And if anyone had doubted the truth of religion, they would not dare to proclaim it. (Spinoza, the 17th century man was one of the very few who dared to do so and was severely punished for it). The Art was sublime, strict, and majestic.

But this way of life could not have lasted forever. The artist wanted and had to become free. In the 18th century, the ideas of atheism began to spread widely in Europe, when several of the philosopher-materialists – the opponents of the religion - began to propagate this ideology, which denied the existence of God. Romanticism was born in the art, which was inspired by the French Revolution of 1789 -1799. It was the French Revolution that challenged respect for Christian moral values and trust in the church. The old way of life was broken. New emotions began to emerge in the music of romantic composers. Such a deep sadness, the expression of mental pain and loneliness as in the music of F. Schubert, for example, the pre-romantic music did not know. And maybe one of the reasons why the music of Schubert was

---

* **Carl Ditters von Dittersdorf** (2 November 1739 – 24 October 1799) was an Austrian composer, violinist, and silvologist (scientist who studies forests). He was a friend of both Haydn and Mozart.

  Seriously, he definitely listened to it. Why give something that won't be used?

  And now imagine a contemporary composer giving his music, and especially in such large quantities, to a congressman or other statesman!

† In this regard, it is characteristic of Hermann Abert's remark that "only together with Beethoven are new trends entering the composer's work: instead of working on commission, the artist is given complete freedom to choose the material and to treat it". G. Abert. Mozart, Part 1, Book 1, pp. 329. (Russian edition)

not acknowledged was such as his music's shocking mood what was not common then yet?

Philosopher-materialists continued to conquer the public consciousness, and in the 20th century atheism became the dominant ideology in the world.

A copy of Prince Esterházy's baryton, on display at his palace in Eisenstadt.

In the 18th century, the ideas of atheism began to spread widely in Europe, when several philosophers, opponents of religion, began to propagate this ideology, which denied the existence of God. Romanticism was born in art, which was inspired by the French Revolution of 1789 -1799. It was the French Revolution that challenged respect for Christian moral values and trust in the church. The old way of life was broken. The most outstanding achievement of it is the teachings of Charles Darwin (1809-1882) about the evolution of species which gave the scientific basis for atheism. (Is Darwin, right? This is not the subject of this book. I will only note that scientific evidence of the inaccuracy of his theory has begun to emerge today). The transition from religiosity to atheism is quite natural. Religion with its isolation and dogmatism could no longer satisfy inquisitive minds. Humankind began to search for the substitution of God in science. But even modern science is not able to explain the world and the place of man in this world. Man has felt his insecurity. This should have been reflected in art.

Music and all the arts from Romanticism to the present day have evolved towards greater dramatization and psychologization in the creative works of their brightest representatives. Themes of unshared love, with a tragic outcome often, fatality, vengeance, anxiety and expectations, premonitions and fear of death have become dominant in art. Music reached the peak of dramatism and tragedy-like quality in the 20th century in the expressionist works of Schoenberg, Webern, Berg and besides them Shostakovich. Ustvolskaya completes this list of names. To deepen and inflame dramatism and psychology, increasingly sophisticated means of expression were required. Harmony became increasingly complicated. These complications weakened traditional modes and their ties with harmony, gradually depleting the system as a whole and destroying classical forms. In the 20th century, in the works of the most radical composers: Stravinsky, Schoenberg and Webern the classical harmony and classical forms were completely destroyed. But their work still preserved the traditional genres such as sonatas, quartets, symphonies, operas, etc... Ustvolskaya destroyed the genres. Although she calls her works symphonies and sonatas (she also has such "genres" as "compositions" which is quite symptomatic; it is like calling culinary products and dishes just food), these genres are quite conditional* in her creative work. Of course, one can explain it by the lack of inclination to compose in these forms and genres. But the lack of interest in them also says a lot. These genres no longer existed

---

*   By Ustvolskaya's definition her compositions are not chamber music, "even if it is a solo sonata". Therefore, it is simply impossible to speak about the transformation of genres in connection with her music whereas sonatas are composed for a solo instruments and symphonies are composed for an orchestra. Galina Ustvolskaya doesn't have an orchestra in the conventional sense. Her works, which are not chamber works, but also are not symphonic, are "equal in rights" and are extra specific in nature. We simply agree with the author's definitions of genres, as we agree with the name of the person given to him or to her at birth.

for her*. In this aspect she is contrary to Joseph Haydn, who created a sonata form by summarizing the experience of his predecessors and contemporary composers, and this was an outstanding discovery of musical Classicism. Ustvolskaya on the contrary, having accumulated and summarized the destructive tendencies of music of the twentieth century and earlier times, completed the defeat of classical genres and forms. The technique which she has chosen does not provide an opportunity for great diversity and it is not adaptable to the creation of extended pieces of music. Each new work was therefore come to existence by her titanic job and her creative resources were exhausted from composition to composition. Her last work, the Fifth Symphony, was completed in 1990, 16 years before she departed.

Galina Ustvolskaya's music is very uncommon and original, but like the music of any of the other composers it has its own roots. It is simply impossible to create an absolutely new music, regardless of any tradition or author, as well as to make an absolute invention that has no analogues. This is against the logic and laws of development. Development takes place according to the principle of continuity where everything new necessarily contains elements of the old. There are no such things as art which has not a succession and music which is written from a "blank page". Both musicians and non- musicians often find analogies with other works by different composers. Ustvolskaya is not an exception. She synthesized Russian and Western traditions. Thematic (melodic) basis of her music has Russian-Slavic and Old Russian origin which can be heard well...

---

* One can recollect Chopin, who almost completely limited his work with piano music. But in the context of the time when everything was in the process of active evolution, it is perceived differently. Chopin's music is not the last music of the era. Ustvolskaya's music is not evolution, but involution and the last, final stage of the entire European music.

Sergey Slonimsky

On the Internet, in an interview given by Sergei Slonimsky* to journalist Yury Shestakovich I have read this:

"I think that the spiritual music which we have now is a little bit... naïve. That spiritual music, which was born in Russia in the Middle Ages, which arose on the basis of the znamenny singing (Russian chant - S. Bokman) which is the unique tri-voice creative work and which is the most complicated and serious art hasn't been continued unfortunately including the works of those composers who are considered as a classics of Russian contemporary music..."

"… hasn't been continued"? Why does he say that? And what about Ustvolskaya? And how cleverly she did it! She transformed the znamenny chant into instrumental music.

I will continue. Atonalism began to be practiced for the first time by the Austrian composer Arnold Schoenberg. The cluster technique, often used by Ustvolskaya (cluster is a group or bunch of notes which are performed simultaneously and more often on a piano by palms and fists) was invented by the American composer Henry Cowell.†

---

*   **Sergei Mikhailovich Slonimsky** (Russian: Сергéй Михáйлович Слонѝмский, born August 12, 1932, Leningrad - February 9, 2020, S.-Petersburg) is a Russian and Soviet composer, pianist, and musicologist. He is a son of Soviet writer Mikhail Slonimsky and a nephew of the Russian-American composer Nicolas Slonimsky.

†   Henry Cowell (1897-1965), an outstanding American avant-garde composer, was one of the most active members of the Temple of the People, a unique theosophical community in Halcyon, California. This Temple exists. Ustvolskaya could not have known about it. What is interesting here is that, in inventing spiritual nonreligious music, she used a technique invented by composer who was follower of spiritual nonreligious Teaching! Cowell invented this technique without regard to the Teaching. This is just a composer's technique.

(Ustvolskaya may have discovered this technique by herself, but even in this case her discovery is secondary. Cowell discovered and applied it the first).

Speaking of Galina Ustvolskaya and about her work and its origin, it is impossible not to think about the importance of Dmitry Shostakovich and meeting with him for her formation. Galina Ustvolskaya fierce denial of Shostakovich's influence on her creativity and on her worldview and life itself cannot exclude the fact of this influence.

Dmitry Shostakovich*

---

*   **Dmitri Dmitriyevich Shostakovich** (25 September [O.S. 12 September] 1906 – 9 August 1975) was a Soviet-era Russian composer and pianist[1] who became internationally known after the premiere of his First Symphony in 1926 and was regarded throughout his life as a major composer.

Shostakovich achieved early fame in the Soviet Union, but had a complex relationship with its government. His 1934 opera *Lady Macbeth of Mtsensk* was initially a success, but eventually was condemned by the Soviet government, putting his career at risk. In 1948 his work was denounced under the Zhdanov Doctrine, with professional consequences lasting several years. Even after his censure was rescinded in 1956, performances of his music were occasionally subject to state

> *(...) Now it is trendy to think that D.D. Shostakovich was a conformist and praised the authorities. Well, he praised them because he did not want to irritate them. But suddenly I am reading a nasty book, whereby the mouth of his woman-student* it has been said that Shostakovich was stingy, that he had not helping to anybody and that he was a mediocre composer and a very ordinary person at all. I do not know if this is really the opinion of the pupil or just the writer of the book has added it from herself, but this cunning ingratitude to their own teachers, and not only to the teachers, but to the Benefactors (!) is also a sign of our time.*

Sergei Slonimsky, as interviewed by Yury Shestakovich, the Internet.

It is known that Shostakovich was inclined toward innovation and bold experiments in his music, but having received formidable shouts and edifications, he was forced to adapt himself to these circumstances and composed music "understandable" to the leaders. He had the ability of creative reincarnation. So here are two composers in music history, the two Dmitry Shostakovich coexisting. One of them was a composer of cute music such as the Festive Overture, the Romance to the movie "The Gadfly" and the Oratorio "Song about Forests". The other one was a composer of complex, extremely dramatic and almost expressionist-like symphonies, such as the Fifth, Seventh and Eighth Symphonies. And the Fourth Symphony, which was performed for the first time only in 1961, a quarter of a century after the premiere (which had not taken place then).

> *(...) Musical instruments were not used in the role for which they were intended. Thus, the piano turned into a percussion instrument (fist blows on the keyboard in the 6th sonata of S. Prokofiev), the violin from a singing, delicate instrument turned into a wheezing*

---

intervention, as with his Thirteenth Symphony (1962). Shostakovich was a member of the Supreme Soviet of the RSFSR (1947) and the Supreme Soviet of the Soviet Union (from 1962 until his death), as well as chairman of the RSFSR Union of Composers (1960–1968). Over the course of his career, he earned several important awards, including the Order of Lenin, from the Soviet government.

*   The hint on the book of O. Gladkova "Music as Obsession"

and knocking one. The clarity and logicality of the harmonic sequences were sacrificed to the arbitrariness and deliberate complexity of the sound combinations, the natural chords turned into "sound-timbers", sounded spots and blots. From the speech of T. Khrennikov* at the meeting of composers and musicologists of Moscow. Magazine "Soviet Music", No.1, 1948, p.54

Tikhon Khrennikov

Unlike Sergei Prokofiev, who was "imported" by the Soviet regime from abroad and who, despite his international reputation had to adapt himself to this regime painfully, Shostakovich grew up and formed as a human and creative person under this regime. Prokofiev's personality has formed in pre-revolutionary Russia, then its evolution continued

---

* **Tikhon Nikolayevich Khrennikov** (Russian: Тихон Николаевич Хренников; 10 June [O.S. 28 May] 1913 – 14 August 2007) was a Russian and Soviet composer, pianist, and General Secretary of the Union of Soviet Composers (1948–1991), who was also known for his political activities. He wrote three symphonies, four piano concertos, two violin concertos, two cello concertos, operas, operettas, ballets, chamber music, incidental music and film music.

  During the 1930s, Khrennikov was already being hailed as a leading Soviet composer. In 1948, Andrei Zhdanov, the leader of the anti-formalism campaign, nominated Khrennikov as Secretary of the Union of Soviet Composers. He held this influential post until the collapse of the Soviet Union in 1991.

in the West, and in these conditions his work, of course, was free from Soviet ideological dogmas from the very beginning. It is even more surprising that under the conditions of total prohibitions and fears, which Shostakovich could not rid himself of until the end of his days, he managed to protect his main creativity.

In the years of Ustvolskaya's studies with Shostakovich, his authority in the Soviet creative environment was great. This could not but have an influence on his students, especially on the closest ones. Georgy Sviridov, a composer who later became a phenomenally successful and widely known one in the Soviet Union studied with Shostakovich at the same time as Ustvolskaya did. He and Ustvolskaya both became students of Shostakovich's in 1937. Both had previously studied with different teachers. Both were expelled from the conservatory. It was Shostakovich who rescued Ustvolskaya from expulsion by accepting her to his class. Sviridov was expelled for neglecting political science. Both were favorites of Shostakovich. Both later resented their teacher for not helping them enough. But here is an interesting peculiarity, which Sviridov did not deny, and Ustvolskaya passionately denied, the fact of creative continuity. And it is especially interesting that Georgy Sviridov had grown from a Shostakovich-traditionalist (which did not prevent him from taking a worthy place in Russian culture and even having followers; a very talented composer Valery Gavrilin being one of them), while on the contrary Ustvolskaya grew up from a Shostakovich innovator, who undoubtedly was innovator in the Soviet environment of the Iron Curtain era. Ustvolskaya went further. She was more courageous in her creative work. But so, it should have been. She was younger. She lived in another era, and she was the representative of another time. Besides, she managed to create her own creative system and philosophy. Both Ustvolskaya and Sviridov - two such different composers - are the satellites of the same planet, the planet by name SHOSTAKOVICH. What powerful creative resources had this man! Unlike Sviridov, Ustvolskaya has no followers.

Galina Ustvolskaya is the last outstanding composer of the 20th century. She completed an entire era of European music with her creative work. It may be objected to: there were and are talented composers besides Ustvolskaya in the twentieth century and later, in our time. Yes, there are. But not one of them managed to express what she did with her music so distinctly, so convincingly, and so mercilessly to express the main feature of this time - its non-spirituality. And, because of it: demonism, fear and destruction, and warning about the painful nightmare, in which Mankind will be involved if it does not manage to return to the simple and wise laws of Life. I think to understand the direction of Galina Ustvolskaya's creativity and to understand the peculiarities of her complicated individuality, Thomas Mann's "complicity" is important in the creation of my book.

I have ventured to assume that Thomas Mann was one of the most readable authors in the intellectual circles of the then most reading country in the world during my youth, during my studies with Galina Ivanovna. His novel "Dr. Faustus" was particularly appealing to composers and musicologists, to all those who study music seriously. The music of the leading Western composers was not played often in the Soviet Union, and this novel created an illusion of involvement in their music. Not without a reason Thomas Mann called himself a musician transformed into a writer. This can be seen in the composition of this novel, and in reasoning about the music of its heroes, which are very witty and entertaining.

Now it is strange to recall, but at first this writer seemed boring to me, and we even argued about it with my friend who also studied with Galina Ivanovna. He admired the novel and simply answered my arguments: "You are not grown up enough for it!" One day in his presence I asked Ustvolskaya who had encouraged us usually to read more, listen more, watch, and see more;

- Galina Ivanovna! What about Thomas Mann? A boring writer as it seems to me...

- Well, do not say so! He is an amazing man!

Sasha did not say anything, but it felt like he was satisfied.

In this novel, Thomas Mann created what seemed to be a generalized image of the genius composer of the twentieth century, Adrian Leverkühn, without specifically implying anyone. He said that it was a spiritual biography of Friedrich Nietzsche. It was Nietzsche who asserted the relativity of any universal sense, truth, verity, which could be relied upon by an artist and a simple human being. Nietzsche had emphasized the significant role of the instinct in man. He was very distrustful of spirituality. T. Mann called his novel "book of the end" not by chance. Reasoning about spirituality, about church and religion are remarkably interesting. How imperceptibly God is being replaced by his antipode and devil . And this is what (or who) is the owner of the present-day mind, art, humankind. And this is not by chance that Leverkühn concludes the deal with the devil to survive creatively.

I "stumbled" over Thomas Mann's letter to Theodore Adorno, in which he fantasizes about the hero's compositional technique and what works he should compose, absolutely by chance, when the book was written, and I had already developed a concept of the creative image of the composer Galina Ivanovna Ustvolskaya. Thomas Mann's ideas, which are set out in the letter, have delighted and alarmed me. I had reread the novel, and I was amazed to find out the resemblance not only of Adrian Leverkun's musical ideas to those of Ustvolskaya, but also by similarities of their natures. As if the writer chose Ustvolskaya as the prototype of the hero of his novel. The types of Adrian Leverkun and Galina Ustvolskaya are similar!

It's a parable novel, and T. Mann endowed his hero with individuality particularly typical for a composer and creative man of the twentieth century. It was as if he had foreseen that a composer like Ustvolskaya should exist! For me this resemblance between the two composers - fictional one and the real one - became decisive, and I have had no doubt that Galina Ustvolskaya was a composer-symbol of the twentieth century and that she was the one who completed it with her creative work.

Every epoch creates its own heroes. And the meaning of outstanding deeds and phenomena in different epochs (times) are different. Our time is a painful "Time of Change" - in ancient Chinese terminology, a time of spiritual digression. But it cannot last forever. It should not be! And so, it will not be! Ustvolskaya convinces us of it by her music. And if Beethoven's works became the life-affirming culmination - the Ninth Symphony - and after it the evolution of music began to change its direction gradually that culmination of another and opposite quality is the music of Galina Ustvolskaya. She destroyed the aesthetics of demonism, bringing it to the extremes and exhausting it. She touched upon the most important and urgent problem of our being - the problem of its (non)-spirituality. And how convincingly it is expressed by her creativity! No edification, statement, or proclamation of the power of Light and Good is as convincing as her unhappy and often terrible music. This is just the kind of music that helps us to realize to what extent spirituality determines the ways of development of Mankind and that only true spirituality will save us. The very fact of Galina Ustvolskaya's creative work, so refined, with such exceptional skill, convinces us that this is yes, the end, finale! But it is not the end of everything - just to the most terrible ones! It is too late to frighten Mankind with the Apocalypse.

Belmont, July 21, 2010, August 1st, 2019.

VARIATIONS ON THE THEME GALINA USTVOLSKAYA

(Introduction)

"...Indeed, the public, which forgets so easily, seldom overlooks anything really remarkable, though I am sometimes tempted to compare it to a herd of cattle, momentarily distracted by the lightning from its peaceful grazing."

-Robert Schumann[*]

But really, not everyone gets distracted, just a few... the most curious.

When I began my composition studies with Galina Ivanovna Ustvolskaya[†] at the Rimsky-Korsakov College of Music, I did not realize how seriously it would affect my life. From our first meeting I sensed how unusual she was. This is why I so clearly remember the details of our meetings, lessons, and our conversations; every one of them was thrilling and significant for me.

During those years she was my true Teacher, the kind of one they call Guru in India. Naturally, it never crossed my mind that I would write about Ustvolskaya. I simply studied, and in those years of apprenticeship, the details of Galina Ustvolskaya's life were of little interest to me. How often are the most mundane details of day-to-day

---

[*]   "Letters of Robert Schumann" ed. Dr. Karl Storck, transl. Hannah Bryant (London: John Murray, 1907), 70.

[†]   In Russian there are a few ways to address a person. They reveal the level of intimacy in a relationship; e.g. "Galina Ivanovna" (literally, Galina, daughter of Ivan) is respectful and formal. This is how a student would always address a teacher, a younger person would call an older friend, unless the older party proposes otherwise, which would usually imply a very close friendship. "Galina Ustvolskaya" is an artistic abbreviation of a full name, but is still formal and is appropriate to use when referring to her as a composer. "Galya" is a diminutive form of "Galina." (note by transl.)

life used to create a sensation in biographies of extraordinary people? But to tell the truth, those details reveal little uniqueness about a personality. No one can describe how an individual is organized from within and where his life and aspirations are directed.

It seemed to me Galina Ivanovna soared somewhere extremely high above life. That captivated and ignited me. Extremely vulnerable and sensitive, she perceived the world differently from most people; she would force her way through life as if through dense and thorny brushwood. Mundane life scratched and wounded her, mutilating her soul…

It would be appropriate to say about Ustvolskaya what Aksakov said about Gogol, one of her favorite authors: "[…] we cannot judge Gogol according to ourselves, we cannot even understand his impressions because, most likely, his whole body is built somehow differently from ours; […] his nerves are thinner than ours: they hear what we do not and they shudder for reasons unknown to us."[*]

Very consistent and always guided by principle in her work, Ustvolskaya had formed her style already in the fifties. At that time in the Soviet Union, not only was her style unacceptable on an aesthetic level, but it could also have been seen as criminal and treasonous by the state. That predetermined her spiritual isolation and financial troubles.

Ustvolskaya's "Grand Duet," written in 1959, was dedicated to Mstislav Rostropovich. But Rostropovich never performed it during those years and there were no discussions about that between the author and the performer. If the performance took place, Ustvolskaya could have been expelled from the Composers' Union and even arrested», say the authors of Ustvolskaya's on-line discography, referring to Rostropovich's memoirs[†]. This may have been the reason Shostakovich did not help Ustvolskaya more actively in building her career. Shostakovich was a courageous man who managed to overcome terrible, deadly obstacles that endangered not only his work, but his life; he spiritually rose above them. Those obstacles served as a powerful motivation for his work and

---

[*]   S.T. Aksakov *The Complete Works* (Moscow: Pravda, 1966), vol.3, *A story of my acquaintance with Gogol*, 201 (Russian)

[†]   Peter Graham Woolf *Galina Ustvolskaya and the Piano*, http//www.musicweb. uk.net/classrev/dec99/Ustvolskaya.htm

some of his compositions shock even more when one understands the circumstances in which they were written. But how should an artist feel when he/she is aware of how much of his/her creative power and talent remains unrealized? Besides, Shostakovich was famous and knew that his music could captivate a lot of people. Unquestionably, this was true heroism. It was heroism that revealed itself in front of the entire world. I am not trying to simplify my understanding of Shostakovich. Not everyone is capable of what he has done. But imagine a composer who cannot publish or perform his/her music; a composer who is only known among an extremely limited number of people. He/she cannot make a living with his creative work but continues to create new and original music. This is how Ustvolskaya is. Her faith and courage reveal themselves differently.

She surpasses many of the innovative works of Western composers by her boldness.

Ustvolskaya's violin sonata was performed before a visiting American delegation in 1958. The delegation included composer Roy Harris, who found the piece "kind of ugly", which, of course, does not add him any honor[*].

Soviet bureaucrats wanted to show the Americans that there was an avant-garde in the USSR, completely ignoring the fact that not every American composer is an avant-gardist. Roy Harris (1898-1979) was not an avant-gardist. "[Harris was] a prominent representative of nationalism in U.S. music. (*American nationalism? – it is something curious! – S. B.*) He came to be regarded as the musical spokesperson for the American landscape [...]. Harris's works are marked by broad tonal melodies and asymmetrical rhythms," reads his biography[†].

Ustvolskaya's music substantially differs from the music of the avant-garde. Avant-garde music is a sensation, not because of *what* it is, but because of *how* it is made. Ustvolskaya's music is a sensation of another kind. Her music is oversaturated with emotion. She breaks aesthetic taboos no one has yet dared to break and allows emotion into her music that no one before her has dared to reveal. This is her

---

[*]   Ian MacDonald *"Music under Soviet rule: Ustvolskaya"*, http://www.siue.eku/~aho/musov/ust/ust.html

[†]   www.royharrisamericancomposer.com

philosophy, and it is clear in her compositions - from the first piano sonata to the fifth symphony. But her music is not only that of frightful emotions. It is an attempt to understand the world more fully, a world that includes apparent forms and habitual feelings, but also something invisible, intangible, and unexplainable, which is equally important to life.

Recently, interest in Ustvolskaya's music has grown significantly. Articles about her and her work are emerging. It is possible to order a CD of her compositions. There is even a Ustvolskaya fan club on the Internet. Many pages of publications are dedicated to the relationship between Ustvolskaya and Shostakovich. Unfortunately, this fact is being overused to advertise Ustvolskaya's work, and the sensation of Ustvolskaya's personality and her music has fallen by the wayside. Her exceptional courage, her unexpectedly daring and sometimes shocking attitude toward things well-known and habitual in life and in music – these are the things that make her personality unique.

She had many students, but no pedagogical method or special approach. She did not teach composition like Arnold Schoenberg, who taught his own twelve-tone system to his students; or, as Rimsky-Korsakov, who gave Stravinsky fragments of his own compositions to orchestrate and then compared it to his own orchestration. It is hard to imagine Ustvolskaya doing something like that with her students. She did not teach her own music or her own technique. She understood very clearly the enormous distance that lay between herself and her students. Had she tried to teach them to her system, she might simply have destroyed their consciousness.

Arnold Schoenberg was an outstanding teacher. When his twelve-tone system was created, he started to teach it to some of his talented students. He believed in the historical significance of his discovery and considered it to be the evolutionary step that was to take over after classical harmony. Ustvolskaya, on the contrary, was not interested in the popularization or theoretical substantiation of her compositional method or her philosophical concepts. And could she do that? Her technique is not due to composing. Her creative method is more philosophical than that of any other composer.

Even the most truthful narration about a personality only creates its literary double; a phantom. There are as many doubles as there are narrators. Only to a certain degree can they help our imagination, but never will they give us a complete image of the personality portrayed. There is a threshold of sincerity, of language, and of genre. As for Ustvolskaya - there is also a threshold of mystery. Yes, the mystery which was created by her.

FIRST VARIATION

The Beginning

I vividly remember my first lesson in the studio of Galina Ustvolskaya at the Rimsky-Korsakov College of Music in the fall of 1968. Almost all of her students were there. It was the beginning of the new school year.

"How old are you?" asked Galina Ivanovna.

"Not too old, just eighteen."

"Well, depends on how you look at it! My nephew is also eighteen. He is married and recently fathered a child."

Her irony was benevolent.

"And you, it seems, came from somewhere south?"

I answered that I came from Zhdanov* where I had completed two years of studies as a bayan (kind of button accordion) major, (from the hometown of the creator of ominous decrees to the city where those decrees were executed!) that originally, I was from Kyiv, where I had not been accepted to a school...

On August 14, 1946, Orgburo of the CK VKP(b) adopted a decree (which was later published in the newspaper "Pravda"), in which the prose writer Mikhail Zoshchenko, was called a "vulgar dreg of literature" and the poet Anna Akhmatova was called a "typical representative of the alien to our people, empty and ideal-less poetry." (Both writers were from Leningrad.) The real author of this decree was probably Stalin himself. This became obvious after the

---

*   It's Mariupol now, Ukraine. Mariupol is the historical name of this city. Mariupol has been occupied by Russian forces since May 2022.

stenographic transcript of the Orgburo's session on August 9, 1946, was published. Stalin was present at the session. There to comment on Stalin's thoughts as well as to announce them to the public was Andrey Zhdanov, a member of the Politburo and an overseer of ideological work. This is how the famous Zhdanov Report appeared in the magazines *"Zvezda"* ("Star") and *"Leningrad."* The Report was published in mass circulation and became required reading in public schools and colleges. I remember it well from the 1949 literature textbook that my father used for his evening classes. I am not convinced that ordinary citizens of the Soviet Union took this report seriously and trusted it. When I asked my father who Zoshchenko was, he told me, smiling, what a wonderful humorist he was. Father did not even remember that there was such a report, even though he must have studied it at evening school for adults.[*]

"Yes, you played your rhapsody superbly at the exam".

"Comrades," Galina Ivanovna turned to the students, "how he played! He is simply a virtuoso on the bayan!"

"It was not a rhapsody. It was a concerto… a concerto for bayan and orchestra," I objected naively.

"Yes, of course, a concerto… concerto, I am sorry…"

---

[*] Via an Internet source I surprisingly learned that Galina Ustvolskaya had been accused of "formalism" as well.

"After the release of the notorious February 1948 Resolution Ustvolskaya like many other composers were accused in Formalism, an abstract, audience-alienating approach to composition". **ustvolskaya**.org/eng

This statement is easy to refute just by looking at Ustvolskaya's Katalogue; 1.Concerto for piano, full string orchestra and timpani (1946). First performance: 15 February 1964, Leningrad. 2. Piano Sonata No. 1 in four parts (movements?) (1947) First performance: 18 December 1973, (*emphasized by S. B.*) Leningrad. And so forth. You can see that no one piece for which Ustvolskaya **could be** accused of "formalism" had ever been performed before February 1948. With this unfair assessment of her work their authors are seeking to raise the status of Ustvolskaya, to make her more elevated, more significant, to add "sanctity" to her. These people do not understand that false statements about person cannot improve the image of her personality, that lies and falsity, if even they cannot always be exposed, always belittle the image of the person they want to flatter. In addition, one, perhaps, single false testimony will make doubtful others, which are true.

The selection committee was listening to me with great seriousness. Only one compact, energetic, and cheerful woman with bangs (later I learned that it was Ustvolskaya) could barely suppress her laughter. I could not even take offense; I was so surprised! Such serious people - not even a smile! But this woman was simply crying with laughter. After I graduated, I reminded Ustvolskaya about her inimitable behavior during my entrance exam and how it intrigued me. She seemed embarrassed and kept repeating: "Is it true? Did I behave like that? Poor Semyon…"

In those years, apart from Galina Ivanovna, composition was taught by Valery Alexandrovich Gavrilin, Vladlen Pavlovich Chistyakov, and Boris Valentinovich Mozhzhevelov, head of the Theory and Composition Department.

For as long as I knew her, I was astonished by her youthfulness. She was of no age.

Once I caught sight of her grey hair. We were both in line at the ticket counter at the Maly (Small) Hall of the Leningrad Philharmonic It was in the spring of 1973, I think. The event was outstanding – Svyatoslav Richter was performing. Galina Ivanovna was ahead of me; not too far, but she did not see me. The line was chaotic, and I was staring at the back of Ustvolskaya's head hoping she would look back and I could say "hello," but she did not turn her head. I kept staring and suddenly I noticed she had grey hair. (Never before or after this incident had I seen gray hair on Galina Ivanovna). Years later, at her house I said something about her amazingly young appearance (by that time we addressed each other in the familiar pronoun "ty".)

!..

"Yes. I am a person without age!" agreed Ustvolskaya.

"But you have grey hair!" I said, remembering my "discovery."

"No, I don't have grey hair," Galya said smiling.

"Yes, you do!" I insisted.

"I do not have grey hair!" Galya continued to smile…

Our conversation started to resemble a Gogolian interlude, but I managed to stop. Almost in time… How naïve I was then!

The impression of youth was reinforced by her almost childish naturalness.*

She was lighthearted, had a profound sense of humor, and could be ironic and sarcastic at times. She was very spontaneous with her students as well. She could make fun of any blunder in a student's work; she could prick student- not maliciously, but seriously enough.

"Semyon, Allegretto is spelled with two "l"'s."

" Right!" - I answer in a hurry to correct the error.

"Of course, it is right," she said smiling, but with some tension in her voice. She then made some other remarks about my work.

"Right," I repeat again, automatically.

"Of course, it is right, Semyon!" The tension was increasing.

"Our Semyon is so extraordinary!" says Galina Ivanovna. "Or, maybe on the contrary?"

"Ordinary?" I asked.

"Uh-huh," says Galina Ivanovna.

This "incident" recalls another interesting episode.

Once, after an exam where I performed well and received a "5" (an equivalent of an "A" – I.B.), Valery Gavrilin called me up and pointed at a place in my score where at the beginning of the line it said *"oboi"* and asked with authority:

-What is this?

I did not understand. Then, Valery Alexandrovich rephrased the question:

"One oboe?"

"Yes, one"

"Oboe," he pronounced weightily and continued:

"And this?"

"?"

---

* Only sometimes was I surprised by her gaze: it was as if someone else was looking through her eyes. A very strange impression.

"One clarinet?"

"One."

"*Cla-ri-net-to. Clarine-tto*; not '*Clarinet-ti*', like you have…"

This unexpected "attack" did not leave a profoundly serious impression on me. They liked my music. I got a good grade. What else? And Gavrilin was right… Ustvolskaya, in whose presence (or, maybe especially *for* her) it happened, seemed a bit hurt.

"Well, this is, you know, nit-picking, I am sorry. His students today performed very poorly, very poorly," she said afterwards when we were alone.

"Speak up. Let us help Tanechka. What shall we do to redeem this forfeit?" - goes the discussion of a student's work.

"Maybe she could compose a fugato here?" someone suggests.

"Figato*…." says Ustvolskaya, scratching her head in contemplation.

"No, this is not for Tanechka. Tanechka, try to compose a short stretto," she says, her face lighting up with a smile. (She had this special, radiant smile - as if she were talking to a child).

"Do you know what a stretto is? Comrades, who knows what a stretto is?" Ustvolskaya asks the class.

"What, does nobody know? Sasha, what does stretto mean?" - She repeats her question to Sasha Kastrov, the full-bodied 4th course student, red haired and shaggy like Gogol's hero Nozdryov. We all giggle nervously. Giggles progress into laughter…

"I know, but I can't explain it," exhaled Sasha, turning bright red from laughter and as if spitting out the words.

"It is, indeed, inexplicable. Like love."

Loud and still nervous laughter heightens beyond any control.

---

* Here Ustvolskaya purposefully mispronounced the word "Fugato" with a reference to the Russian slang-word "figa", which could be interpreted as "nothing" (note by transl.)

Today, Ustvolskaya is strangely giggly. She explains that on her way to school, a bunch of Young Pioneers boarded the streetcar she was in. (It was Young Pioneers' Day, a holiday in the former Soviet Union.)*

"There was a young trumpeter. He blew his trumpet the entire time. So ridiculously he blew…" Galina Ivanovna continued to laugh as she thought of it.

"Ira got music?" asks Galina Ivanovna.

"No… I just got out of bed." Small and plump Ira answers seriously, adjusting her glasses with the index finger.

Students are chuckling.

"Well, that is certainly something to share," says Ustvolskaya, chortling.

The teacher's questions continue.

"What music do you know and like?"

"Shostakovich."

"What, precisely?" Shostakovich can be different, you know. He has «Fonariki» and «Cheriomushki»."†

"The Fifth Symphony," I say.

"More?"

"And the Eleventh…"

INTERLUDE

Galina Ivanovna very often mentioned "Fonariki" ("Flashlights" – I.B.) with irony, as an example of the bad taste. I did not know this song; I only knew that it was written during the war. Intrigued, I went to the audio library and listened to it. It seemed banal, especially compared to the large works of Shostakovich. Of course, if this song

---

*   *The All-Union Pioneer Organization named after V. I. Lenin*, abbreviated as or the *Young Pioneers*, was a mass youth organization of the Soviet Union for children of age 9-15 that existed between 1922 and 2992. Similar to the Scouting organization of the Western world, pioneers learned skills of social cooperation and attended publicly funded camps.

†   "Moskva - Tcheryomushki" - operetta by Shostakovich

were written by a composer-songwriter it would be totally different. It would have to be judged differently.

It is important to understand why the prominent composer of the 20th century Dmitry Shostakovich composed this song and other music of this kind. I shared my thoughts with Solomon Volkov. I called him in New York and asked what he knows about this song. And here is what I learned from him. It turns out that this song was written on commission from the Ensemble of NKVD(!!!) (Peoples Commissariat of Internal Affairs, grandmother of KGB-I.B.) Yes, there was one. And it was organized on the initiative of Lavrenty Beria himself. It did not exist for long, only 1940-1947. The idea behind this ensemble was that it was supposed to "outdo" the famous Alexandrov Song and Dance Company. Invited to work there were: director Sergey Yutkevich, playwright Nikolay Erdman, artist Ryndin and young Yuri Lubimov, future founder, and artistic director of the Theater on Taganka. It is hard to imagine that anyone could refuse such an "offer". Erdman was even freed from a camp. This is how this little song "Fonariki" on the verses by Michail Svetlov came to existence. It was written in 1945 for a show called "Victorious Spring". Incidentally, it was already the third commission to Shostakovich by this group. Did Ustvolskaya know about this?[*]

Shostakovich's own assessment of his operetta Moskva-Tcheremushki is well captured in his letter to Glikman on December 19, 1958:

"Dear Isaak Davidovich,

I am behaving very properly and attending rehearsals for my operetta. I am burning with shame. If you have any thoughts of coming to the first night, I advise you to think again. It is not worth spending time to feast in confidence, all I must tell you.

---

[*]   "I'm staying here to finish the piece for the NKVD Song and Dance Ensemble", letter to Isaak Glikman of 10.14.1942. In the comment to this fragment in Russian edition of these letters (in English version such comment absent) Glikman wrote: ""Probably Dmitry Dmitrievich did not attach much importance to his work, which he worked on in Moscow. Otherwise, he would have called it and briefly described it". *Isaak Glikman, Story of a Friendship: the letters of Dmitry Shostakovich to Isaak Glikman, 1941-1975, transl. Anthony Phillips, (Ithaca, N.Y.: Cornell university Press, 2001, 79; ПИСЬМА К ДРУГУ, Издательство «Композитор», С.-Петерсбург, стр. 47, 48.*

I press your hand warmly.

D. Shostakovich"

"And what classical music have you heard?

"Few good musicians went to city Zhdanov. They mostly played second-rate music."

"Which is that I am curious?"

"Well, Vivaldi for example…"

"Did you hear? Vivaldi, it turns out, is a second-rate composer!"

I am very embarrassed.

"Who is your piano teacher?"

"Baumstein, Gennady Ilych."

"Ah, Genya? Very well. You should take piano very seriously, says Ustvolskaya with great authority."

"Too often composers are out of luck because of their poor piano skills. "Even the talented ones, even the talented," she repeats.

(I should note that Ustvolskaya herself composed without the piano and held optional "table sessions" with her students regularly.)

I received my first "homework assignment."

Ustvolskaya did not assign "homework" in the typical sense. According to her, a student composer should not only fulfill a creative goal, but also be its initiator. Of course, if someone needed a hint, Galina Ivanovna gave one. More often, however, an exchange of ideas took place.

In this case, obviously, I needed some impulse since I was only starting and did not yet know anything at all. Galina Ivanovna never gave prepared "recipes," but she always had an idea about how to direct and organize the research. She seemed to be teaching by not instructing.

"I will ask you to bring me, by next Monday, a polyphonic piece in free form and another one on a folk tune, also in free form. I am

---

*   *Isaak Glikman, Story of a Friendship: the letters of Dmitry Shostakovich to Isaak Glikman, 1941-1975, transl. Anthony Phillips, (Ithaca, N.Y.: Cornell university Press, 2001, 79*

usually at school on Mondays and Thursdays from four o'clock on. On Wednesdays we will be writing at the table - also at four. Write down my phone number. If you have questions, call. Only do not call me, please, at eight in the morning, as Sasha once did."

Plump and red-cheeked, with dense and wild "Nozdryov's" hair and sideburns, the senior student Sasha Kastrov giggled in embarrassment…

I was excited by the lesson, and I left class being charged with my teacher's wonderful energy, but with absolutely no idea how I was going to manage my assignment.

A week flew by. I was in an anxious fever. It was difficult to find the solitude to compose something in the dormitory. To find an empty room during the day at the college was unthinkable. And there was this uneasy feeling of necessity to do whatever I can do (or else I am in trouble), compose anything at all, forgetting the originality. And so, I decided to write down everything that came to mind, just so I could finish my "homework." At least it would be clear that I did not loaf around. I had a thick music book, which I had filled almost completely with writing by the designated Monday.

Galina Ivanovna was sincerely surprised by the amount of work. I played and she was turning the pages, saying:

"Go on… go on… next one… Is that all?"

"No, I have more…"

"Did you use up the whole music book?"

"Uh-huh…"

"Hold on, this once again, please… I will accept this."

"Do you like it… personally?" I asked timidly.

"Well, some things I do not like even in Tchaikovsky. That is not the question. I accept this. It is enough."

Noticing my fussiness, she asked:

"Are you in a hurry?"

"Yes," I say, - I am going to a concert at the Hall at the Finland Railway Station.

"What concert?"

"Shostakovich."

"Do you really like his music so much?"

"Yes."

"Well, it seems to me all is not bad for the beginning. I think it will work".

The concert turned out to be unimpressive. The ensemble of violinists, under direction of Ilia Spielberg, played the Romance from the "Gadfly" and something else of the sort. Choral Poems on the Verses of Revolutionary Poets were performed... The Piano Quintet appealed to me more. I thought, what a strange composer. I came to hear SHOSTAKOVICH but heard Shostakovich.

It turns out, Professor Isaak Glikman was also at this concert. Shostakovich in his letter to Glikman from September 24, 1968, wrote:

"Dear Isaak Davidovich,

My thanks to you for your letter with its description of the concert in the Leningrad Concert Hall. The student choir of the Conservatoire does sing very well, and I am glad that they impressed you." [*]

I hear irony in this letter. To whom or what is it directed?

---

*   Glikman, *Story of a Friendship,* 154

SECOND VARIATION

♫

First Test

I passed my first winter exam with excellence. I am not saying this to brag, but to better explain the dynamic in my relationship with Galina Ivanovna. She was incredibly pleased with me and did not hide it[*].

"The test board asked, Is this really the same Bokman, the one who came to us half a year ago?"- She said with pleasure. I, of course, was also proud. I believed in myself. But my belief had another side. My confidence grew; I befriended with some jolly crowd and began to spend much time in idle conversations, playing cards past midnight, dreaming up all kinds of "projects" that would never be fulfilled, and so on. I did not worry about composing -- there was enough time before the summer examinations. Ustvolskaya sensed this at once. One day, she asked me if I had music, and upon hearing the complacency in my "no", she spoke frankly, without sparing my ego.

"Do you know what snobbery is?"

"No," I said, sensing a trick and starting to feel how my face was getting hot.

"See, you do not know. You are so nice and so curious: who is with whom, who has whom… But am I interested in you? Can I, let us say, talk to you about Remarque or Hemingway and how they are different or similar, and why? And who is Thomas Mann? What do you know about Gauguin and Van Gogh, and their relationship?"

"Well, it is something… some sort of post-impressionism," I said uncertainly.

---

[*]   Almost all these pieces were included in the piano album "Humoresques" which you can listen by YouTube: Simon Bokman "Humoresques" - YouTube

"Not some*thing*, but some*one*. 'Some sort' is unsuitable! You must say 'I don't know'! All those social circles with all those conductors!"

"There is even one stage director," I added.

"Yes, yes... they are certainly the emptiest people, these stage directors! So, precisely this type of friend will not teach you those things! Composers have always been the most educated people of all... Languages must be learned, at least two..." "I am learning"

"Which one, I'm curious?"

"German."

"Let's speak", said Ustvolskaya cheerfully, and she suddenly pronounced some short phrase.

"Was?" I tried to parry off limply.

"Sour kvass",˙ said Ustvolskaya, bursting into laughter.

---

*   Kvass: a traditional Russian beverage (note by transl.)

THIRD VARIATION

About Humor

There is no humor in her music, but her music has a special aesthetics. It is an aesthetics of fire. One does not play game with the fire.

In life she is very witty. Once, I dared to tell her in class that I did not like her Second Sonata (nonsense, of course). Galina Ivanovna, I remember, only shrugged her shoulders, and said: "They did not want to publish it. During the discussion someone asked, «Why quarters? Aren't there other values available?»" She laughed as she told the story. "Then, another one got up to defend me: «I have known her for a long time. She is very skilled and can write not only quarter notes, but eighth, and even sixteenth ones»."

Her expressions are small humorous masterpieces. It is worth memorizing them like aphorisms.

A student brought in a new composition. The music is absolutely "Scriabinesque," hard to distinguish from Scriabin himself.

"Well, what can I say?" pronounced Galina Ivanovna. "Music is here, the author is absent."*

❊ ❊ ❊

"Hurry up, finish this piece. What is there to perch on? This is not the «Queen of Spades», and Tchaikovsky wrote that in forty days…"

---

* Ustvolskaya does not like music of Scriabin. Shostakovich did not like this composer either. According to Maxim Shostakovich, he described Scriabin's music as a mixture of Theosophy and perfumes. *Shostakovich in memories of son Maxim, daughter Galina, and archpriest Michail Ardov. Zakharov,* Moscow, 2003 (Russian edition).

"Galina Ivanovna, do you compose without an instrument?"

"Yes, Olechka. It is notably, isn't it?

"Uh-huh… Really, always? Without an instrument at all?" the maiden asks shyly.

"No, if I'm writing for piano, I have a sit for a bit", smiles Ustvolskaya.

"And what do you write at the moment?" The curious girl student continued her inquiries further but blushing and lowering her eyes.

"Myself about, Olechka… I am writing about myself," says Ustvolskaya, smiling radiantly.

I was leaving for the army and had come to say goodbye. Naturally, I was sad.

"There, in the army, Galina Ivanovna, I'll forget about music and become a bast shoe" *

"You don't look like a bast shoe; more like an *elegant* shoe", objected Galina Ivanovna, pronouncing "elegant" with relish, seriously, but with laughter in her eyes.

"Right, comrades?"

The students agreed and nodded their heads laughing.

I am calling Galina Ivanovna from Kaliningrad. (After I had graduated, I was living there at the time.) She invites me to come to Leningrad. I am hesitant.

"Well, worried about the money? Life is more precious than money."

---

* A Russian idiom implies a simple, uneducated person (note by transl.)

"...They are saying I do not value and do not love anybody besides myself and that I look down on everyone. It is not true. I do not like the fools - that is true; I like the smart and the talented ones!"

However, thinking recently about the music of Ustvolskaya and about music in general, I stumbled over a thought that, indeed, the absence of humor in her music is a unique case in music history, and this puzzled me.

Galina Ivanovna taught that to compose funnily and humorously is not only difficult; it is risky. The discussion had come up because of an idea I had had to compose comic music. "You want to laugh at something or someone," Galina Ivanovna warned, "but in the end, you will be mocked instead."

I am going through the names of prominent composers. Not all of them are humorous and cheery, but at least irony, grotesqueness, or lightheartedness is present in their works. Moreover, *Scherzo* (a joke) has become a traditional movement of a classical symphony; that is, a part of the symphonic cycle, determined by the classical regulations. It seems that, whether you want it or not, if you decide to write a symphony, you must have a sense of humor. Funny? - Not at all. Life is diverse on the outside as well as on the inside. There must be a place for joy. How can one manage without it?

> How often we mourn, I and you,
> Our fates, and their pitiful ways,
> But, friends, if you only knew
> The cold and gloom of future days!*

These prophetic lines of Alexander Blok could serve as an epigraph to Ustvolskaya's music. She is simply unable to rejoice in her music. Why? I have been asking myself this question for a long time. The answer may lie only in the music itself. An artist cannot go against himself and compose something without seeing a need for it. It means that this dark mood and this feeling of despair possess her so much that they overwhelm all other thoughts and moods.

---

*   Alexander Blok (1880-1921), transl. S. Bokman, edit. A. Glaser

Her music is a voluntary constraint and ban she imposes on herself, her life, and her work. It naturally leads to the loss of immediacy and spontaneity. She is not fully in her music and her music is a fight between herself and something invisible, yet extraordinarily strong and dreadful. Who wins? Galina Ivanovna liked to say, "to carry bricks is a thousand times easier than to compose music."*

Carrying bricks, wearing fetters - these are, perhaps, suitable images of what her work is to her.

> But, friends, if you only knew
> The cold and gloom of future days!

A composer thinks about the future, but the sources of their reflections are in the present.

---

*   I'm looking for a comparison between Ustvolskaya and the mythological Sisyphus. Remember, there was a character in Greek mythology who tried to break the laws of existence defined by the Gods: he had to roll a heavy stone on the mountain, while stone, barely reaching the top, rolled down, and do it forever? Ustvolskaya, like Sisyphus, rebelled against the laws of creativity, intending to create stylistically and aesthetically completely new music, moreover, the music which is not life-affirming, which is also contrary to the laws of cosmic construction, and for this, like Sisyphus, was punished by incredibly hard creative work. Ustvolskaya herself talked about composing of music in the same way: Sisyphus' labor! It's simply amazing how she gives herself away with that word expression! She also loved to repeat that the carrying of bricks is easier than composing of music.

FOURTH VARIATION

♪

The Pedagogy

I decided to write a song. Some poetry by a former prisoner of the concentration camp Sachsenhausen was published in a supplement to the "Ogonyok" magazine. My father, who was a prisoner of war, was very touched by one of the poems.

> I will return to you, my Russia,
> To hear the murmur of your forests,
> To see your blue rivers... etc.

He said: "You are a composer. Write music to this poem." (Later on, the songwriter Arkady Ostrovsky, in collaboration with the poet Lev Oshanin*, did write a song based on this poem.) I took my father's request seriously and began composing. I thought it turned into quite a decent Soviet song. And so, I brought it to Ustvolskaya.

"Why did you decide to write this?" was her first question. "Do you feel somehow close to these lines?"

"This is a poem by a prisoner of a concentration camp," I explained.

"So what?"

"My father was a prisoner..."

"Is that so? Your father was in a concentration camp? That is terrible. But Semyon, how can you feel this through your father? Your father, perhaps, could write music to this poem, but not you. I cannot, for example, feel anything through my mother..."

That was my only experience in songwriting.

---

*   Lev Oshanin and Arkady Ostrovsky were a very popular songwriting team in the Soviet Union in the 1960's (note by transl.)

Ustvolskaya often said that she was not a teacher, but she was a brilliant teacher indeed. Without inventing a teaching method, she was a school herself. Possessing such unusually attractive creative energy and charm that made her influence almost hypnotic, she did not let this influence extend too far. She found ways to excite, to ignite, and to provoke interest. She used to say, "What an amazing profession we have!" and pointed to the wall where composers' portraits were hung. "These are, you see, our colleagues - Bach, and Mozart... the wonderfully beautiful Mozart... (It is known that Mozart was not beautiful in life, but somehow in many of his portraits he looks like a dandy) "...and Beethoven..."

Giving someone the task of writing a programmatic piece, she would say: "There is nothing wrong at all with writing program music. So many great composers did it. Grieg, for example, wrote program music all his life. And what about Stravinsky?"

"Tchaikovsky," said someone in the class.

"Yes, Tchaikovsky, that's right, and Glinka, and Mussorgsky..."

Quite often students asked what in modern music she considered to be the most avant-garde and which system one ought to choose for himself. Ustvolskaya would answer invariably: "Do not think about it now. If you have talent, it will stay with you. Meanwhile, it is more important for you to take and to accept. To love or dislike something, one needs to know it. I, for example, do not like Shostakovich. And auntie Manya, my neighbor, does not like him either." (I doubt that she knew her neighbors, even by face.) "But we do not like him for varied reasons. Go, see the 'Golden Cockerel' from the gallery, see 'Boris,' see 'Petrushka'* at the Small Opera House. Be sure to do so. Read the classics."

I remember a conversation between Ustvolskaya and a student who had discovered a compositional system and was working on it. Her music was becoming increasingly monotonous. Ustvolskaya suggested that the student should not be so meticulous.

---

*   Opera by Nikolai Rimsky-Korsakov, "Boris Godunov" by Mussorgsky, Stravinsky's famous ballet. (note by transl.)

"But is it bad if a composer found something of his own?" exclaimed Ira.

"Think about Beethoven," calmly, but weightily said Ustvolskaya, "who said when he was dying that only then did, he understands how to compose."[*]

Students also asked her about serial music, whether it is possible to study the technique and whether she could help with that.

"I can, of course, but why do you need to tie yourselves to any particular system now? Why do you need somebody else's system? Invent your own. I am, you know, inventing my own system," she said smiling. (In my memory, it was the only occurrence when Ustvolskaya referred to her own music.)

"And what about tonal harmony?"

"It had been developing, like a human, from generation to generation. And the time was completely different."

She warned her students against citing folklore and other composer's music. "That is for people who can't write anything on their own," she said. (This was likely a jab at Shostakovich. At least that was how I understood it back then.) However, when I was looking for a theme for my final composition and was in doubt because I wanted to make use of the Schubert's "Organ-grinder," Ustvolskaya somehow cheerfully took the burden from me by saying: "Why not? Stravinsky can – why can't we?"[†]

Having noticed a resemblance between her own music and a student's composition, she strictly remarked that she does not like it when someone writes "like her."

"Shostakovich really liked it when others wrote 'like him,' but I do not" says Ustvolskaya. "Do you know Sviridov's Piano Trio?" she

---

[*]   In this conversation, Ustvolskaya showed pedagogical flexibility and tact. In those years of relative liberalism students' experimentation was not punishable, but it was not encouraged either. In Ustvolskaya's studio, this tendency existed and at one of the exams the student in question received a comment from jury, wishing she would not to get carried away with "formal" techniques which are, in a manner of speaking, for authors who are not so talented, and who use them to mask their incompetence.

[†]   This piece was properly edited in 1994. It is possible to listen to it in YouTube.

continues. "I, honestly, cannot tell it from Shostakovich's Trio. So, Shostakovich praised this Trio a lot.* One must search for his own style. There was such composer, Gurilev†, - do you know his music? He was not Glinka, of course, but still, he went down in music history..."

"Can you work simultaneously on several compositions?" Ustvolskaya unexpectedly asked. (We were walking towards the Composers' Union).

"No," I said.

"I cannot either. Some do two, and even three compositions at once, but I cannot."

I feel proud of her trust and of her "either" ...

My philosophy has changed radically since then and I not only work on different works at the same time, but also on different projects in different activities. This method is very productive. Creative energy is unified, and inspiration can flow from one deed to another one. Just as the fire of one match can ignite a forest, so the creative fire of one act can ignite the lights of others. It is important to catch the rhythm of alternating activities. Thinking never stops. But thoughts should be constantly organized.

Ustvolskaya is not very wordy or eloquent; she does not like twaddle. The terseness of her speech is akin to her music. Her speech is aphoristic, clean, and very competent, devoid of superfluous or strange words. Her diction is clear, proper, and crisp. Sometimes she would lack the words to express certain nuances and would say, apologetically, "I hope you understand me?" Or, speaking about a student's music, "Well, what can be said about it? It may be... or may not be... Do you understand what I am trying to say?"

---

*   Isaac Glikman in his commentary to Shostakovich's letter of January 12, 1946 wrote: "In conversation with me, Shostakovich lavished praise not only on Sviridov's First String Quartet but also his Piano Trio. He did much to obtain a Stalin Prize for the latter in 1946." (Glikman, *Story of a Friendship*, 31)

†   Alexander Gurilev (1803 – 1858), a student of John Field, became a well-known composer of songs and piano pieces, but died in ignominy. Today his songs are still performing in concerts in Russia and they are studiing by the music students. (Note by transl.)

She knows a lot, but she is not an "intellectual." She does not juggle dates and quotations. Her knowledge is not there to flaunt. But she likes to check students sometimes.

"So, the Rubicon has been crossed," she said, meaning that the work has moved out of its "dead point" and started to happen.

"Do you know what the Rubicon is?" she continued.

"It, I think, was a boundary river in ancient Italy that Julius Caesar crossed as he started a war."

"Well done, you do know."

Ustvolskaya is fluent in German and me, wanting to show off, once memorized a large excerpt from an ancient German epic that inspired Richard Wagner. I read it to her. She fervently praised me and my memory, saying: "How could you memorize all of that? This is an Old German dialect!"

I was not modest and said that I thought if I happened to be in Germany, in a month, perhaps, I would speak German fluently. To that Ustvolskaya objected heavily, "Well, no! I would, perhaps, be fluent in a month, but you - hardly!"

She was neat and dressed simply, but very carefully put together her outfits. She wore bright sleeveless dresses with a blouse or a sweater underneath; or blouses and skirts not too short, not too long. She had short hair and bangs. She looked young.

"It doesn't work, I can't write, I don't like what I wrote…" ran a general stream of student complaints to which Ustvolskaya reacted sympathetically. She remarked that it is a normal condition for a composer and "if you like your music for an hour," she said laughing, "then you can keep it."

"One must work constantly. Tchaikovsky said that a composer must compose music regularly, the way a shoemaker stitches the shoes."

From Tchaikovsky's letter to K. K. Romanov*: Ever since I started to compose, I set it as my goal to be in my work like the greatest music masters - Mozart, Beethoven, Schubert - were; that is not to be as great as they were, but to be as they were composers in the manner of shoemakers rather than barons. (Our Glinka, whose genius I, of course, am not going to deny, was an example of the latter.) Mozart, Beethoven, Schubert, Mendelssohn, and Schumann composed their immortal creations absolutely the way a shoemaker stitches his shoes, which is day to day work and, for the most part, made to order. Were Glinka a shoemaker instead of a baron, - instead of his two (although outstanding) operas he would have written fifteen, and in addition to those, some ten symphonies. I am ready to cry with vexation when I think what Glinka would have given us were he not born a noble person before the time of emancipation. [...]. I am irrevocably convinced that a musician, if he wants to realize his potential, should cultivate the craftsman in himself; [...] Rather, for all of this, a significant role is played by our distinct inner creative organization, and that what for one is agreeable, for another does not work at all. Most of my fellow composers, for example, do not like to write on commission; I on the other hand could never be as inspired as when asked to do this or that, when I am given a deadline, when someone anxiously awaits the completion of my work.†

Ustvolskaya, of course, is not an "indolent composer." She may not have many compositions. However, it is not because of laziness, but because of a difficult standard to which she holds herself. Tchaikovsky became inspired when someone was anxiously awaiting the completion of his work. But, of course, one must consider the kind of commission. Tchaikovsky's opera "The Queen of Spades" was commissioned by the Mariinsky Theater and approved by the emperor himself.

And what if no one is awaiting its completion? Moreover, what struggle a creator must undergo simply because he cannot fully share his growing knowledge, talent, and experience. Misunderstanding,

---

*   K.K. Romanoff was a Great Prince and a poet. Tchaikovsky wrote romances to his poetry.

†   P. Tchaikovsky, *The Complete Works*, (Moscow: Musika, 1977), vol. 15b, *Literary Works and Correspondence,* 148-149

cruelty, and crudeness make him suffer no less than physical pain. And one must find energy for creative work.

"…Precisely like a shoemaker, from day to day! You must do paper dirty because of notes and gradually it will become easier to compose." Thus spoke Ustvolskaya for whom composing was painfully difficult.

"Don't be afraid to shorten music, apply surgical procedures," also one of her pieces of advice. She never corrected anything in her students' compositions, but sometimes helped with "surgeries." She said, having heard the music, "So… I think we should perform a surgery. I would cut… (Turns pages) this, (turns again) that… and you could start (turns pages back) there, even from here (points with her finger). Try, play as I said and see what happens…"

After praising me for a good critique of a composition we heard in class, suddenly, completely unexpectedly she turned her praise into reproof. "You judge others so well, 'not in the brow, but straight in the eye'. Why is it that you are not as demanding of yourself as of others, ah, Semyon? Why, if you do understand everything so well, you do not accomplish your job well?"

This was how Ustvolskaya trained self-reliance. She did not try to "endow" students with her knowledge and experience. One had to learn to take it from her.

Once I asked: "How should I understand art? Are there, perhaps, some special qualities for which an artist is appreciated?"

"Ah, go to the Rembrandt room at the Hermitage, look at his paintings, and then in the neighboring rooms see the works of his students and other Dutch contemporaries. You will see a great similarity between those painters and Rembrandt. But something makes them different. What? If you can understand that you will understand the main idea of art."

I rushed to fulfill this "assignment" and very scrupulously investigated all the Rembrandt there was at the Hermitage at the time. I went to the rooms with other paintings of the same era. They were remarkably similar, indeed. I did not understand what it was I had to see and walked and walked about the rooms. I was tired. It was time to go, and I still had not figured it out. Much time passed. To ask Ustvolskaya it felt embarrassing. I returned mentally to that wondrous "task" time to time. The sorrowful image of the blind father embracing his poor prodigal son, kneeling in front of him ragged and exhausted, appeared in front of my eyes repeatedly. There was such deep and sincere repentance in that painting. And what a wonderful, mysterious, and sorrowful image of the old father… This ecumenical parable, so highly and touchingly expressed by Rembrandt, moved me tremendously. And suddenly, I understood: I do not remember anything besides this painting! There is something besides mastery that the artist puts into his work, and not everyone possesses that "something." Art, if it is real, thrills. It is so simple: *art must be thrilling!*

Ustvolskaya never asked me whether I went to the Hermitage or did the other things she suggested; she never asked what I saw and what I understood. Never. That, as I get it, was one of her pedagogical

---

* I've long noticed that it's as if there's some sort of pact among today's more and less successful as well as established composers to ban brightly colored emotional music. A contract of mediocrity?

I wonder and marvel at some of the "innovative" trends in contemporary art: why is throwing pianos on stage in Mozart's "Don Giovanni" is a great thing to do in this production? Why is the music of contemporary composers is so boring? (I can't talk about all of them, but only about those who are widely publicized). Why are modernized opera productions, works of sculpture and painting so ridiculous and meaningless? These trends are become very common and therefore, habitual.

One day, while "browsing" the Internet, I came across a curious document. It's called "THE 45 COMMUNIST GOALS AS READ INTO THE CONGRESSIONAL RECORD, 1963". Personally, I was particularly interested in items: 22, 23 и 25.

22. Continue discrediting American culture by degrading all forms of artistic expression. An American Communist cell was told to "eliminate all good sculpture from parks and buildings, substitute shapeless, awkward and meaningless forms."

23. Control art critics and directors of art museums. "Our plan is to promote ugliness, repulsive, meaningless art."

25. Break down cultural standards of morality by promoting pornography and obscenity in books, magazines, motion pictures, radio, and TV.

It seems to me that the adjective "communist" in this context should be taken symbolically: there is a certain force that influences all life processes not only in America, but all over the World. The coincidence of these processes points to this. (Read the entire document - it's freely available - and evaluate which ideas are global.)

But that power is weakening. This is exactly what the availability of these materials indicates.

principles: not to instruct, but to give direction, following which a student would discover the answer; especially in personal creative work, where a student's personality must emerge fully, his own actions and initiative are important. Students should be able to set a creative problem and work independently toward its resolution. So, in this sense, Ustvolskaya did not have a pedagogical method, (she called methodical pedagogy "handholding.") And there were, indeed, some students who asserted that Ustvolskaya did not teach at all.

Rembrandt, "Return of the Prodigal Son"

FIFTH VARIATION

It is Curious.

She was not the kind of teacher who would wish her students would outgrow her, or the kind of teacher who presented her students with her portrait as a prize for excellent work. It seems to me she could not imagine that anyone could compete with her in composition. This belief in herself and her work, and in this gigantic "I AM," helped her withstand her internal struggles and life's temptations. It is precisely this quality that makes Ustvolskaya so attractive. Are you able to compete with her in creative aspiration, courage, spiritual fortitude, and her faithfulness to her chosen path?! How could she withstand the spiritual terror that prevailed in the country for many years, when everything around her sounded so different?! For a student, her example is absolute. But such fortitude was hard internal work. I know because I saw how sometimes her dissatisfaction broke through in irritation: "Our little Gavrilin is going to Paris. There his music will be very appropriate now among all those matryoshkas and balalaikas," she remarked cuttingly.

"Galina Ivanovna, did the composer Boris Tishchenko study with you?" I asked.

"The composer Boris Tishchenko studied with me," she said teasingly, and I could hear that my question was not very pleasant.

"Why are you asking? Many studied with me..."

"Well, he is such a popular composer..."

"Boris Tishchenko is popular? Kolker is popular! Pozhlakov is popular!" (Leningrad songwriters, popular at the time)

"Well, famous," I clarified.

"Boris Tishchenko is famous?" She exclaimed.

"Pozhlakov is famous! Kolker is famous!"

After a short pause she continued: "He, by the way, used to say that he got everything from me, here, at the college... I went through hell with him. He wrote like Chopin, then like someone else... I wanted to expel him... His mother came... told me how talented he was... in physics, mathematics," recalled Ustvolskaya, nervously shivering. She could not stand dealing with the student's parents.

She sometimes helped some of her former students. I remember at least two incidents when her former students found themselves in critical situations at the conservatory. They went to her for help, and she intervened. One mediocre student got a "three"* on his senior final composition exam. He cried, and Ustvolskaya pitied him and wrote a letter of recommendation to a provincial conservatory.† Not only was he accepted, but he was also looked upon very differently from other students. He eventually built a serious career in that town.

She was a very conscientious, sensitive, and clever teacher. About her absences Ustvolskaya always told in advance, unless she was sick, which was rare. She did not like being late and was angry when other teachers were late. She did not, however, run her studio on an exact schedule. Everybody simply knew that Ustvolskaya is in from four o'clock on. No one knew exactly when she would leave because she would stay as long as was necessary to hear and talk to everyone and answer all the questions. It was different with the "table practices." There everybody had to come at the same time - everyone was given the same theme. How moved she was during those practices! "Quiet... People are creating, writing music," she would say.

She enjoyed her students' accomplishments... if they remained *her* students. It was the joy of watching a child still doing things awkwardly, not yet quite right, but already like a grown-up. But then, later... Could she commend even one of her former students, for exceptional talent, interesting music, or personality? I do not know whether they did not

---

*   An equivalent of a "C" (I.B.)

†   In the Soviet Union, letters of recommendation were issued by a graduation committee to the most successful students. Without such a letter it was virtually impossible to be accepted at the Conservatory. In this case, Ustvolskaya's name played the trick. This was quite an exceptional gesture on her part. (Note by transl.)

exist at all, or simply no longer interested Ustvolskaya. Most of her students went on to continue their studies at the conservatory and became dependent on their new teachers. They were no longer *her* students. And yet, I was surprised and disappointed to read, in a book by O. Gladkova, how Ustvolskaya speaks about her own pedagogical career: "I worked at the music college for a long time, about thirty years, but I taught only to sustain myself and I do not suppose that I trained dozens of famous composers. Those were trained at the conservatory."[†]

Discussing some young Leningrad composers, she once said that could not single anyone out. "Everybody is excited about Banshikov. I do not know. He is talented but untidy and unscrupulous. He does not know how to sort his ideas…"

Was Galina Ivanovna, right? If one measures success by fame and recognition, then yes. (Ustvolskaya never considered fame to be a true criterion of success. Does luck and success always accompany the lives of creatively inquisitive people?) I remember, sometime in the 80's I heard a radio show about the music of Alexander Knaifel, one of the young composers of the 70's. They played oratorios. Something in them was engaging, but to really know and to understand the latest music from the first listening, especially on the static radio, is not easy.

I became acquainted with the music of Gennady Banshikov at the premiere of the opera *"Lubov and Silin"* in 1969. (Solomon Volkov wrote the libretto, based on Kozma Prutkov's plot.) It was an "opera-skit." Despite my skepticism at the time, I could not resist an ecstatic reaction to this play. The plot is full of character and the libretto is witty, but Banshikov's compositional and instrumental creativity and the emotion in his music also deserve admiration. And the stylistic diversity typical of Banshikov was in place there. It was an extraordinarily strong statement.

---

*   O.Gladkova , *Galina Ustvolskaya: Music as an Obsession,* (St.-Petersburg: Musika, 1999), 34

†   Once, no teacher but Ustvolskaya came on time to a composition exam held at the college. This outraged her: "That's how they do everything: work, compose, everything!" I remember one incident when I happened to be late to a meeting at her house. She was very upset and it affected her mood to the very end of my visit. As far as I can remember, it never happened again.

There are examples in music history of how a student in search of his path and in search of an innovative approach becomes more non-traditional, more radical, and bolder than his outstanding teacher. This happened with Balakirev and his students, the infamous "Mighty Five". One of the master's former rebels, Rimsky-Korsakov, turned out to be not a leading innovator, but rather an "unfashionable", and even conservative, composer in comparison to his younger contemporaries. His student Igor Stravinsky was more radical in his creative work.

It is, however, impossible to be much more radical than Ustvolskaya. As a teacher, she knew how to awaken talent. There was a sensation in her personality; it seems as if much was revealed to her, but those revelations were ending in her, and were limited to her creative process, without further continuity or development. This is a strange contradiction of her personality. In truth, however, her philosophy brings an end to all philosophy, and cannot be continued or developed any further. This is why she cannot have disciples. Of course, the evolution of music is not and never can be exhausted. Where must it go from there? – This is the question Galina Ustvolskaya poses to us with her creative work.

SIXTH VARIATION

♪

Music on Commission

Often, in her remarks, she would connect creativity to time. "Now it is impossible to compose one work for thirty years and then be reworking it for another ten years," said Ustvolskaya. "This is a different time." During a class discussion about Bach someone was amazed at how, having a huge family (it seems as if it is well-known that Bach had two wives and twenty children) which he supported, he managed to write so much ingenious music.*

"And he even had finding time for party! The time, however, was different."

Ustvolskaya spoke briefly about the things she knew very well, and it was clear that her knowledge was not merely bookish. Later, I read in one book that a unit of time had different lengths in different eras

---

*   J.S. Bach could hardly afford himself the luxury of spending long periods of time, such as a few years, working on any one composition while, for example, as the Director of Choir and Music in Leipzig he composed a new cantata every week. In literature there is frequently mention of Bach having many offspring - he had twenty children from two wives. And officially that number is correct. We should note, however, that Bach never experienced having all twenty in the household at the same time. His first wife Maria Barbara Bach whom he married in 1707 - she was his cousin - gave birth to seven children, three of whom died as infants, and then ultimately at the time of her death in 1720 there were four in the family: a girl and three boys, two of whom, Wilhelm Friedemann and Philippe Emmanuel, became famous composers, and Philip Emmanuel even surpassed his father's glory. In 1721 Bach married for the second time, to Anna Magdalena Wulken. In 1730 Bach already had seven children - three from his marriage to Anna Magdalena. Of the thirteen children to whom Anna Magdalena gave birth, seven died; at the time of Bach's death "of his twenty children "only" nine were living - five sons and four daughters". (The third son of the first marriage, Bernhard died in 1738). "The eldest son of Anna Magdalena, Gottfried Henrich was of weak intellect".

Albert Schweitzer. JOHANN SEBASTIAN BACH. Volume I, VIII. *Bach in Leipzig,* pp. 144, 145. Dover Publications, Inc, New York

indeed. A comparative analysis of a time scale revealed that our year is shorter than a year in the eighteenth century and even shorter than in the seventeenth.

"Go ahead, learn how to make a form," said Ustvolskaya as she was instructing me to write variations for piano. "It is a 'commission.' Learn to write on commission, or else you will be asked to write for a play, and you will say: 'I don't write this, I only write funeral marches...' In the Union[*] there actually was a composer who only wrote funeral music," Ustvolskaya said to the laughing students. Turning to me again, she continued: "Stravinsky, for example, wrote on commission his whole life…"

…Stravinsky, Bach, Beethoven, and Mozart... Joseph Haydn was a famous commissioned composer, who served the Esterházy family for about thirty years. He was even required to compose music to be played between dinner courses! Through the eighteenth century there was no unordered music in Europe at all and musicians were musical craftsmen and employees (servants, even) of the rich, or the church.

"Haydn was the conductor of the court orchestra for Prince Esterházy, to whom he was under obligation for the entire output of his creative powers; and it is more than a mere symbol that he had to appear at the concerts in Esterház and Eisenstadt dressed in a lackey's costume."[†]

This truly was spiritual serfdom! Undoubtedly, Haydn was a well-to-do man, but imagine a composer as gifted and as acclaimed as Haydn living today. The profits from the sale of his music would bring in billions. Of course, such demand for classical music today is unimaginable. Compared to even the most recent past, interest in spiritual achievement is tremendously low. And, of course, the highly demanding cultural consumption by just a few exceptionally educated and influential people of the 18th and earlier centuries is captivating in its own right.

---

[*]   Composer's Union – S.B.

[†]   *Alfred Einstein Music in the Romantic Era, (New York: W. W .Norton & Company Inc., 1947, 12*

Even Mozart, who became a "free artist" after 1782, did not write music for an imaginary public. He wrote to order "for different kinds of ears, except for the long ones," as he put it.

As A. Einstein writes, "[Mozart] wrote piano concertos so long as society esteemed him as a virtuoso, and ceased to write them when it neglected him; he wrote no operas "for eternity," but only when he had an order for one. In 1785 Anton Klein, a very influential public official in Mannheim, asked him to compose music for one of his libretti; but Mozart refused, if a performance was not assured. All of Mozart's works were pieces written to order or for a definite occasion. Only, it should be noted, the order usually roused his own inner impulse."*

It is commonly believed that the great masters of the past had intelligent and educated patrons with good taste, but was that always so? There was the XIX Century already, and you will see how the world started to be changed step by step. Here is an excerpt from a letter that Beethoven wrote in 1817 to his publisher George Thomson in Edinburgh. The topic was the Beethoven's arrangement of the Scottish folk songs. Beethoven was already the author of eight symphonies and the opera "Fidelio," works that brought him international recognition.

…Is it your request that they be about <u>as easy to execute at the keyboard as the songs already written for you up to now?</u>†‡

With these nineteen airs I shall make up six characteristic overtures with accompaniment of two violins, a viola, and violoncello, or only with a violin and a violoncello according to <u>your taste</u>. As for the seventh overture, which you wish to insert in the collection of Scottish songs, I must know whether it is to be drawn from the Scottish songs themselves, and from which ones. You have doubtless noticed that in all your commissions <u>the pleasure of serving you has transcended my interests</u>, as I have prepared the accompaniments for quartet, trio, or duet <u>at the same price</u> as the solos and <u>the long songs as the short</u>‡

---

*   *Einstein Music In the Romantic Era, p.13*

†   Here and below emphasis by S.B.

‡   *New Beethoven Letters* translated and annotated by Donald W. MacArdle and Ludwig Misch, (University of Oklahoma Press: Norman, 1957), 208-209

Stravinsky said that he most often received commissions for music that he wanted to write. However, the orchestration of "The Rite of Spring" was motivated by the fact that Diaghilev expanded the orchestra and the musicians needed work. Stravinsky did not plan his work for a big orchestra, but it turned out to be a great ballet!

"At this Berlin meeting Diaghilev encouraged me to use a huge orchestra for The Rite of Spring, promising that the size of our ballet orchestra would be greatly increased in the following season. I am not sure that my orchestra would have been as large otherwise." [*]

Arnold Schoenberg, while living in Hollywood, was summoned to write a movie score. He did not decline, but requested a record $50000 "which, to my delight, turned out to be too much, for it would have been the end of me," - he wrote in 1936 to Alma Mahler-Werfel. [†]

> *But if I were somehow to survive the task, I could subsist on this honorarium - at least modestly - for a few years, which would allow me to live to finish at least those compositions and theoretical works that I have already begun...*

And Shostakovich, coquettishly, wrote to Isaak Glikman about his work on movie scores, which he differentiated from his primary compositions.

> *[...]I am working hard, but not composing anything. I hope that this is only a temporary malfunction in my modest and insignificant talent.* [‡]

Ustvolskaya did not like to compose on commission. To please a patron, she, in her own words, "has too somehow please herself." But this was an impossible task. I happened to hear her skeptical opinions about writing for the cinema or theater more than once. I grew ever

---

[*]   *Memories and Commentaries. Igor Stravinsky and Robert Craft, (London: Faber and Faber Limited, 2002, 89*

[†]   Schneyerson, *Articles on Contemporary Foreign Music. Essays. Memoirs. "Arnold Schoenberg – Musician and a Man",* (Moscow: Sovetsky Kompozitor, 1974), 191

[‡]   "Letters to the Friend", letter of January 12, 1946, the publishing house "Kompozitor", St.-Petersburg, 1993, p.72 (Russian).

more convinced that it was something indecent and secondary. To a certain degree it is so, but composing is also a craft (see above what G.U. said about it herself) and it is a paid job.

In her monograph of Ustvolskaya, Gladkova writes: "Ustvolskaya could write easy and engaging music (her early compositions which were not included in the Catalogue speak for themselves), but she did not strive for this," (as if she purposefully wrote music that was difficult and non-engaging! – S.B.) "She did not take commissions; she preferred to live inconspicuously and in poverty (?!)"*

How inspiring! Has this been read by Ustvolskaya?

To support her words, Gladkova quotes Shostakovich's letter to Glikman where he mentions Ustvolskaya as one of the potential authors for a commissioned movie score. Shostakovich writes, "I don't think that Ustvolskaya would be able to please the director of the film." The quote is followed by Gladkova's commentary: "In her life, Ustvolskaya did not know how to "please" anyone and, frankly, never wished to do so."

But this is not about servility! Incidentally, Ustvolskaya loved to repeat Tchaikovsky's phrase that a composer should write music just as a shoemaker makes shoes – regularly, day to day. This comparison is also valid in a different aspect: if a shoemaker makes his shoes for a customer, he should *want* to please the customer. And how, may I ask, can this be different? What customer would prefer a creative approach to his order?

But, even more importantly, Shostakovich meant something quite different in his letter. It is apparent if one quotes letter in a broader context:

"The important thing when writing music for a film is that composer and director should be soulmates. [...] I do not think that Ustvolskaya would be able to give the director of the film what he needs, although she does need to earn some money. However philosophical one's attitude to poverty is, in the end it becomes unbearable. I have never considered either self-deprecation or self-aggrandizement to be valuable personal qualities."

---

*   O. Gladkova, *Galina Ustvolskaya*, 42

In his commentary to this letter Glikman writes: "Galina Ustvolskaya was at the time living in exceedingly difficult [financial] straits. Her refusal to participate in the film stemmed from a degree of innate modesty almost self-abnegation."[*]

Exaggeration serves no good purpose:

> "For my part, I would like to say: never, at any time, even during the academic years at the Conservatory, which I spent in the class of Dmitry Dmitrievich, was his music not close to me, as well as the personality of Dmitry Dmitrievich. I would say more harshly: I did not accept his music, as in subsequent years, and, unfortunately, the very personality of Dmitriy Dmitrievich only aggravated my heavy, negative attitude to him. I do not think it is necessary to write in detail on this subject".
>
> -G. Ustvolskaya, January 1994, fragment of the article "Galina Ustvolskaya and Shostakovich", the Internet.

I told Galina Ivanovna how I almost received a commission to write music for a play. "Luckily, it did not work out," I said; to which Galina Ivanovna unexpectedly cheerfully said: "Too bad, you could have earned some money." She then remembered how she wrote music for a scientific film and received an unbelievable sum of money before the 1961 reforms – 30 000 rubles. Much later, she was suddenly asked to come to the studio again to receive an honorarium. "I thought it was a mistake, but it turned out that they translated the film into Mongolian and repeated the payment. "I spent almost all of that money on the taxi," she remembered with pleasure[†].

---

[*]   Glikman, *Story of a Friendship,* 87, 274

[†]   I should mention to the reader that in the former USSR back in the late fifties (1959-60, around that time) when Ustvolskaya got such honorarium personal car prices were around:

Moskvich-401 - 9 000 rubles,
Moskvich--402 - 15 000 rubles,
Moskvich--407 - 25 000 - 27 000 rubles.
GAZ M20B Победа ("Victory")- 16 000 rubles

It would have been too expensive for Russian "middle class" then, and very few people had the means to buy a personal car, almost nobody.

Undoubtedly, different composers are different people with different personalities, and what is unacceptable for one is decent, natural, and normal for another. ("What is good for a German is death for a Russian" goes a Russian proverb.) There is still a common belief that ballet music is applied music and not a serious art. Igor Stravinsky proved otherwise and did so convincingly. Verdi wrote operas. Chopin was the "poet of the piano…" There is no reason to fault them for this. Every artist paints the world—a world that could not be painted with a single color -- in his own manner. However, could Ustvolskaya talk to a patron the way Beethoven did? (Beethoven, who was known as harsh, proud, independent, and uncompromising.) Undoubtedly, she could not.

"…Compose a simple and clear theme with five or six variations. Do you know what it is? The theme, perhaps, be a single voice…"

I started thinking.

"I like your theme," said Ustvolskaya when it was done, "only it is too difficult for variations. I do not know how you are going to write on it." And I did not know myself. I struggled with it. When I came to class Ustvolskaya asked:

"Got any music?"

"No, I said."

"You try and compose another theme? This is a difficult one, although it is possible to work with it. I could write twenty or thirty variations. But for you, it is a bit like the labor of Sisyphus. You have to learn to do yourself some slack. I personally do same myself sometimes, too."

"I can't compose another theme and I don't know what to do with this one," I confessed, frankly.

A semester went by. A catastrophe was brewing. I came to the exam without music. Ustvolskaya explained to the jury that I worked a lot, watched, listened, and even read, and that I was, obviously, overwhelmed with information; but that she was confident that these difficulties were temporary, and I would work everything out. The jury listened to her and gave me a suspended "four"* for inner growth. But the problem

---

*   An equivalent of a "B" (note by transl.)

remained. Before the school break Ustvolskaya said to me: "Look, I am not a teacher. I can, of course, point out different composers' works, and you can "spy" on them to figure out how to do this. But I will not do that. There is a composer Yevlakhov* at the conservatory. He shows his students Beethoven's sonatas in class. He is already sixty years old, and he *still* teaches this way... Dmitri Dmitrievich† said: 'We do strange things.' Yes, strange things... keep searching."

And I, as I usually did after such conversations with Ustvolskaya, rushed to "search," electrified and excited...

I was extremely nervous and decided to stay in Leningrad for the winter holidays. I called my parents in Kyiv, informing them of my decision. They were terribly upset, but what was to be done? The axe of expulsion from the school hung over me.

I was alone in an empty room with two naked beds and in a half-empty dormitory, which, due to renovations, smelled of paint and of whitewash. Sometimes fragments of conversations echoed through the long and resounding corridor, someone's footsteps approached and receded...

I actually tried to "spy" on Beethoven and Stravinsky - things seemed to have come to a standstill. Once I stepped out to smoke and met Volodya Kitayev, a theory major who was a year ahead of me. He was surprised and glad that I had not left for vacation. (He grew up in an orphanage and had nowhere to go.) I told him of my sorrows, as they say in Russian fairytales. And what do you think? Volodya recounted an episode from Glinka's autobiographical 'Notes' (a book I had not yet read), which had to do with Glinka's studies with Dehn. Dehn had given Glinka a long theme for a fugue and Glinka could not work it out. "Then Dehn showed Glinka how Handel developed this theme. Rather than using the whole theme, he had extracted a fragment," Volodya told me.

---

*   Evlahkov, Orest Alexandrovich. Warsaw, 17 Jan 1912 - Leningrad, 15 Dec 1973). Russian composer and teacher. He graduated from the Leningrad Music Technical School in 1936 as a pupil of Ryazanov, and from the Leningrad Conservatory in 1941 as a pupil of Shostakovich. In May 1941 he made his début as a composer with the Piano Concerto, performed by Moisey Khalfin and the Leningrad PO. He was appointed in 1947 to teach.

†   Shostakovich (note by transl.)

How everything turned and transformed in my head! The following week I wrote four variations and hurried to call Ustvolskaya*. She received me at home. She praised my persistence and asked what else I was doing.

"Reading"

"Whom?"

"Leskov."†

"Good writer."

INTERLUDE

I continue to contemplate the strange, little known, difficult to understand, but significant phenomenon - the COMPOSER USTVOLSKAYA. Working on this book, I began to understand what my own creativity should be, in what direction I should go.

---

*   These Variations later became the first movement of the Sonatina, which I later composed, already in the second year of school. Subsequently, this Sonatina was seriously edited by me, and when Igor Stravinsky left this world in April 1971, I dedicated this music to his memory. It can be heard in the U-tube in my performance.

†   Nikolay Semenovich Leskov (1831-1895), Russian story teller, novelist, and journalist; also wrote under pseudonym of M. Stebnitskii. Shostakovich's ill-famed opera "Lady Macbeth of Mtsensk District" is based on Leskov's story. (Note by transl.)

SEVENTH VARIATION

♪

Jubilee

Under conditions of total coercion, the conscious is stifled and, due to an inner sensor or survival instinct, never really allowed to open and reveal itself. In an artist, if he/she is honest, inner disagreement with the system and refusal to obey it results in isolation and, therefore, in building his/her own system in life and in art.

We were approaching 1970. In keeping with the "Highest Orders" the country was preparing to celebrate the 100th birthday of Vladimir Lenin. Creative and artistic unions were preparing for the event. The conservatory and the college were naturally involved and "set into motion." Once, Ustvolskaya announced that we, the students of her studio, must take part in the composers' contest dedicated to the occasion. "It would be better, perhaps, to use a text," she suggested. "Look in the papers. Sometimes you can find poetry there that is not bad."

I did not take this assignment seriously. Ustvolskaya, however, asked me and other students every week to tell her about what was being prepared "for Lenin." I sensed (by then I understood her a little) that all this "Lenin-mania" was not particularly to her liking. Once, in reply to her question I asked, smiling, "Are you writing as well?" Unexpectedly, Ustvolskaya answered rigidly "*WE* are not you! You are a student!" I felt ashamed, but she, I think, was a little frightened that rumors about her students (and, by extension, herself) sabotaging such an "important" event would go where they should not. The same day I rushed to the public library on the Fontanka river to find a text. I found a poem by Ilia Erenburg* that left me dumbfounded.

---

*   Erenburg, Ilia (1891-1967), Russian/Soviet writer, publicist, and poet. Although he began as a poet, he became most famous for his prose.

On the Boloto stands Moscow. Waiting.
It wants to join the ferocious killing.
They must endure as on a Great Thursday.
Noisy roosters already crow,
Horses' urine has yellowed the snow,
The air is thick with bonfire smoke.
From churches a gloomy buzz is emanating,
Women are waiting, waiting…*

The poem was called "Pugach's Blood." Ustvolskaya admired the text but doubted that it was suited for the occasion. "How do you find such texts? I would write to this myself!" "Go ahead and write, please," I offered magnanimously. "Thank you, Semyon. 'I have my own whiskers'†." (She often noted my ability to find good texts. I did not yet know then that I would someday write poetry). I told her about my idea, and that I wanted to set it for a female voice.

"Which one?"

"Soprano"

"Maybe a man's voice would better suit this text?"

"No, soprano, I think, will be better. Also, I want an oboe, piano, and choir… a men's choir. I can show you the oboe part right now and some bits of the piano part."

"Well, I don't know," said Ustvolskaya after listening to fragments of yet uncomposed music.

"It is hard to understand it that way. And you yourself, it seems to me, do not yet understand what you want to do, although I like your oboe… Comrades, what else might we say here? We have some sketches. And does he have enough mastery? How can we redeem this forfeit?" she asked, smiling, turning to the class. It was obvious she was not angry with me.

---

*   Translated by I. Behrendt, A. Glaser, A. Zeyliger

†   A Russian idiom implying "I am quite capable myself" (note by transl.)

71

INTERLUDE

Nikolay Uspensky's *Samples of Old Russian Singing Art** was published in 1968 and Ustvolskaya's Twelve Preludes† were published the same year. I bought both editions simultaneously at "Rhapsody," a sheet-music shop on Nevsky Prospect. In modern notation, Old Russian chants look just like Ustvolskaya's notation. This similarity and the simultaneity of their appearance bothered me. Eventually, I dared to ask Galina Ivanovna whether she was inspired by the Old Russian music and borrowed from it her system of notation, particularly for the Preludes. She answered that she arrived at it differently.

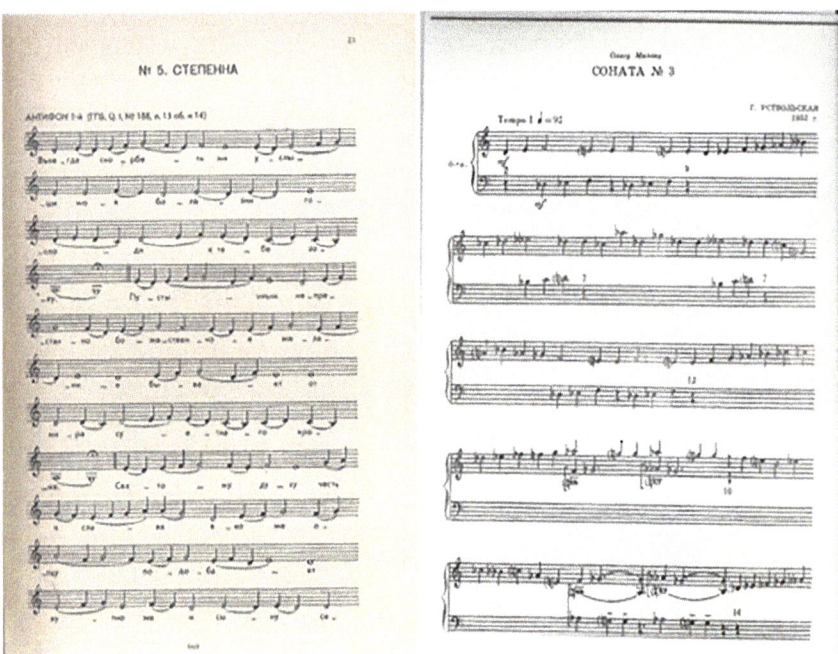

A page from the book "Samples of Old Russian Singing Art" by Nikolai Uspensky and a page from the Third Sonata by Ustvolskaya. There are similarities between these fragments, although the distance between them is several centuries. This Sonata is dedicated to Oleg Malov.

---

* N. Uspensky, *Samples of Old Russian Singing Art*, (Образцы Древнерусского певческого искусства), (Musika: Leningrad, 1968).

† Ustvolskaya, *Twelve Preludes for Piano,* (Musika: Leningrad, 1968).

In their "ancient" modality, some of the preludes actually resemble the old Znamenny chants.[*] The American pianist Maryann Lee declares that Ustvolskaya built her "spiritual style" and her special notation system based on the Znamenny chant.[†] I can neither argue nor support this statement. I simply do not know, although I do understand that every new discovery is based on something.

Ustvolskaya's music is not religious and does not fit into a single genre. But in its asceticism and sternness, it is undoubtedly closer to the Russian orthodox tradition than, for example, to the traditions of the Catholic Church. I do not believe in happenstance and am convinced that every incident is consequential and preconditioned, but we do not always consciously recognize it. And while the simultaneous publication of the two works in the same place proves no logical succession, the coincidence hints at a certain relationship between the two. I also know, however, what creative intuition is and what amazing discoveries can be made with its help. Creative work is such a mysterious process! It can reflect the most unexpected and sometimes contradictory tendencies, be they momentous or rather stable. It is a complex mixture, an alloy of something comprehensible to no one; at times, the artist himself is unable to fathom his creation, having received it from on high.

Is Ustvolskaya religious? She does not practice any religion. However, she undoubtedly believes in some Higher Power, which she calls the Spirit. (It seems to me; she does not call it God because it is a religious term; and to say "I believe in God" would attest to being religious.) Her faith, though, as it is refracted in her music, contains a fear of the Superior, of the "world to come" and of the unknown. Her supplications for Forgiveness, Serenity, and Grace are remarkably close to the Russian orthodox tradition, which portrays God as a menacing and punishing judge. Punishment is for sinners, of course, but who is sinless?

---

[*] A particular type of Russian chant, slow moving and lengthy. Its name derived from the old Russian word for "sign" – "znamya". It was originally written down using a series of signs above the liturgical text. (note by transl.)

[†] Lee, Marian. *"Galina Ustvolskaya: The Spiritual Works of a Soviet Artist."* Ph. D.diss., (Peabody Conservatory of Music, 2002)

In the Soviet Union, the church was officially separate from the state, according to the Constitution. However, everyone living in the country knew that in reality religion was prohibited. A religious citizen could not build a serious career, study at a prestigious institution, or find a decent job. Houses of worship were under close surveillance. During religious holidays, they were patrolled by the police and KGB agents. Nevertheless, despite prohibition, interest in religion and religious symbolism was growing. In the seventies, many young people began attending churches and synagogues, especially during holidays. Naturally, the authorities did not accept this. Raids took place. Activists from the "conscientious youth[*]" under the direction of "senior comrades[†]" came to churches to reveal "those, who lack political consciousness" and put their names onto special lists.

The large-scale movement toward religion was not, however, a discovery of faith, at least for the majority. It was an expression of protest, freedom of thought, disagreement with the system, and the rule of Soviet ideology. Ustvolskaya's spiritual works, apart from her special connection with God, are an expression of inner protest. (The score of the Composition "Dona Nobis Pacem," for example, could not be published with such a subtitle.) They are a challenge to the system, a reaction to oppression. Such art could only appear under the conditions of the Soviet Union. Imagine an American composer who writes spiritual music. (It does not matter whether it is religious or not.) Would it be a sensation?

---

[*]   A sarcastic reference to the young people, who worked for the regime. (note by transl.)

[†]   KGB agents (note by transl.)

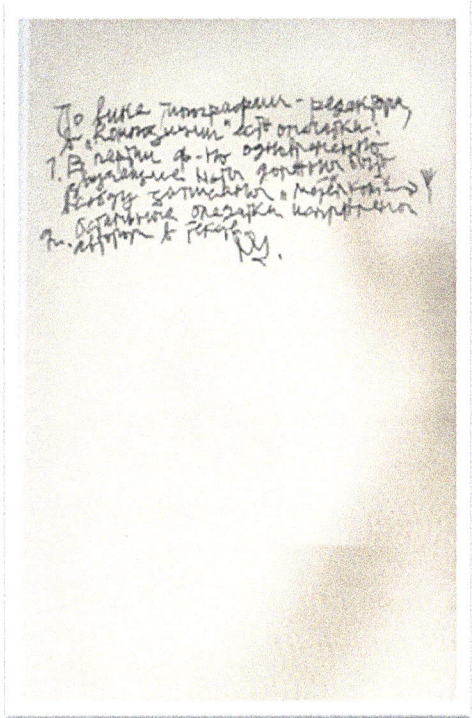

Translation:

"Due to the fault of the printing House and editor, there are misprints in the Composition: In the piano part, the notes that sound at the same time must be written everywhere as the "brush". Other typos corrected by the author in the text." G.U. The editor of the Composition was Vadim Veselov. When Galya was inscribed this score music for me, she used to say irritably: "Why did the editor make such a mess of it?!"(...) "I won't work with Veselov anymore!"

Translation:

"To Senya – Galya". Date in Russian manner: 22.II.78. As you can see, Composition "Dona nobis Pacem" ("Grant us Piece") was published without this title.

EIGHTH VARIATION

♩

Shostakovich

I am staggered by Ustvolskaya's spiritual fortitude. One must have enormous courage and faith to choose such a difficult and unique path. But there were, perhaps, people in her life who sympathized with her, helped, and supported her...

Attempts to speak about Shostakovich with Galina Ivanovna were unsuccessful. It was not a "forbidden topic," but any question, remark, or phrase, containing his name, was interrupted by a dismissive hand gesture and a phrase "Ah, this is not interesting" or "why are you interested in this?" I felt embarrassed about my curiosity – really, why am I interested? So, I taught myself not to bring it up again. It became natural.

Although the presence of Ustvolskaya's music in my life was rather insignificant, her uncompromising personality and her conviction ...were fascinating and captivated me. Shostakovich, on the other hand, was widely performed and propagandized, but the way I saw it back then, he seemed entirely compromised.

His official status in the country was, I think, one of many trials in the composer's life. Stalin's regime with its decrees and harsh critique of Shostakovich's music perpetually threatened the composer's life, but at the same time elevated his "ratings" as an *artist – intelligent* in the eyes of the intellectuals of society. His rehabilitation, on the other hand, provoked suspicion. It was a different era. The generation that had lived under Stalin had grown old, many had passed away, and the youth of the 60s-70s looked at things differently - who knew what was really happening back then? Even Muradeli have been implicated, as well as many others, so it is not because Shostakovich was so original, Stalin simply gave free rein to his rage. Moreover, Shostakovich made things far more complicated by composing official works. People called him the "Court Composer of the Central Committee." It is only now, after several books have been published containing documents about the true reasons and circumstances in which certain works were composed (e.g. Glikman's *Story of a Friendship, or* Volkov's *Shostakovich and Stalin*) that one begins to understand in what a monstrous atmosphere and under what terrible circumstances this man was saving his work. Much has been revealed that we did not know. Besides, for several years he held important positions, was a deputy and gave public speeches. In other words, he was a semi-official figure. His music did not seem to me progressive and daring enough. But every so often, Ustvolskaya would say something that showed her inner connection with Shostakovich, which was quite painful. When I, "no longer a student," asked her, "no longer a teacher," to listen to my music and to help with advice, she answered ironically, with a question: "And who should I show mine to? You see, even Dmitry Dmitrievich* is no longer a judge of it..."

Once, Galina Ivanovna assigned the "invasion theme" from Shostakovich's Seventh's Symphony as a theme for our "table practice." Some amusing "knick-knacks" came out and we all had great fun.

Ustvolskaya is cited in Gladkova's monograph as having said something fascinating about Shostakovich's *Seventh Symphony*:

"Once in 1939-40, Shostakovich visited me and told me that he had almost finished the Seventh Symphony. He needed to finish writing the coda and to correct some things; he mentioned that he did not know what the best way was to name it: 'The Lenin Symphony' or 'Lenin's Symphony' – Dmitry Dmitrievich respected V.I. Lenin very much and had always wanted to dedicate one of his compositions to him."†

It turns out that the symphony, which is known under the title "Leningrad" was almost completely written before the war. Shostakovich wanted to dedicate it to Lenin and Ustvolskaya viewed this critically. But to understand this fact completely, one must understand that during those frightful years, for those who disagreed with Stalinism, "Lenin's" meant "not Stalin's." Knowing this original idea, one can

---

*   Shostakovich (I. B.)

†   Gladkova, *Galina Ustvolskaya,*.31

perceive the Symphony as anti-tyrannical, although it does not cease to be the symbol of the Leningrad Siege and World War II for Russians. Here is what Shostakovich says about it himself:

"'The Seventh Symphony' had been planned before the war and consequently it simply cannot be seen as a reaction to Hitler's attack. The 'invasion theme' has nothing to do with the attack. I was thinking of other enemies of humanity when I composed the theme.

"Naturally, fascism is repugnant to me, but not only German fascism, but any form of it is also repugnant. Nowadays people like to recall the prewar period as an idyllic time, saying that everything was fine until Hitler bothered us. Hitler is a criminal, that is clear, but so is Stalin.

"I feel eternal pain for those who were killed by Hitler, but I feel no less pain for those killed on Stalin's orders. I suffer for everyone who was tortured, shot, or starved to death. There were millions of them in our country before the war with Hitler began.

"The war brought much new sorrow and much new essence destruction, but I have not forgotten the terrible prewar years. That is what all my symphonies, beginning with the Fourth, are about, including the Seventh and Eighth.

"Actually, I have nothing against calling the Seventh the Leningrad Symphony, but it's not about Leningrad under siege, it's about the Leningrad that Stalin destroyed, and that Hitler merely finished off.'"[*]

Ustvolskaya told me how, when she learned that Shostakovich had joined the Party, she tore his portrait into pieces (Shostakovich's present to her) and flushed it down the toilet. "So, perhaps he believes in it," I suggested. "That is right! He is an old man now and believes in *all that*!"

Professor Isaak Glikman writes that when he visited Shostakovich in the hospital where he was recovering after breaking his leg, he was struck by hearing Shostakovich say several times: "Probably God is punishing me for my sins, for instance, joining the Party." Shostakovich considered his joining the Party to be a downfall. Glikman writes about it in detail in the commentary to Shostakovich's letter of July 19, 1960. "The utter fearlessness Shostakovich exhibited in his creative and artistic life coexisted with the fear Stalin's terror had bred in him. Small wonder that, caught in the toils of years of spiritual enslavement, in his autobiographical Eighth Quartet Shostakovich gave such dramatic

---

[*]   Solomon Volkov *"Testimony. Memoirs of Dmitriy Shostakovich"*, New York: Sixth Limelight Edition , 1999, 155-156

and heart-rending voice to the melody of the song 'Was killed by the hardness of bondage'."*

So, what kind of a person was Dmitri Shostakovich in reality? Was he the "conscience of the epoch" or a hidden dissident? Was he a communist idealist, who was forced to join a Party that committed violence, but a true believer in idealized communism? Was perhaps Ustvolskaya not so wrong in saying that "he believes in all that"? (He has wanted to dedicate his Seventh symphony, which he had begun composing before the war, to Lenin, but we should aware that on this time in the mind of people who hated Stalinism Lenin was a symbol of struggle against Stalin!) Was he adjusting to the situation by composing his Eleventh and Twelfth symphonies and his Ten Choral Poems on Verses by Revolutionary Poets? It seems to me, none of the above. I also think that no one really knew the true Shostakovich, because he was too closed to the outside world. (And did he know himself?) Therefore, the assessments of him made by different people are equally fair and unfair. He lived a frightening, but creatively full life and suffered most of all from the underutilizing of his composer's energy. Maybe this was the reason for his mysterious disease: severely traumatized mentally, he lost control over his body. He is a martyr and an idol of his time, and I admire him and sympathize with him. I can say this now, however, but back then…

On the walls of the college hallways hung composers' portraits; all good-looking, hair neatly combed, with an illustrious saying under each of them. For a few years, I walked by those portraits many times daily and read: Mussorgsky: (…) truth, no matter how bitter; bold, sincere speech with people—these are my leaven, these are what I want, this is where I am afraid of missing the mark." (And he really had not "missing the mark."!) Glinka: "Music is created by the people and we, composers, are only arranging it." (This is my favorite saying when I am arranging someone else's music.) Under Shostakovich were the words: "People need all kinds of music – from a simple song to Beethoven's sonatas."

"…Is it really necessary to try yourself in everything and leave your trace everywhere?" says Ustvolskaya of Shostakovich. "Once, Soloviev-

---

*   Glikman, *Story of a Friendship,* note 36. p. 93

Sedoy* said to me: 'It is a hundred times more difficult to write a song than your stupid symphony because everybody will sing the song!!' OK, I will not argue, but why is it 'stupid'? I wonder whether I could write a song? No, perhaps not...Or maybe I could write something, after all?" says Galina Ivanovna pensively.

"One day I am walking down the street and see a poster. In big letters it reads: **'KHOVANSHINA,'** then in smaller letters, but still quite large: **'Shostakovich.'** I am all confused. I come closer and read: **'Laureate of the Lenin prize, Hero of the Soviet Union...'"**

"Socialist Labor," I correct her.

"What is the difference?! I then read, **'Artist of the People'** and only after that, in exceedingly small letters, **'Mussorgsky.'** Now I understand: this is Mussorgsky's Khovanshina, edited by Shostakovich. As if poor Mussorgsky had not already been edited so much that we do not really know him at all; but couldn't they, at least, print his name properly?"

I saw that poster on Matveev Pereulok. (Matveev Lane).

About the cycle "From Jewish Poetry"

"The Jewish public is sobbing during the performance of this music. SOBBING! But is it good to have this provincial flavor?"

"Mahler did it too," I remark.

"But not like that, not like that." Ustvolskaya is saying fervently.

"And is it good for the Jews that it's written LIKE THAT?"

"The Jewish theme, like a red thread, embroiders all of his work; like a red thread..."

"Why?" I asked.

"I don't know, I don't know," said Galina Ivanovna.

"I can, of course, *assume*..."

What exactly she could assume I never found out. I received an explanation from none other than Shostakovich himself:

"I think, if we speak of musical impressions, that Jewish folk music has made the most powerful impression on me. I never tire of delighting

---

*   Vassily Soloviev-Sedoy, popular Soviet songwriter

in it, it is multifaceted, it can appear to be happy while it is tragic. It is almost always laughter through tears.

"This quality of Jewish folk music is close to my idea of what music should be. There should always be two layers of music. Jews were tormented for so long that they learned to hide their despair. They express despair [through] dance music.

"All folk music is lovely, but I can say that Jewish folk music is unique. Many composers listened to it, including Russian composers, Mussorgsky, for instance. He carefully set down Jewish folk songs. Many of my works reflect my impressions of Jewish music.

"This is not a purely musical issue; this is also a moral issue. I often test a person by his attitude toward Jews. In our day and age, any person with pretensions of decency cannot be anti-Semitic."[*]

In her book *Amazing Shostakovich,*[†] Sophia Khentova mentions Shostakovich' relation to Vladimir Lenin through his mother Maria Alexandrovna Blank, whose father was a Jew. This may be precisely what Galina Ivanovna was alluding to when she said, "I can, of course assume…" Ustvolskaya is not antisemitic. She is an anti-Shostakovich. And the style of her music is anti-Shostakovich to a certain extent. But, in the process of refuting Shostakovich through her work, Ustvolskaya is paradoxically continuing and developing his style, because she builds her denial on his music.

By denying Shostakovich, Ustvolskaya continues his tradition in her own way because her denial is based on his work!

I did not know anything about Ustvolskaya and Shostakovich's relationship during my student years. Today, some of her statements sound to me like repercussions of her disagreements with the former teacher. A relationship can get in the way of clear perception and overshadow the personalities; for many years, my perception of Shostakovich was overshadowed by Ustvolskaya's.

After the première of Shostakovich's Fourteenth Symphony on October 1, 1969, in the hall of Leningrad Capella, we had a class

---

[*]   S.Volkov *Testimony,* 156-157

[†]   *Amazing Shostakovich,* Variant: St.-Petersburg, 1993,p.21

discussion. Almost everyone had been to the concert. We, the men in the class, were judging the work very strictly. Ustvolskaya even observed that: "The boys are judging it very harshly. But could you do something similar? It is a symphony, after all, a large work..." (Now I understand that our perception was unwillingly preconditioned by Galina Ivanovna's attitude towards the author of the symphony. Perception can be manipulated.)

-...It does matter to Shostakovich what others say about him. Any opinion is important to him, regardless of who it comes from; you, or any other person from the street. He hears, of course, they say he is old and has outwritten himself. So, he puts out a whole battery of percussion just to be a bit more contemporary, a bit trendy. I, personally, dislike this very idea: 'No, not all of me will die..." ("Why can Pushkin say this, but Shostakovich can't?" I think now.) ...there is an eclectic choice of texts... And when after the performance, limping suffering author with a cane himself approaches the stage and making a bow, so of course, there are wild applauses...

I did not know about the terrible disease of Shostakovich. Ustvolskaya, I think, must have known. In this context her statement is even more shocking.

INTERLUDE

How did Galina Ustvolskaya begin her career as a composer? Was she ever a beginner? (Once, I asked Galina Ivanovna about it. She made a scabrous joke but did not answer the question.) Who were the musical and non-musical heroes and idols of her childhood and youth? Who had the most noteworthy influence on her? How were her views and opinions formed? Who were her favorite and least favorite teachers, in life and in music? I hoped to receive the answers to O. Gladkova's monograph on Ustvolskaya.[†] But the book does not answer these important questions because Ustvolskaya herself does not offer any answers. To me, Gladkova's book is valuable primarily because, in what

---

[*] Ustvolskaya is ironically referring to the famous poem by Alexander Pushkin, "Memorial" (note by transl.)

[†] O.Gladkova, *Galina Ustvolskaya – Music as an Obsession*, (Musika: St.-Petersburg, 1999).

is written (and what is not) I can clearly see Ustvolskaya's personality the way I remember her. It is interesting that in Gladkova's monograph, the chapter about Ustvolskaya and Shostakovich's relationship, which quotes Victor Suslin's slanderous letter about Shostakovich to Ustvolskaya is followed by the chapter about Ustvolskaya's Octet. Shostakovich left the hall after the performance of Ustvolskaya's Octet because the piece had such a strong effect on him that he could not listen to the second half of the concert. Shostakovich's authority is a serious argument: Shostakovich himself left the hall?! Gladkova refers to Sophia Khentova's book, *Amazing Shostakovich*. The wonderful pianist Maria Karandashova, who participated in that performance, also told this story to her students.

Suslin wrote in the aforementioned letter that "not every student can brag that a teacher uses his themes in his compositions," purposefully neglecting the fact that by doing so, the great composer gave credibility to young Galia Ustvolskaya, who was then just beginning her path. Suslin's letter betrays his clear desire to please Ustvolskaya. But one should not please anyone by discarding the truth. Galina Ivanovna, who hates servility, should have been an example for Mr. Suslin.

Below are fragments of letters from Dmitry Shostakovich, the teacher of Ustvolskaya to his student, Boris Tishchenko, who was also a student of Galina Ustvolskaya. Bright memory to all of them...

---

*   *Amazing Shostakovich,* Variant: St.-Petersburg, 1993

17.IV.1970

Dear Borya!

[...] I read with intense pleasure your admiration of the Trio of Ustvolskaya and admiration for her works. I know and love her Trio, the Violin Sonata, the Twelve Preludes, and many other works. A. K. Lyadov (composer) once said: "Pushkin is a great phenomenon. Someday the entire world will say so" (I quote, perhaps, not very precisely). I believe that Ustvolskaya's creative work will gain worldwide recognition for everyone who cares about real music. [...]

Yours D. Shostakovich

9.II.1971. Moscow.

Dear Borya!

[...] Yesterday in the House of Composers was the Leningrad concert. I listened to the first section, i.e., the Second Violin Sonata of Prigozhin, the vocal works of Arkhimandritov and Octet of G. Ustvolskaya.

Octet made such an impression on me that I could not force myself to listen to the second section, although there was the Fourth Quartet of W. Basner, which I know well and which I love very much, and romances to the words of G. Lorka by Salmanov.

Octet exhausted me and deprived me of strength for further listening. Surprisingly beautiful and strong music. [...]

Yours D. Shostakovich

I was touched when I read how Shostakovich loved his disciples.

NINTH VARIATION

Influences and Succession

"**[...]** I must humbly confess that I was brought up in awe of the venerable public and that I do not see any kind of indignity in pleasing it, in keeping with the latest trends, and that is what differentiates me from the proud thinkers and poets of the new generation who haughtily disregard the opinions of their contemporaries, wishing however to be leaders, and going their own way, not caring whether or not they have listeners – This first confession brings up another -- more daring one – so be it: I confess that I (in literature) am an absolute skeptic, if not worse – and that all of Parnassus's sects are the same to me, each exposing its advantages and disadvantages -- Isn't it possible to be truly a poet without becoming an inveterate classicist or a fanatical romantic. Forms, rites – must they absolutely enslave literary conscience (?) [...]."

[Alexander Pushkin A draft of a letter to N.N. Rayevsky]*

Did Shostakovich influence Ustvolskaya and her creative thinking? Ustvolskaya's personality is original. It is no coincidence that Shostakovich had to stand up for her before the conservatory's authorities, and if not for his defense, who knows how different her life would have been. Once, she was almost expelled from the conservatory. Ustvolskaya told this story to the class when a student asked, "What if a teacher is not a very nice, or even a dishonorable, person? Should the student stand up for himself and how should one do this?"

---

*   Pushkin *Letters* edited and annotated by B.L. Modzalevsky, (State Publishing: Moscow, Leningrad, 1928), 2:29-30

The grammar in the Russian original of the letter is far from flawless. (It is a known fact that at the time of Pushkin, Russian aristocracy was more fluent in French than in Russian.)The translator attempted to preserve the original "flavor" of the quotation. Alexander Pushkin wrote in Russian with grammatical mistakes. Ustvolskaya adored this. She also adored and was amazed by Mussorgsky who wrote "non-existent notes for double-bass".

Ustvolskaya's answer went something like this: "A well-mannered person should be able to manage a good relationship with anyone he is close to. I studied with many: with Gnessin[*] and with Steinberg[†], and I had good relationships with everyone." She smiled. (It is true; Ustvolskaya had a good rapport with people. It is no surprise that she worked at the College under different directors for almost thirty years.) "They once gave me a 'two'[‡] in composition and Shostakovich took me into his studio. He came up to me and said: 'Galya, don't cry, I'm accepting you in my studio...'[§] But I did not cry. I just stood there quietly with my back to the wall..."

Reminiscing about her studies with Shostakovich, Ustvolskaya once noted that at that time not everybody sought to study with him. "And me? I was interested, I suppose," she was recollecting.

(In those years, when I started to study with Galina Ivanovna, not everyone wanted to go to her class also. Valery Gavrilin was the most popular among the teachers of composition in the music College regarding the success of his "The Russian Music Notebook").

Ustvolskaya did not try to copy her teacher. I believe that. But being Shostakovich's student, she must have experienced his pedagogical influence. He was a demanding teacher.

"Once, Shostakovich reassigned me to his assistant to study all of Beethoven's symphonies, sonatas, and quartets; all the keys, primary and secondary themes - absolutely everything. Can you imagine? It

---

[*]   Michail Fabianovich Gnessin (1883-1957), Russian composer, a student of Rimsky-Korsakov, Liadov, Glazunov.

[†]   Maximillian Oseevich Steinberg (1883-1946), Russian composer, a former student, son-in-law and an admirer of Rimsky-Korsakov. He was a teacher of Shostakovich also.

[‡]   I cannot help not mentioning that, in my opinion, Ustvolskaya was expelled not because of mediocrity, but because at that time she already tried and composed music which was unappropriated for academic tradition. Otherwise, Shostakovich would not be interested in her as a student.

[§]   Shostakovich helped Ustvolskaya later on as well. He defended her from attacks made by her colleagues at the Composers' Union. Already in America, I read his statement about Ustvolskaya: "I am convinced that the music of G. I. Ustvolskaya will achieve world fame, and be valued by all who hold truth to be the essential element of music." (Ian McDonald Music Under Soviet Rule: *Ustvolskaya, "The Lady with the Hammer"*, http://www.siue.edu/~aho/musov/ust/ust.html)

was so painful. I asked Dmitry Dmitrievich to spare me from it. He said: 'Galya, you should go through this…' Just you wait, I will give you a similar assignment and then you will get a test – then you will know…" she added jokingly.

In 1940 Shostakovich was a prominent composer who had gone through many tough things; he had already written his Fifth Symphony and the opera Lady Macbeth. Ustvolskaya, at this time was just… Shostakovich's student. She was 21. This sequence of events is impossible to argue with. (I can hear a cheerfully ironic exclamation from Ustvolskaya: "So what? I was already a genius then." Once, when I asked her for a photograph, she did not want to give it to me and joked: "Why don't I give you the picture of myself as a five-year-old girl instead? I was already a genius then.")

Does Ustvolskaya emulate her teacher? No, she does not, and this is as it should be. Only an untalented student copies and imitates his teacher, and a wise teacher would not want to have a student like that. "A son can be unlike his father in everything, except for one secret feature; but this very feature makes son and father alike," said Alexander Blok[*]. A true student does not imitate his teacher, but develops, expands, and perfects the inherited traditions. Orchestration principles are one example. It is unimportant that Shostakovich's use of orchestra is traditional, as a rule, and Ustvolskaya did away with orchestra in her music completely. Their compositional principles and their traditions are the same - not the "coloring" of music with various instruments, but an organic and artistically convincing writing for specific instruments. It is impossible to say about such music that it is "orchestrated" because it is written for these instruments or for that orchestra. Ustvolskaya was very precise to her students' music when it came to so-called orchestration, the choice of instruments. She liked to ask provocative questions like: "Why did you use a clarinet here and not a flute? A flute can play this…" or "this is not very convincing. It tempts me to use a not good word, one word which I do not like. The word 'formalism;' as though this is a formality… as though this may or may not exist…   Do you understand what I am trying to say?"

It is a very deep tradition. Rimsky-Korsakov taught it to his students.

---

[*]   Alexander Blok, *Lyric Poetry. Theater.* (Moscow: Pravda, 1982), 3.

It is, moreover, insignificant whether there are stylistic similarities in the works of Ustvolskaya and her teacher. The rejection of tradition is rooted in tradition. One cannot confuse the author of "The Rite of Spring" with the author of the "Golden Cockerel," although the inheritance is undeniable.* How else can one pass on the experience? It is conveyed from teacher to student, from one generation to the next. A student can also be influenced by the esthetic preferences of his teacher. In this case, the influence of the teacher is replaced with the influence of another artist, whom the teacher considers to be a great artistic example. For Ustvolskaya and Shostakovich, such an example was the great Gustav Mahler. Ustvolskaya was recollecting that she saw tears in Shostakovich's eyes while listening to Mahler's music. (She herself caught "mahleria" - this is how Ustvolskaya referred to her "obsession" with Mahler - during her student years, and when she started teaching, she would listen to his music with her students). Ustvolskaya and Shostakovich also had literary interests in common. They loved Gogol, Leskov, and Chekhov… It is also curious that their method of composing was similar: thinking the music through to the smallest details, and only then writing it down at the table. (Galina Ivanovna sometimes wrote her music sitting on a couch and holding a manuscript on her lap). According to the Gladkova's monograph, in response to the question of whether Ustvolskaya edits her works she replies:

"No. My written works were often put away for a long time. But if after that they did not satisfy me, I destroyed them. I do not have

---

* To understand how artistically close Stravinsky was to Rimsky-Korsakov, one should listen to the opera *Mlada* by the latter. *The Rite of Spring* was undoubtedly anticipated by this Great Russian composer's work. It is interesting that Stravinsky seems unaware of this. He writes, "I was guided by no system whatsoever in *The Rite of Spring*. When I think of the other composers of that time who interest me, Schoenberg, Berg, and Webern, their music seems much more *theoretical*. And it is supported by a great tradition. Composing *The Rite*, I had only my ear to help me. I heard and I wrote what I heard." (*Memories and Commentaries*. Stravinsky and Craft, 94)

But that's the thing: a composer's ear cannot be totally "pure". A lot gets "stuck" in there, often unconsciously, and later, sometimes after many years, it comes out all mixed and melted down into something else. It becomes new. Interesting also is Stravinsky's confession about how naturally and organically he composed this music. What is important is not the system, but the talent, which dictates a form of expression. Live creative energy must flow freely in the desired direction.

drafts; I compose without an instrument, at the table. All is thought out so thoroughly that all that is lefts is to write it down."* Undoubtedly Ustvolskaya has taken this method from Shostakovich, learned it from him.

I find thematic material in some of Ustvolskaya's compositions to be like Shostakovich's. In the Piano Concerto, for example, or in the symphonic poem "The Lights in the Steppe," and even in the Preludes, and (it is hard to believe), in the Fourth symphony…

In her book "Galina Ustvolskaya. Music as an Obsession," Gladkova allowed an inaccuracy in her analysis of this symphony. She writes: "The only movement of the symphony varies three motifs. First – b-e-f, is played at the beginning by the trumpet, second is introduced by the piano – g-f-e-d, and the last is the "dead end octave". It is unclear from the text which octave. In the score it is e5-eb6 on the trumpet. But the Bb trumpet - as Gladkova mentioned correctly listing the instrumentation - is a transposing instrument, which means that the concert tones it performs are one whole step below the written notes: a-d-eb and d5-db6. Otherwise, the trumpet motif and the piano motif do not correspond.

Although the thematic material may be similar, the difference between the two authors is in how they work with their material. This is important and it makes them the opposites of each other. The first movement of Shostakovich's First Symphony, for example, resembles the music of the Scherzo "Sorcerer's Apprentice" by Paul Dukas. So, I wonder: what if Dukas himself developed his theme in the manner of Shostakovich? How would it be enriching his composition! But he did not, and could not have, and did not even wish to do so. And Shostakovich, when he was nineteen, could not and did not want to compose differently either. Shostakovich imitated Dukas somehow, but, to a much larger degree, he found a completely new direction. This is exactly how innovative ideas are getting birth. Everything new is a continuation of something old. Everything new, consequently, has own roots.

---

*   Gladkova, *Galina Ustvolskaya*, 29

In her book "Amazing Shostakovich", Sophia Khentova tells the story of Ustvolskaya's relationship with Shostakovich. Undoubtedly, they had a very deep connection… but it is known that from love to hate is only one step. Something happened, something destroyed their relationship…

S. Khentova writes: "…Meetings were happening in Leningrad where Shostakovich had been often. This is what Galina Ivanovna Ustvolskaya talked about them on May 14, 1977, after it all became a distant past:

'For a long time, I lived in a communal flat together with my parents; Dmitry Dmitrievich did not come there. But when I moved into a flat on Blagodatny Pereulok, he, when in Leningrad, came often. I lived there for fourteen years, during which our close relationship took place… We would go out of town. Once, we were walking in the woods and suddenly he scattered money between the trees! It was early spring. Snow was melting a little. He loved snow. When the snow melted, he became sad. Twice I visited his dacha in Bolshevo… We walked a lot. At that time, U.F.O. was a popular conversation topic. Once he saw in the sky a flying dot and said: 'there is a flying saucer. There are people in it.' He was very impressionable.

'After the premiere of the Song of the Forest, we came to the hotel Evropeiskaya, where he was living at the time, and he started sobbing with his face in a pillow. There was vodka and snacks on the table. He drank a little and quickly calmed down. He sometimes liked to stimulate himself a little with alcohol but was never drunk.'

sinfonie nr. 4 · symphony no. 4
(1985/87)

galina ustwolskaja
galina ustvolskaya
(*1919)

*) Cluster mit der Handfläche. / Play cluster with the palm of your hand.
**) Cluster mit dem Unterarm. / Play cluster with your forearm.
***) Cluster mit Handfläche und Unterarm. / Play cluster with your hand and forearm.

Shostakovich taught Ustvolskaya as he instructed other students, without favoritism. She did not yield to the influence of her teacher. She thought, *'The best course of life is to experience everything for oneself. I studied music. But it was not based only upon Dmitry Dmitrievich's recommendations. A prepared "menu" did not work. I played by myself. A couple of times we played four hands, but not in class, in his apartment; he had then already moved to Moszhaiskoye Shosse, later renamed Kutuzov Prospect. He gave me Mahler's symphonies. He lent to me Stravinsky. I listened to his arrangement of Stravinsky's Symphony of Psalms.'*

Like other students, Ustvolskaya showed Shostakovich what she composed. He praised and admired her work and found some inspiration for himself; it showed particularly in his Fifth quartet where he included a theme from the finale of Ustvolskaya's *Trio for Clarinet, Violin, and Piano*. 'He told me: 'you are a phenomenon, and I am a talent.'

'He could get overly excited. Once, he said that contact with me makes him better. However, he never helped to publish my music, and never helped to have it performed.'"

After the death of his wife, Nina Varzar, in November 1954, Shostakovich seriously considered marrying Galina Ustvolskaya. He told his children about it. In an interview with Khentova, Ustvolskaya remembers,

"He wanted to bring me closer right away. He wrote many, many letters. When I had my tonsils removed in the clinic of the Academy of Military Medicine, he wrote two letters a day. A nurse was amazed: 'who is this boy who writes to you?' There could have been more letters if I were more communicative… He signed them, 'Your Mitya' and requested insistently that I call him Mitya. I could not do that and signed my letters 'Galia Ustvolskaya'… He liked it when I spoke German. I translated the Farewell song from Mahler's "Das Lied von der Erde" for him. He wanted to learn German but could not. He asked: 'Why don't you want to marry me?'"

After Shostakovich divorced Margarita Kainova, his relationship with Ustvolskaya was resumed. Khentova writes,

"One of the autographed copies of his "Satyrs" was presented to Ustvolskaya with the signature: *'To the dear Galia Ustvolskaya from the loving D. Shostakovich.'* It is dated April 6, 1961. By that time,

Ustvolskaya had gathered a unique collection of autographs: the Fifth quartet, the cycle "From the Jewish Folk Poetry," the cycles on the verses of Pushkin, Preludes and Fugues for piano, opera "Gamblers" … Her meetings with Shostakovich began again. She also experienced a tragedy. In 1960 she lost her husband, the composer Yuri Balkashin, who suddenly died of suffocation in Repino, at the composers' resort.

She and Shostakovich were both lonely, but Ustvolskaya still refused marriage."[*]

Shostakovich and Ustvolskaya belong to two different epochs of Russian and Soviet history and culture. Shostakovich's career began during a period of general elevation, enthusiasm, and a time of belief in revolutionary ideas and their promising future. Like Beethoven, who worked under the influence of the ideas of the French Revolution in 1789, Shostakovich'style was determined in large part under the influence of the October Revolution of 1917. Their ideals faded with time, but the creative pathos determined by them remained in the works of both composers.

Ustvolskaya's youth was a time of repression, though it did not touch her personally, but hurt the consciousness of the thinking part of society.

Shostakovich was very socially aware. Stalinism strongly affected his views. Shostakovich's music is the expression of an inner protest and a fight. The composer deserves profound respect for fighting for his music under conditions of complete totalitarian control. The Fifth Symphony, written in 1937, is a brilliant example and confirmation of this. Even now it has not lost its esthetic attractiveness, but in those years, it was received as a very bold work in its language and content. A student of Boris Asafieff, Natalia Petrovna Rozova, who taught European Music History at the Rimsky-Korsakov College of Music, attended the premiere of the Fifth symphony at the Grand Hall of the Leningrad Philharmonic in 1937. She told us (she liked to reminisce, and we took advantage of it when we wanted to distract her from a question or a test) that the musical language of the symphony seemed very daring and even – just imagine–the symphony was not

---

[*]   Khentova, *Amazing Shostakovich,* 154,155

understandable to everyone. The opera "Lady Macbeth of Mtzensk" seemed more understandable.

Natalia Petrovna Rozova and me in my 1st year in the college, 1968.

After a concert at the Grand Hall of the Leningrad Philharmonic where Mravinsky conducted the Fourth symphony, I carefully told Galina Ivanovna about my impressions; the music had captivated me. I thought that Galina Ivanovna would not want to share in my excitement. But she said with certain pathos: "He was purer back then after all!"

His premieres were always treated as major cultural events. Ustvolskaya is secluded. Her music is performed infrequently even now, although there are no longer any formal prohibitions on the popularization of her works. They existed during Soviet times. The music of Shostakovich is impulsive and eclectic, Ustvolskaya's - rational and selective. She is akin to an ascetic hermit who performs rites and incantations understood only by a few.

INTERLUDE

If we do not comprehend the present, it is impossible to understand where we are headed and how to build the future. (And how important it is to understand that!) Art has become so complex that sometimes it is almost impossible to tell true art from intermediate gimmicks. One must listen very carefully and for a long time to discern between the two. Sometimes it takes years. (Is there enough time to listen carefully?) Performers could and should be more sensitive to help listeners be more discerning. But many performers ignore contemporary music for that reason – they do not understand it. They prefer classics. Classical music seems easier to comprehend. It has always been this way. What we now call classical was not always understood by its contemporaries. Now there are specialists in Bach, Mozart, Chopin, the impressionists…

Instrumental technique is like a sport. But there is a significant difference between the mastery of performing and pure sport. It is the philosophy of performance, which requires an ever deeper understanding of the creative process and its goals. Sports also have their philosophy, but their development cannot be as significant throughout the ages. Take runners, for instance: they still run as they have run for thousands of years. A performer playing 'classical' music is like a runner, continuing to cover the same route. This is also important for music because the landscape of time that frames its own "route" is ever changing. A temporal landscape – this is what is new for a performer of an old repertoire. (This is why, paradoxically, those interpretations and methods of playing that were common at time when those works were written are now considered to be obsolete and specialists continue to discuss the matter.) However, we need new roads – in life and in art. These must be paved and opened. A performer who does not understand contemporary music cannot really understand classical (sometimes mistakenly referred to as 'traditional') music, because all classical music is, at its root, innovative.

To play Ustvolskaya's music is difficult emotionally and physically. It must not be "interpreted." A performer must study the score with great attention to all the author's remarks and notation. Nothing is superfluous. Ustvolskaya carefully thinks about every articulation, every dynamic; metronome markings are everywhere and there is no opportunity for interpretation. Of course, if the performer is talented, his personality will enrich the music, but one cannot purposefully "rethink" it or play it in a different tempo or use different dynamics. Ustvolskaya is decisively against the "interpretation" of her music.

I should mention that regarding Ustvolskaya's demanding performance of her music, Artificial Intellect is the best performer, what is incredibly significant! Intellect is neither soul nor heart!

Once, during a lesson, somebody briefly called her out of the room. Ustvolskaya quickly left. She returned shortly.

"It was a pianist, Oleg Malov. He wants to play my music," she said. I could sense the excitement in her voice.

Ustvolskaya's encounter with Malov was almost ideal. He had bought the score and had become interested in playing it. He found Ustvolskaya and they began to collaborate.

Oleg Malov is, certainly, one of the most consistent and thorough performers of Ustvolskaya's music. I remember that Galina Ivanovna was pleased with his participation in the performance of her Compositions, and his performance of the Third sonata, which is dedicated to him.[*] However, listening to a recording of her piano sonatas by Markus Hinterhäuser[†] convinced me that a talented musician can find new colors. It seems to me that Hinterhäuser is trying to soften the roughness of this music through a more delicate tone production.

---

[*] In Gladkova's monograph, Oleg Malov is not mentioned among the performers of Ustvolskaya's music. According to Marian Lee's IREX research report, "Ustvolskaya rationalized this oversight by the fact that Malov plays her music "badly" and that she now officially supports the pianist Reinbert de Leeuw and Frank Denyer as proper interpreters of her music. The truth to the omission is more likely due to the souring of the relationship between Ustvolskaya and Malov several years ago, and it was probably understood by the biographer that he not be mentioned." (Marian Lee IREX research report http://www.irex.org/programs/iaro/research/lee.pdf)

[†] I should say proudly regarding Mr. Markus Hinterhäuser that when I wrote this note in First Edition of this book, I did not know this wonderful musician in any aspect, and I could not flatter him as a boss of" Salzburg festspiele" because he was not appointed yet at this time.

TENTH VARIATION

♪

Strong nerves. Success. Khrennikov

I valued the opportunity to be around Galina Ivanovna very much and still think of my studies with her as the great luck of a lifetime. I loved talking with her. Forget talking – just being near her! I felt lucky if she were alone in the classroom and we could chat. She would ask me to open a window – even on a freezing winter day; she often was overflowing, overheated from within and in need of more air. ("I don't know what to do with myself," said Ustvolskaya of herself.) Sometimes, I shall confess, I was simply freezing and asked for permission to smoke – it seemed warmer that way. Permission was granted. What did we talk about? It seems like nothing, really. Only, after such soulful encounters I always felt elevated, and there was nothing more wonderful in the world then creative work, that I must compose, and that there was a lot to be done…

Knowing that sometimes Galina Ivanovna came to school earlier to have lunch in the school eatery, I tried to be there at the same time. Once I decided to treat her to a dessert. "But how can you treat me, Semyon? You are a student!" she objected. "But Beethoven never forgot his teacher Joseph Haydn," I rebutted. "…and despite the fact that he was not his student anymore, he never missed an opportunity to treat him to a cup of coffee – sometimes with cream and sometimes with something a little stronger." Galina Ivanovna laughed, nodding agreeably. My gift was accepted.

While serving in the army, I tried to see Ustvolskaya during my infrequent leaves. I wrote to her and called her at home. Once, after some mischief, I ended up in the guardhouse. On my next leave I rushed to see Ustvolskaya at school.

"Did they really just lock you there and leave you alone inside?"

"No, there were others too…"

"But still, locked!"

"Well, there was a peephole in the door where the guard looked in once in a while."

"You are an iron man, Semyon, with strong nerves. I do not know what would have happened to me if I were there."

"But what was there to do?" I thought…

("Strong nerves" was not a compliment from Ustvolskaya, nor were such epithets as "healthy," "cold-blooded," "vigorous," and "glowing with health.")

"However, the work of a poet, as we saw, is absolutely incommensurable with the order of the outside world. Poets' goals are, as they say, broadly cultural," said Blok in his famous speech about Pushkin. Topicality does not get along well with true creativity. Of course, here we are talking only about the Soviet era when art was "monopolized" by the Party and its "actuality" was determined by its ideology and politics. But actually, true spiritual meaning and the timeliness of culture in any given era always had an important value in the works of talented artists.

In a talented artist, creative intuition and a "commissioned" (or ordered) motive (and it does not matter whether this "order" comes from within, or is a specific given assignment,) create a split between the two worlds, the inner and the outer. It results in allegory, (as in Blok's "The Twelve,"* where one cannot really tell whether it is written for the Revolution or against it;) or, at worst, it results in ambiguity, tastelessness and pettiness. These qualities became typical of Soviet art. Some examples of such art penetrated our consciousness so deeply that we do not notice their unmasking double meaning. They became "classics." For example, how should one understand the following verse by Mayakovsky: "I clean myself under Lenin…"? (It is a fact that Mayakovsky's love for Lenin, which he expressed fully in his poetry, was not mutual:

---

*   *The Twelve* is a revolutionary poem by Alexander Blok, first published in 1918. It is deeply symbolic that this first Soviet poem became the last work of the great Russian poet never to become Soviet.

"Comrade Pokrovsky!* …I am asking you to help in this struggle against Futurism etc. Lunacharsky[†] allowed the editorial board (alas!) to publish Mayakovsky's "150, 000 000". *("One hundred fifty million" is the title of poem – S. B.)* Is it possible to stop it? We must stop it. Set such conditions that no more than twice a year and no more than 1500 copies of those Futurists can be published." May 6, 1921).[‡]

Or Nikolay Tikhonov's[§] "We could make nails of people like that! You would not find stronger nails than that!" And they did, indeed, make nails out of people!

Ustvolskaya managed to save herself as an artist by taking little interest in the surrounding world; she did not let it in. Not everyone could do that. Once you began serving and became an official artist, it was difficult to change the situation. This was an excruciating problem for the big talents.

But Galina Ustvolskaya was both encouraged and seduced by the stimulations at the beginning of her journey. She could have made

---

* Mikhail Nikolayevich Pokrovsky (Russian: Михаил Николаевич Покровский; August 29 [O.S. August 17] 1868 – April 10, 1932) was a Russian Marxist historian, revolutionary and a Soviet public and political figure. One of the earliest professionally trained historians to join the Russian revolutionary movement, Pokrovsky is regarded as the most influential Soviet historian of the 1920s and was known as "the head of the Marxist historical school in the USSR". Pokrovsky was neither a Bolshevik nor a Menshevik for nearly a decade prior to the October Revolution of 1917, instead living in European exile as an independent radical close to philosopher Alexander Bogdanov. Following the Bolshevik seizure of power, Pokrovsky rejoined the Bolshevik Party and moved to Moscow, where he became the deputy chief of the Soviet government's new department of education, the People's Commissariat of Enlightenment.

† Anatoly Vasilyevich Lunacharsky (Russian: Анатолий Васильевич Луначарский, born Anatoly Aleksandrovich Antonov; 23 November [O.S. 11 November] 1875 – 26 December 1933) was a Russian Marxist revolutionary and the first Bolshevik Soviet People's Commissar (Narkompros) responsible for the Ministry of Education as well as an active playwright, critic, essayist and journalist throughout his career.

‡ V.I. Lenin. Complete works, v.52 (Moscow: Izdatelstvo Politicheskaya Literatura, 1958, 179-180)

§ Nikolai Semenovich Tikhonov (Russian: Николай Семёнович Тихонов; 4 December [O.S. 22 November] 1896 – 8 February 1979) was a Soviet writer and member of the Serapion Brothers literary group.

a career. Bylina* "Stepan Razin's Dream" on the text of the song of the Ural Cossacks "Oh, not evening, but not evening" for bass voice and symphony orchestra (1949) opened the season of the Great Hall of the Leningrad Philharmonic four times in a row, conducted by Nathan Rachlin with the premiere. Later - Evgeny Mravinsky. Isn't this a success? Profoundly serious success. And the incentive for further promotion...

"In 1949 Khrennikov officially attacked the young composer Alexander Lokshin using formulations of one of Stalin's most notorious ideologists, Pavel Apostolov. In his speech Khrennikov contrasted Lokshin "modernist" style with the bylina Stepan Razin's Dream by Galina Ustvolskaya which he considered an ideal example of true national art. Khrennikov's speech aroused great indignation in Mikhail Gnessin who accused him of duplicity: not daring to criticize Lokshin in a professional environment, Khrennikov attacked him ideologically from his position as a leading Soviet official. After this ideological campaign Lokshin was excluded from academic circles. (from the article "Khrennikov", Wikipedia)

I happened to hear a recording of her symphonic poem "The Lights in the Steppe" about the development of virgin lands. Galina Ivanovna and I listened to this music at her house. She was in a good mood and being recollecting that Shostakovich praised this work a lot, saying "Good job, Galya!"

In a Soviet Music Encyclopedia, in the entry on Ustvolskaya, the works that are listed are those in the style of Soviet Socialist Realism. I did not know those compositions and asked Galina Ivanovna about them: "What is 'A Man from the High Mountain,' 'Hero's Feat'... Ustvolskaya answered smiling, but firmly:

---

*   Bylina or starina (Russian: были́на; pl. были́ны byliny; also ста́рина; pl. ста́рины stariny) is a traditional East Slavic oral epic narrative poem. Byliny songs are loosely based on historical fact, greatly embellished with fantasy or hyperbole to create their songs. The word *bylina* is derived from the past tense of the verb "to be" (Russian: быть byt') and implies "something that was." The term most likely originated with scholars of Russian folklore; in 1839, Ivan Sakharov, a Russian folklorist, published an anthology of Russian folklore, a section of which he titled "Byliny of the Russian People," causing the popularization of the term. Later scholars believe that Sakharov misunderstood the word bylina in the opening of *Igor' Tale* as "an ancient poem." The folk singers of byliny called these songs stariny (Russian: старины) or starinki (Russian: старинки) meaning "stories of old" (from Russian: старь star')

"There are no such works!" *"But the Encyclopedia,"* I started, but could not finish. Ustvolskaya did not let me.

"There are no such works! I took everything back and destroyed them! I even took them back from the Music Archives!"

I also heard the recording of her Children Suite. Such "encyclopedic" information and recordings, of course, gave a wrong, incomplete, and inaccurate idea of her creative image. This is a completely different Ustvolskaya. In this music her individuality is not shown clearly. And it was not research of herself of course. At the same time, quite opposite works were composed. For example, the Piano Concerto. The time was very cruel, and the artist's compromise was sometimes just payment for saving one's life. But later Galina Ivanovna prohibited herself from such compromises.

INTERLUDE

They are not memoirs. Of course, I am recollecting. But when I am thinking about the past like that I tend to analyze and generalize. I do not want to be the one to hold back the reader's initiative. I wonder what conclusion this narrative can lead you to. Nevertheless, the point remains: Ustvolskaya is an outstanding representative of the 20th century! Why? Her personality, her art and her philosophy reflect the typical features of the individual creator of that time: both personal and artistic. Yes, she belongs to the 20th Century, and the 21st one should be another life, another person, and another creativity. Not at once, of course, but the Creator is the voice of the era. And he is its forerunner!

ELEVENTH VARIATION

♫

TV. Peiko. Solzhenitsyn

With time, a true artist becomes lonelier and lonelier. Fewer and fewer people are able to really understand him/her and his/her work. So, who is he/she working for? For himself. "For God," some would want to correct me. No, he/she works for himself, but through his/her work he/she becomes closer to God. Real creativity is God given. The result of such collaboration is the person, grasping the Truth; he/she prays through his/her work, intuitively sensing the knowledge entering him/her in an invisible ray. He/she constantly expands the frame of consciousness, pushing the threshold of Mystery further away, penetrating it more deeply, grasping more, but not uncovering it…

She is not a social person. It is absolutely impossible to imagine her at a social event in an evening dress with a glass of champagne in her hand. She "moved" her birthday from June seventeenth to July seventeenth to avoid visitors and phone calls. (By July, she was already on vacation.) I believed it and regularly sent her birthday greetings to this incorrect date. She limited her social life because social relations burdens and torments her.

One day, on February 13, 1974 - you will understand why I confidently name this year and date - I visited Galina Ivanovna. She was animated and a little bit worried. She said with a little embarrassment: "Semyon! I bought a TV set. That is how far I have fallen". It felt as like she was happy to buy it. We were talking, and Galina Ivanovna was periodically approaching the screen, switching the channels. The "Time" program showed Solzhenitsyn's arrival in what was then West Germany. So, it is possible to name not only the date - on February 13th Aleksandr Isayevich (more precisely -

Isaakievich) Solzhenitsyn was deported - but also the time of my visit: around 9 pm.

There were only very few people who could understand her and with whom she would share her views. From time to time, she would praise some individuals, but later she would drastically change her opinion about them. Some day she was cheerfully praising certain Veselov, (I did not know who he was then), saying what a wonderfully pure person he was, that he was the only one she could share herself with, that they have perfect mutual understanding. Some time passed. Ustvolskaya has telling me:

"Veselov called me once and asked: 'Could you, Galya, take part in a concert with me? In the Union they said that if Ustvolskaya agrees, they would organize such concert.' Imagine, a man calls me, to woman, and asking…"

"But Galina Ivanovna, isn't Veselov* only person with whom you can share yourself?"

"Who told you that?"

"You said it yourself."

"I could not have said such a thing!" she said angrily.

Or, once, she told a story about how in Moscow, composer Nikolay Peyko had a reception at his house.

"As a composer, he is certainly nobody," said Ustvolskaya. "But how a wonderful person he is!"

Sometime later, I went to Moscow and met with Peyko to discuss some personal matters. He invited me to his home. But the meeting was unproductive, and he made a repulsive impression on me.

---

*   Veselov, Vadim Fedorovich, 1931-1990. Leningrad. Was a pupil of G. Ustvolskaya in the college by R. Korsakov. Graduated from the Conservatory in 1959 in the class of Yuri Balkashin. He was the musical editor of the Leningrad branch of the publishing house "Music", where he edited the works of G. Ustvolskaya as well. C. Slonimsky: "It's very offended that such a defenseless, really melodic, innermost composer as V.F.Veselov is completely forgotten". http://www.youtube.com/watch?v=TV6Htg3N4qI

"You know, this Peyko is such a … strange person," I said to Ustvolskaya, unable to find out the right words to describe him.

"Why did you go to him?" Galya asked.

"Well, I thought he could help. You said he is a wonderful person."

"I said that? I could never have said such a thing! He is a fool!"

The necessity of talking to strangers burdened her. She told me that in the summer, when she and her husband went on vacation, most often to Lithuania, they would buy four train tickets instead of two to avoid having strangers in their compartment. Once, I dared to borrow Ustvolskaya's technique. My wife, daughter, and I traveled from Kaliningrad to Moscow by train. I bought four tickets to buy off the whole compartment. "We'll travel in comfort," I thought. But the conductor could not come to peace with our comfort. "Look, a bunch of nobles! I do not know where to put people and there you are, three on the four berths! I will give you a passenger, just so you know!" The same thing happened at every station. It was a trip!

Students loved Ustvolskaya. There were various attempts to invite her over, which was unthinkable. One girl from Ustvolskaya's studio invited Galina Ivanovna and the whole studio to a party. Her parents had a house outside the city. (I must say that this was exactly what Ustvolskaya "loved" the most – having to meet and talk with the parents of her students.) It happened in May, just before Victory Day. No one promised that they would come, but no one declined either. Ustvolskaya did not object. Afterwards, it turned out that the family was preparing for the visitors, and for Ustvolskaya coming especially. The table was laid, but nobody showed up. "But Semyon, how could they expect that I would come? It means that they do not know me and do not understand me at all…" To her, "to know and to understand her" is the main point in her relationship to other people.

INTERLUDE

Is human brotherhood possible? All people possess the same natural qualities, which make them similar. However, the prevailing of some qualities over others makes us different, sometimes irreconcilably.*

Religions have attempted to raise the awareness of brotherhood. Indeed, there is some sort of brotherhood among the representatives of one religion. But each religion, often controversially interpreted, claims exclusivity and the highest knowledge of the meaning of life, therefore disconnecting people more and more. Thus, the call, "Be embraced, millions!" does not reach their consciousness. Note that neither Christians, nor Muslims, not Jews, not members of some party, but simply MILLIONS! This call does not reach the millions. It is muted by other calls and screams.

Were Beethoven and Schiller idealists or prophets? In any case, altruism is the ideal and the law of the spiritual world. This is why the Ninth Symphony lives on.

.

---

* "A man can describe his joys and his torments. We believe that he feels like us (although, there is no proof to this. This is an interesting example of believing in the non-scientific.") (K. E. Tsiolkovsky *Monism of the Universe. The Cause of Cosmos.* (Novosibirsk, CO "Detskaya Literatura", 1993,) 10

♪

666 — The Number of the Beast!

This variation is important for understanding Galina Ustvolskaya's ideology and of her faith. It would be good to listen to her symphonies, from the Second to the Fifth, ahead of time. You can also try listening to them as a background to this narrative. The effect will be interesting.

"All who really love my music should refrain from theoretical analysis of it. Galina Ustvolskaya" [*]

This seems like a strange request. Strange, because particularly those who take an interest in Ustvolskaya's music would want to understand it better and would be thinking about it. Naturally, others who are indifferent to her work will not bother. This is natural! I am not trying to analyze Ustvolskaya's music. Let musicologists do that. My analysis is that of a listener. I write about her symphonies because they are peculiar in their philosophy. Ustvolskaya's music, in my understanding of it, represents a struggle to find the truth. What is the result? The *Twelve Preludes,* for example, or even the *Octet* are quite different works from symphonies. Drama is present in those wonderful compositions. There is even a certain delightful romanticism in the *Preludes,* but there is none of the endless despair, fear, loneliness, and even hopelessness that are present in her symphonies – her most recent works.

> *And I saw, and behold, a pale horse, and its rider's name was*
> *Death, and Hades followed him; and they were given power over a*

---

[*] Gladkova *Galina Ustvolskaya,* Surprisingly, the request is being violated by this book itself. I sympathize to its author O. Gladkova. She undoubtedly wrote this book, overcoming restrictions and prohibitions. And it turned out to be a useful book.

*fourth of the earth, to kill with sword and with famine and with pestilence and by wild beasts of the Earth.**

Even a deep-rooted atheist prays in the face of danger. Ustvolskaya's last four symphonies are like the prayer of a person who is experiencing a terrible misfortune. Here are the terror and fear of vanishing and nonexistence, a need to be heard, and a lack of faith in any chance of finding peace and harmony. Her loneliness is unmatched. The four symphonies form a complete cycle. The music is frightening and... decorative in some way. You see the dark and stern faces of saints from Orthodox icons, and paintings of Hell and the Last Judgment come to mind.

Now the seven angels who had the seven trumpets made ready to blow them. The first angel blew his trumpet, and there followed hail and fire, mixed with blood, which fell on the earth; and a third of the earth was burnt up, and a third of the trees were burnt up, and all green grass was burnt up. The second angel blew his trumpet, and something like a great mountain, burning with fire, was thrown into the sea; and a third of the sea became blood, a third of the living creatures in the sea died, and a third of the ships were destroyed.†

"Seven trumpets..." Why couldn't they be the Ustvolskaya's "orchestra"? The homogeneous ensemble of angels causes an association with similar ensembles of Galina Ustvolskaya. She has no music for seven trumpets. But she has music for eight double basses. There are 6 trumpets in the Second Symphony... There are also 6 flutes and 6 oboes (!?!) Three sixes: 666!!! The Number of the Beast! (I don't believe in this symbol, but this is how it's defined by the Bible. We cannot change it). There are trombone and tuba and drums – a bass drum and a snare drum, and the piano. Nevertheless, the Three Sixes of brass are separated from the rest of the instruments

---

* The Holy Bible. Revised Standard Version published by Holman Bible Publishers for Cokesbury, 1982. Revelations 6:8

† Revelations 8:6-8

by their tessitura and by the position in the music score. And the music itself is pushing the mind to such an interpretation.

These are incredibly special works, even for Ustvolskaya. They are like musical icon painting. In all four symphonies, texts do not play a constructive role. From the musical standpoint, these works could exist without words. However, the composer needs the words. Interestingly enough, they do not help to bring forth the meaning of the compositions, but as if trying to mask it. The symphonies are allegorical. The words contradict the musical content of the symphonies and that is why, it seems to me, the composer needs them to be heard and understood. In the Fifth Symphony, for example, the old Slavic text of the prayer "Our Father" is translated into modern Russian. In the Second Symphony, the persistently repeated words, "bliss, truth, eternity" can be perceived as cries of despair that make one doubt the very core of these concepts. The listener hears panic and terror.

> *The third angel blew his trumpet, and a great star fell from heaven, blazing like a torch, and it fell on a third of the rivers and on the fountains of water. The name of the star is Wormwood. A third of the waters became wormwood, and many men died of the water, because it was getting bitter.*[*]

In the Third and Fourth symphonies, the listener hears despair in the supplication: "Jesus the Messiah, save us!" This despair comes from a fear that no one will hear, and no one will save. The last symphony is a staggering epilogue. The words of the daily prayer "Our Father" have a simply diabolic musical background. The prayer's pathos is ironically reinterpreted in the music. The Fifth symphony is very sharp and caustically sarcastic. This is a unique example of the grotesque in Ustvolskaya's music.

> *The fourth angel blew his trumpet, and a third of the sun was struck, and a third of the moon, and a third of the stars, so that a third of their light was darkened; a third of the day was kept from shining, and likewise a third of the night. Then I looked, and I heard an eagle crying with a loud voice, as it flew in midheaven,*

---

* Revelation 8:10-11

"Woe, woe, woe to those who dwell on the earth, at the blasts of the other trumpets which the three angels are about to blow! *

With the words "For Thine is the Kingdom, and the power, and the Glory for ever and ever! Amen," the diabolic bacchanalia reaches its apogee. "Routine" blows on the wooden cube, as if someone were nailing a lid on a coffin†, complete the work. God did not hear. And death is the only salvation from the brutal torment and suffering.

These four symphonies were not conceived as a cycle; their "evolution" into a cycle reflects the evolution of the consciousness of the composer. O. Gladkova asserts that Ustvolskaya's style has no evolution. This is not true. One must listen carefully to understand clearly that her music changes; it becomes darker and darker. Compare, for example, the *Twelve Preludes* and the *Sixth Piano Sonata,* or *Compositions* and *Symphonies.* The technique, invented by Ustvolskaya, does not change, however. Like Gogol, who tried to save himself through fasting and prayer from impending danger, known only to him, Ustvolskaya prays. In this regard, the Third and the Fourth symphonies come close to a type of religious music. Those prayers are like the final desperate attempts to draw back disaster.

Here is religious standard text in the Fifth symphony, but there is neither piety nor humility; not even a supplication. There is only bitter irony and sarcasm. Such music cannot be called religious. Neither is it spiritual. It does not contain the light or hope that spirituality implies. So then is there a God, a Spirit, or a Higher Consciousness? And what powers rule the world? And is there serenity, intellect, truth, joy, and what are they? Music reaches the threshold of consciousness, beyond which there is either absolute darkness or the all-penetrating light – who knows.

---

*   Revelations 8:12-13

†   Here are interesting details! The Second Composition "Dies Irae" has written for eight double basses, a wooden cube and a grand piano in 1972-73. The Fith Symphony, 1990 for oboe, trumpet, tuba, wooden cube, violin and reciter. But, as K. Bagrenin, Ustvolskaya's widower told me, neither verbally, nor in writing did G. U. ever decipher the meaning of the "cube" either in Symphony or in Composition. To the question: "what does it mean?" she just answered: "it is necesarry so". It's obviously, the meanings of the "cube" in both - composition and the Symphony are coinciding. And this long box which is titled as a cube is vision mistake. It is more alike coffin!

Once, at Ustvolskaya's apartment on Gagarin Street, the conversation turned to Beethoven and his Ninth Symphony. "But is it really good: 'be embraced, millions?' she suddenly asked." I did not know what to say, because her question seemed so strange and unexpected to me. I thought that Galya was joking, but she had not even a hint of a joke in her eyes then.*

Then from the smoke came locusts like the power of scorpions of the earth; they were told not to harm the grass of the earth or any green growth or any tree, but only those of mankind who have not the seal of God upon their foreheads; they were allowed to torture them for five months, but not to kill them, and their torture was like the torture of a scorpion, when it stings a man.†

---

*   In fact, the Finale of the Ninth Symphony, its "Ode to Joy", is the end of the Apocalypse, which during Beethoven's lifetime had not even been heating up properly yet. It is heating up now! And we know that it will end with the Victory of Light. And Beethoven had known it even earlier! This is the true Great Prophecy! And here's an example of how long it takes to mature the understanding of truly great ideas. Beethoven is the greatest of the Prophets. How can you compare invented baseless Ustvolskaya's "spirituality" (that's right - in quotes!) WITH Beethoven's greatest visionary gift! I was at the birth of this Ustvolskaya's concept: not religiosity, but spirituality. It was 1978, in Ustvolskaya's apartment on Gagarin Street. In one of our meetings, probably we were talking concerning her music, and she repeated it like a mantra several times: spirituality without religiosity! And it was obvious that this "discovery" delighted her. It wasn't a discovery. It was her INVENTON! Why didn't I mention this episode in the first edition of the book? I forgot it among many other details. But there was another significant reason. Ustvolskaya was alive when I wrote this book, and I knew that such a detail would be very unpleasant to her.

†   Revelations 9:3-5

Painting of Heronimus Bosch

She sharply feels the presence of destructive powers in the world, in life, and in space. This frightens and depresses her. Music helps her to free herself from these tribulations, eases the sufferings caused by the absence of harmony in the world. In Goethe's novel *The Sorrows of Young Werther,* the hero dies from hopeless love. He shoots himself. This novel depicts a love story of Goethe himself. The influence of Goethe's novel on his contemporaries was so great that it created a suicidal "fashion" - many young people in Germany committed suicide soon after the book was published. But Goethe did not shoot himself. He shot his double, his phantom Werther and thus freed himself to survive.

That is why her music is overflowing with manifestations of dark powers and elements. She does not serve these powers. Her personality is such that she cannot serve anything or anybody at all; her religion is in herself.

The darkness thickens before dawn and Ustvolskaya's music is, for me, a proclamation of renewal.

> *And I took the little scroll from the hand of the angel and ate it; it was sweet as honey in my mouth, but when I had eaten it, my stomach was bitter. And I was told, "You must again prophesy about many peoples, nations, tongues, and kings.*

What if we suppose that a Higher Intellect exists, after all? What if we suppose that God is not a literary character or a metaphor, not a dealer- or merchant-God whom we go as far as to instruct: "forgive us our debts *as we forgive our debtors*" – some God this is! What if there is a God who does not punish, but rather a God-creator, a highly organized system of conducting the universe? What if humanity drives itself into a dark corner through ignorance and by refusing to abide by the laws of the cosmos? To believe in a Spirit, in a Higher Power joyfully and openly is to serve it with your creativity. I do not hear this in the music of Ustvolskaya. Maybe her philosophy is to show how terrible the world in which we live is. But her music is a part of this world. Isn't she aware of that? Naturally, I am far from the kind of primitive understanding of music in which a major key connotes light and joy and a minor key implies darkness. (The means of expression are important, but they do not determine a composer's philosophy. One's philosophy is determined by the composer's works with its material.) Does the question, then, have to do with a carefully crafted style, which Ustvolskaya discovered and could not leave behind? This is a serious question because if the attitude changes, the music also changes.

A seriously ill person sits by the window. Suddenly, a huge black raven comes, perches on the cornice, and starts to bang on the window with its beak. The glass is about to break, but he keeps banging and banging. What a terrible clatter! It is frightening and

---

*   Revelations 10:10-11

the man by the window wishes for only one thing – for this noise to stop. He is starting to suffocate and… wakes up. How good that it was just a dream. So, relieved! But gradually one begins to understand that this dream came not without a reason, that it came to tell him something, but what?

Ustvolskaya's art is apocalyptical. She knows that this world is dying. It dies from its gloomy ignorance. It dies without realizing it and how a new World is born in it. Ustvolskaya's four symphonies are a requiem for the outgoing world.

Bokman hears her music as 'a requiem to the dying world,' which is as good a motto as any, but his gloss is naïve (or candid, according to taste) and as marked by the clichés of Soviet musicography (…)

David Fanning, MUSIC & LETTERS, OXFORD academic

Everybody can see now how many different events of the current time really show that this "world is dying" and that its dying cannot be ceased.

What may you say now, Mr. Fanning?

The cycle of compositions of Galina Ustvolskaya. maybe also perceived as the Illustrations to the Apocalypse. Symphonies are the continuation and deepening of the theme and its fuller disclosure. It is such a crying, which has grown to Universal scale. The persistence with which Ustvolskaya prophesies in these works suggests an association with the cry and the prophecy of Yurodivy from Boris Godunov, an opera by M. P. Musorgsky. But here the author himself, Galina Ustvolskaya, acts as an irrational exalted prophet.

Creativity in the new era must be different. If art and science unite with the Belief, religion will cease to be a dogma. It will become living knowledge that does not need to be interpreted and clarified. Humanity will cease to be afraid of death. Does an artist need such knowledge? Ustvolskaya once ironically noticed that the moon ceased to be a symbol of love after it was visited by people. A very witty remark! But the problem is not on the Moon. The problem is to find her a worthy artistic substitute. The artist is a tireless seeker of truth. What is it? Who will give the answer? We need to wake up the Spirit in Man, and he will be able to answer.

INTERLUDE

What is the music of the future? Does such music exist? It exists only as a metaphor. Many have been "labeled" with this high-flying term: Composer of the Future. There was Beethoven, there was Wagner, and Scriabin, and Stravinsky…Listening to the works of these composers will convince you that their music represents their respective eras in a worthy manner. Incidentally, not a single artist, no matter how ingenious he is, and no matter how well he imagines the future, could overcome the bounds of his time. It is common to say about an innovative artist that his work represents the future and was composed for the future. This is true only in the sense that the artist is always ahead of his contemporaries in his awareness and understanding of the present. Contemporaries are unable to comprehend the present, so well encapsulated in a work of art. Absorbed in our everyday problems and concerns, we do not notice and are not, ourselves, aware of the time in which we live. We do not ponder over it. But art always lives on the peak of the epoch. An innovative artist who is searching for a new language, form, style, or topic, who is striving for artistic persuasiveness and truthfulness cannot break the bounds of time he is in. Therefore, the keenest works are the works that are spiritually and esthetically timely. Such is the music of Ustvolskaya, a composer of the Epoch of Collapse. Her contemporaries are not always aware of this. Their understanding is behind hers.

Are there composers who reflect their time in their music as fully as possible? Those do not exist either. Rachmaninoff and Stravinsky are both composers of the twentieth century; they were neighbors physically and musically. And in our consciousness, they belong to the same epoch. Every artist is valuable because, having learned something important about life, he expresses it in his work. And after time has passed, we reconstruct the past – their time – according to their works. Everyone's contribution is particularly important here. Composers write the soundtrack for the era. We can hear clearly how time sounds now and how it sounded before. The arsenal of creative methods and techniques is changing and widening. The methods, with which composers of the past expressed emotional experiences akin to ours, seem so naïve now! The methods grow old, but the impact remains. Music brings the time in which it was created closer to us. Music captures time. Future generations will hear the music of Ustvolskaya and say, "What a terrible time it was." "What happened - happened," we will say from the far-off present.

THIRTEENTH VARIATION

♪

Heroism and Demonism

I bought the score of Ustvolskaya's First Symphony in Kyiv at the "Noti" shop on Khreshchatyk in 1972. I remember how pleasantly surprised I was, as if I had suddenly seen an old friend. It was inexpensive and there was only one copy, which maybe was the only copy to arrive at the store, since the total number of printed copies was 200. And what was it doing in Kyiv, anyway?

I bragged to Ustvolskaya, of course.

"Really? Even I do not have one, but you do. People ask me for a score, and I cannot send one. Study it a little. There are things to look at," she said. I looked at it and then, later, presented it to the author, Galina Ustvolskaya.

In 1970-72 I served in the army. The director of the Military Song and Dance Ensemble was Yuri Petukhov, once one of the boy-soloists who participated in the first performance of Ustvolskaya's First symphony – so mysterious are the intersections of people's lives. He recollected warmly that after every rehearsal, he, and another boy-soloist each received a chocolate bar from Ustvolskaya.

During my service in the Ensemble, I called Galina Ivanovna. Once, I called and learned that she had just lost her mother.

Galina Ivanovna did not talk much about her family. Having no children of her own, she adored her nephew and his family (an analogy with Beethoven comes to mind), but these relationships were not stable. Her relationships with relatives had never been simple, even when she was a child. Could it be that the roots of her style have their beginning in her childhood? Her music is, in my perception, at once infantile and catastrophic. But it is an incredibly special infantilism. It is the infantilism of a stubborn, cranky, and unjustly offended child, who has been deprived of fun as a punishment. And so, this child protests in a childish way: "I will, I will! I will with fists, and with elbows, I will bite and scratch!" I sense this kind of infantilism in the Fifth and Sixth Piano Sonatas and in the all-pervasive stubbornness of her style. This is an innate quality, and it is extraordinarily strong. Experience of her own poor childhood is reflected, I think, in the First Symphony, which is based on the children's poems of Gianni Rodari. Children's psychology is close and understandable to her. She once said, "A person's age does not matter to genius. A child draws a plate of semolina porridge, and the plate of semolina is black! Cream of semolina – and black? Ah, it is because it is not delicious!"

This child's way of thinking is so akin to Ustvolskaya's own philosophy! She likes herself when she is a little girl age. Already then, she was not like everyone else.

When I had finished serving in the army and returned to my studying in the Rimsky-Korsakov College, I resumed composing "Pugach's Blood." When the work was ready, I started to look for performers to make a recording for the upcoming exam. But to find a soloist who could sing it seemed an impossible dream. I dared to ask Nadezhda Yureneva, a prominent Leningrad soprano who brought many new works of Russian composers to life. She premiered Poulenc's mono-opera La Voix Humaine in the Soviet Union and Shostakovich's cycle on the poems by Blok in Leningrad. She taught at the Conservatory and to my huge surprise and immense joy, she became interested in my music, agreed to sing it, and even arranged a recording at the conservatory's recording studio*. For me, a student, this was undoubtedly great luck. I easily found the rest of the performers – it was prestigious to participate in an ensemble with Yureneva. I hurried to share the news with Galina Ivanovna and found her in the college eatery. There, over a cup of tea, I broke the news. She seemed surprised and reacted with a phrase, the meaning of which is still unclear to me. "Well, Semyon, well, Semyon…" she said, either critiquing or evaluating me. Seemingly she was not happy with my success. Why?

"Do you think I should not have gone to Yureneva?" I was perplexed.

---

*   Everybody who is interested may listen to this composition om You Tube.

"No, why not?" she said pensively. "Did you tell her that you are my student?"

"Of course. I started with that. I said that I am a student of Ustvolskya."

"Oh, all right then. She agreed because you are my student... Well, Semyon, well, Semyon." Later, after listening to the recording with me at the college recording studio, she said: "Great performance... I wish my music were performed like yours." And we took a taxi to her house where we drank Champagne that we had bought together because I happened not to have enough money. While on the road, Sasha Fridman, a student of Ustvolskaya, who was also with us, admired the text of Ehrenburg, saying that Yevtushenko*, of course, in "Execution of Stepan Razin" took advantage of the coloring of this poem. Ustvolskaya agreed. As she was paying the taxi driver, Ustvolskaya asked for the change, which the driver "forgot" to return. She said, "Unfortunately, I am not rich. But I will be rich yet, will be rich..."

---

* **Yevgeny Aleksandrovich Yevtushenko**, (born July 18, 1933, Zima, Irkutsk oblast, Russia, U.S.S.R.—died April 1, 2017, Tulsa, Oklahoma, U.S.), poet and spokesman for the younger post-Stalin generation of Russian poets, whose internationally publicized demands for greater artistic freedom and for a literature based on aesthetic rather than political standards signaled an easing of Soviet control over artists in the late 1950s and 60s. Dmitry Shostakovich composed his 13-th Synphony with poems of **Yevtushenko** He also composed the Symphonic poem to his "Execution of Stepan Razin".

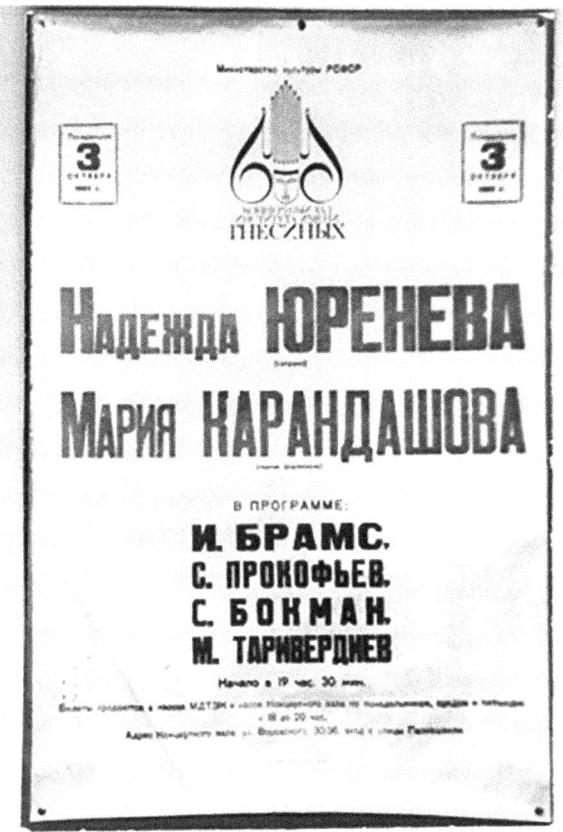

This is a poster of Nadezhda Yureneva's concert in the Great Hall of the Gnessin Institute, Moscow, on October 3, 1983. In this concert, along with Prokofiev, Brahms and Tariverdiev, she performed "Pugach's Blood" with the participation of the Institute's choir, an oboist student and the outstanding pianist Maria Karandashova. It was a great performance!

INTERLUDE.

I cannot help feeling ecstatic about this woman. Her talent is abundant. Her absolute unselfishness, devotion, and generosity put her in one line with the prominent Russian patrons of the arts and activists of the Russian culture. I am convinced that Nadezhda Yurievna Yureneva will be remembered and honored and that her name will remain in Russian cultural history.

Nadezhda Yurievna was disappointed by the comment of Isaak Glikman on Shostakovich's letter of 8.12.1967, as recorded in Glikman's *Story of Friendship*. Glikman wrote that Yureneva had run away from her own wedding. During one of our phone conversations, she told me this story.

N.Y.: Sasha Uteshev and I were invited to professor Michail Semyonovich Druskin's house to celebrate the New Year. There was Arapov with his wife and daughter, and the Druskins... I do not remember whether Galya Ustvolskaya was there. (Of course, not! - S. B.) There was a huge table – it is impossible to remember everyone. Next to me was Glikman. Michail Semenovich [Druskin] said, "Nadiusha, have you already understood that next to you sits the under-the table footsie player?

Glikman was rubbing my knee, and I did not know what to do and how to behave. He was our professor, and I was just a post-graduate student. I do not remember how I found a way out... It was very unpleasant...

S.B. Why did Glikman write that you ran away from your own wedding?

N.Y. Because I did not marry Sasha. But I did not have any plans to marry him... It was his, Glikman's, opinion that I was so frivolous...

S.B. Nadezhda Yurievna, please tell me about the preparations for the performance of the Blok cycle. I heard it was not particularly simple.

N.Y. Galina Vishnevskaya was very unhappy that I was going to perform this cycle in Leningrad. She was causing all kinds of trouble for me. It started after Poulenc. [Mono opera *La Voix Humaine* – S.B.] I sang Poulenc first because she did not show up for the rehearsal. At the administration offices of the Grand Hall, they said: "If Vishnevskaya is not here, let Yureneva perform." People came to the concert to hear Vishnevskaya, but I was singing instead... It was an enormous success. Vishnevskaya made a scandal to Rozhdestvensky - why did I sing? And she did not let me sing with him again. I performed with Rozhdestvensky only once after that. And suddenly, I received a letter from Shostakovich, in which he proposed that I sing his cycle based on the poetry of Blok... So, Vishnevskaya and Rostropovich came to

Leningrad with the express purpose of performing this cycle before I did, which they did at the Small Hall of the Conservatory.

A humorous incident took place during one of the rehearsals of Poulenc's *La Voix Humaine*.

Nadezhda Yurievna was nervous. Her part was difficult, and entrances were complicated. However, she found her way around it. In one place, she chose the oboe part to be her prop. Yureneva unmistakably found the right pitch listening to that part. But once, the oboist missed his entrance. Yureneva could not sing without hearing the expected "hint" from the oboe.

"What happened?" Rozhdestvensky inquired sternly and stopped the orchestra.

"Please forgive me, Gennady Nikolayevich," said Yureneva looking confused. "The oboe did not come in…"

She wanted to explain to the conductor why it was so important to her to hear the oboe part, but the delighted conductor turned to the orchestra and exclaimed, "A singer!!! And she noticed! This is how well one must know the score!" And the orchestra applauded.

With Nadezda Yureneva in the Moscow subway, 1997. On the left – my wife Olga.

FOURTEENTH VARIATION

A True Artist. What does it mean?

Galina Ivanovna told me once how she started teaching at Rimsky-Korsakov College: "I didn't know how to teach then. We played Mahler's music, and we played a game of chess. They wrote "table" works. *(composing without instrument at the table – S. B.)* And I was saying: "One should compose as a genius!"

Humility is not pitiful, and it is not nothingness. Humility is a dignified service.

Is Ustvolskaya a meek person?

She is utterly demanding of the performers of her music. She can take away her music if the performer does not understand it correctly, or if she simply does not like him. She can refuse to participate in a concert with a composer whose music she considers unsuitable for such proximity. The same goes for publishers – she was upset when an editor "improved" something in her notation. She believes in the exclusiveness of her talent and her personality. She is too proud to wage a trivial battle for leadership because the precedence already belongs to her. I wanted to dedicate one of my works to her, over which many creative tears were shed, and I was immensely proud of the result achieved at that time. I received a letter from a friend, who explained to me that, as per Ustvolskaya's request, dedication was impossible; she could only accept one from a person of her equal. I was stunned. I was stunned not because Ustvolskaya did not consider me an equal or worthy of her; I was absolutely astonished by her selectiveness. A gift, some trifle, could be accepted even from a child if it comes from the heart! Besides, she did not reply to me herself, but in a royal gesture assigned it to someone else. If Ustvolskaya did not want to talk with someone, or the topic of the conversation was unpleasant to her, she would ask someone to speak for her, answer the phone, or be an intermediary. In an on-line article preceding Ustvolskaya's discography, I read about her interview with a journalist Thea Derks, which was conducted on her behalf by Victor Suslin, although both, the composer and the journalist are fluent in German and Russian. I could not help a smile.*

Concerned about the long absence of one of her students, to whom she was in a very warm relation at the time, she asked me in a phone conversation (I called her, I do not remember what it was about) to find out what was wrong with him. "I don't know what to think" - I have heard how Ustvolskaya's voice was worried in the phone pipe. "I was already going to write a letter to him. With my own hand! With my hand, you see! It is unsuitable for me to call him. There are his parents there. I cannot talk to them".

But I remember, I was most of all amazed by this "with my own hand".

Ones, on my visit to Galya, she was terribly upset, drank a valerian. All because she and Kostya, her husband, could not share the time. Both had to be composing. Kostya was writing songs.

"He's gone slammed the door! I'm left here with a slammed door! He's putting these his... small scribblers. (*harmonic symbols* - S. B.) I can't see it! This... graphomania! Well Semyon, but I do not compose such music like he does!" Kostia, a former student of her, wrote songs, and it was strange to me, that someone who is so close to Galya could write that kind of music. But they were together – husband and wife – two such different people. I replied that, of course, Kostia's work may not be great, but if it was important to him, she ought to have been more considerate of it. Ustvolskaya was surprised that I did not support her and, obviously, not expecting such a reply from me, she looked perplexed †.

---

*   *Music Under Soviet Rule: Ustvolskaya* http://www.siue.edu/~aho/musov/ust/ust. html

†   I once accidentally slighted Kostia. He was very cordial with me, but I stood him up, not purposefully, but from a lack of experience and simple-heartedness. He deeply hated me. I wanted, but could not, explain myself to him. He did not want to see or talk to me. Moreover, he also forbade Galya to see me or to have any contact with me and I did not learn about it right away. It is hard to imagine what a terrible onslaught she had to withstand considering her fragile and easily injured nature. Thus, my

"There is a Mozart and a Salieri in every poet," wrote the poet Osip Mandelshtam.* I agree easily with this statement. An ingenious artist *"Mozart"* sometimes becomes his own opposite, the jealous "Salieri." He is completely immersed in his work, demands understanding and attention from those around him. He does not even notice how he sometimes "poisons" their lives. The witty Bernard Shaw was certain that a "true artist would rather let his wife be hungry, kids have no shoes to wear, and his seventy-year-old mother work until she drops, than to work himself at anything besides his art."† Arnold Schoenberg considered himself to be under-appreciated even by admirers about whom he said: "…Hindemith, Stravinsky, and Bartók are, if not above me, at least on the same with me level. They [the admirers] have too many idols…"‡ Did not he understand that in art and culture (from Sanskrit "cult" – "service" and "Ure"- "light," "Service of Light") there can be no preferences! Valuable are all, serving the noble ideals, Culture and Spirit. Evgeny Pasternak, the son of the famous Russian poet, in an interview, was asked, "Did your father try to influence you in some way?" He answered simply: "No, the only thing he taught me was not to disturb him when he worked."§

INTERLUDE

What does "new" mean in art? Does the significance of a creative expression resides in its newness? Yes and no. Yes, because if an artist cannot find new colors, why does he create? No, because striving for newness can lead to the loss of genuineness. One can search only within oneself – not outside, but inside. ("I know that I am not Bach. But I am not an Offenbach either!" Rossini supposedly said.) And if

---

every visit, phone call, or letter became reason for a terrible rebuke from Kostia. (I learned about this later.) Eventually, Ustvolskaya gave in. The incident with Kostia happened in 1978. I received my last letter from Ustvolskaya in 1982.

*   Nadezhda Mandelshtam "My Will", New York: Silver Century, 1982, p. 37.

†   Bernard Shaw, "Man and Superman," a comedy with philosophy. Internet, knijky.ru/books/chelovek-i-sverhchelovek. (Russian)

‡   G. Schneyerson *Articles on Contemporary Western Music. Essays. Memoirs.* Moskva: Sovetsky Compositor, 1974, p. 206.

§   *"Zalozhnik Vechnosti v Tretiem Tisiachiletii"* Russian newspaper "New Life", San Francisco, June, 2004

there is nothing interesting going on, it will be – uninteresting. But the method of expression is also important. A style lends conviction. This is where an artist sometimes starts balancing on the edge of a knife. He finally finds a system in which to envelop his originality. He makes a discovery. And then what? He keeps exploiting his find. How long can one do this? Until the system runs itself out. Then this artist starts repeating himself, his style fades and loses attractiveness. It is sometimes exceedingly difficult to give up one's discovery. It is the artist's possession, his property. But composers have done this to preserve the naturalness, freshness, and emotional attractiveness of their style. Bach did it. He was not opposed to borrowing someone else's music and arranging it in his own way. He took from Scarlatti, Vivaldi, Couperin, and from many other, lesser known, composers. (The theme of the well-known Italian concerto belongs to Muffat, whose name does not say much to contemporary listeners.) In the 20th century, Igor Stravinsky, in search of a modern style, "invented" musical neoclassicism, the main idea of which is borrowing from classical styles and sometimes even from the content of classical music itself. A furious opponent of Arnold Schoenberg and his serial technique, he started to compose using this system at the age of almost seventy! It is amazing that he remained an innovator his entire life!

Sometimes it is difficult to determine whether some music is unconsciously influenced by another composer, or it is a conscious "borrowing." Composing using someone else's model can ease and speed the process. Composers of the past did this when they had to compose fast and much. Stravinsky's neoclassicism is perceived as a discovery because of the stylistic contrast: music of the 20th century "in clothes" of the distant 17th and 18th centuries. But the method itself is not new. In Tchaikovsky's Swan Lake two numbers of the second act – the first Scene and the Dance of the Little Swans – seem to implicate Franz Schubert. The prototype of the Dance would be the quite popular Moment Musicale #3. Moment Musicale is written in the key to f minor. The Dance of Little Swans is in the key to f#-minor. The two pieces have almost identical introductions. Thematic and rhythmical relation comes through. Themes in thirds and the use of grace notes make them even more like each other.

Moments Musicaux

Schubert
Op. 94, No. 3

Allegro moderato

Moment Musicale #3, excerpt

The Dance of Little Swans, excerpt

For the "Scene" such prototype would be the main theme of the first movement of the Eighth ("The Unfinished") Symphony. In this case the similarities are even more obvious. Besides the "common" key (b-minor) and the themes, the texture, and even some details in the orchestration are similar! Both the Scene and the Symphony start with the string tremolo. Schubert's tremolo is melodic, and Tchaikovsky's tremolo is static. Both themes are performed by the oboe. The Scene from the Swan Lake seems to be a variation on a theme from the Schubert's Symphony. Schubert's lyricism is dramatized in Tchaikovsky. But Tchaikovsky barely thought he made any kind of discovery. He did not, but Stravinsky did - such a joke of history! But what is even more interesting is that Tchaikovsky's individuality is not lost or in any way diminished because of similarity of his music to Shubert's one. It is also very interesting to note that Tchaikovsky's Children's Album came out under this title: "Children's Album. A collection of light pieces for children. Imitation of Schumann". Tchaikovsky was not ashamed to admit to imitating Schumann without fear of damaging his individuality. (The mention of Schumann was later removed anyway, wishing to "save" the reputation of a great composer.)

For Ustvolskaya such a path would have been unacceptable. Her character is such that she cannot willfully use someone else's discovery, although she, unconsciously does it anyway.

She admired Stravinsky. She spoke of him to our class in 1969. "He is so lively, and short – shorter than me…" she said to us, "And so witty! And what music he writes these days! He is now writing masses. May God help you to write in your twenties the way he writes now, at almost ninety"

And then: "He gets ill a lot, but he wears a huge silver cross around his neck, which protects him…"

I remember listening to Stravinsky's Symphony of Psalms in class, following the score. I was turning pages late and Ustvolskaya was getting nervous and kept saying: "Turn, Semyon, turn! No, not there!" After listening, she said, "How can one compose anything else after such music?"

Ustvolskaya's violin sonata was performed at a meeting with Stravinsky, organized by the Composers' Union during Stravinsky's visit to Leningrad in 1962. But I cannot imagine that the author of the sonata fell on her knees in front of the prominent composer, kissing his hand like Maria Yudina* did, or posed next to him for photographers and journalists wishing to capture herself next to a celebrity. She "has her own whiskers." That is her view of the world.

I remember how she admired Anton Webern, a disciple of Schoenberg, for his devotion to the doctrine of the twelve-tone technique. She admired his consistency and his strictness, which surpassed even that of his teacher. "How he must have struggled!" she exclaimed. "You know, he only has an hour worth of music!"

Ustvolskaya admired Webern because he was a consistent and stylistically "pure" composer. Those qualities are in tune with her own idealistic model. She struggled too, and this is why she does not have much music. She is extremely strict and consistent in using her "post twelve-tone system," as I define it. And if we watch the evolution of her style, we will notice that it changes towards more strictness and harshness, in her technique, as in her philosophy. Having chosen such an exceptionally difficult path, it is impossible to be very productive. But this is the true essence of the creative process. It is shaped by life

---

*   Maria Yudina, (1899 – 1970), a great Russian pianist, also known for her unmatched eccentricity.

itself and the life of an artist in particular. That is why in art there cannot be a single, exemplary right decision. Every artist is right in his way. Whether we agree with him or not does not help us to find the truth. Any creative achievement requires a great strain, sometimes the utmost strain. This is a necessary condition for true creativity. If during this exertion, an artist makes a discovery, it will be contained within the work itself. Where is the discovery in, say, any one of Chopin's Mazurkas? Or in a Mozart's piano sonata? I know there is much literature dedicated to these problems. But do they really exist as problems? Ingenuity is unexplainable.

I am going to say something terrible. Neither Haydn, nor Mozart, nor of course Bach ...were innovators. It would have been too dangerous. "In earlier centuries, the idea of misunderstood genius was not only unknown; it was inconceivable. The artist produced for his own time for the purpose of immediate consumption, hence the vast amount of music written during the three centuries between 1500 and 1800" (Einstein, "Music in the Romantic Era", 16)

Undoubtedly, innovations appeared in classical music. Otherwise, no development is possible. But those innovations never challenged the listeners' minds. An artist was dependent financially on the public and commissioners. "...and when Haydn and Mozart exceeded the ability of their day to understand their music, they tried to conceal the fact."[*] This tells us that at that time High art was in high demand. Another shocking conclusion might be that what is new in art is simply a new talent and that is all. And yet," one must write ingeniously "! - as such Ustvolskaya proclaimed.

The work on this book helped me to see what principles are inviolable in art, have always been such and will live as long as the world inhabited by us! And even without us. Because Creativity lives even outside of us.

---

[*]   Einstein, *Music In The Romantic Era,* 14

This photo portrait is a good likeness of how I remember Ustvolskaya when I was her student.

INTERLUDE

"A thought uttered is a lie." (*Fyodor Tyutchev*). Yes, it is! And we must carefully choose words that retain at least a grain of truth. I was writing this book for myself. I had no publisher/customer. I wrote it during Galina Ivanovna's lifetime. It was difficult for me to write because I knew that she would not like it! She would take this book against herself. But, in fact, that is not the case at all! Ustvolskaya, it seems to me, did not understand the meaning of her creative work herself. That is heroism! But which one? Yes, she wrote for years for the desk drawer! She wrote bold music in deprivation, without regard for critics or even listeners! There is nothing to say about "culture" officials who only in quotation should be mentioned have nothing to say! But I believe that Galina Ivanovna's feat is not that at all. She managed to destroy the aesthetics of demonism with her extremely radical music!

It is impossible to write such kind of music after her! It will be boring and banal! Musical means of expression for showing such emotions are completely exhausted by her music, and such creativity becomes irrelevant. It is very symbolic, as the world is tired of such experiences, both in life and in art. If it is not good for art, it is unsuitable for life as well. And in order to survive, in order to safeguard life on the planet, art must be changed! We need to create! We must be looking!

FIFTEENTH VARIATION

Non-chamber Music Style. Musical Fascism.

The amount of music composed, as well as the number of years lived, does not have a significant meaning because the product of life and work is not a single piece of art, but the person himself. Creative work and life are two mutually enriching processes. One composition or one year of life can completely change one's worldview. Either process can be quite painful; one embodies another. Otherwise, life loses its meaning.

Those who associate Ustvolskaya with Modernism and Avant-gardism are simply wrong. Modernists and avant-gardists are composers for whom novelty and unconventionality is their end goal. Ustvolskaya's music is different. It does not seem to be thought up. It is a very thoroughly contemplated philosophy, a certain attitude towards the world and life. The originality of her music is determined by her own originality, by the unconventionality of her understanding of the incidents of life. This is why straight-forward analogies about the origins of her musical style are impossible. But any artistic event is a continuation, even if it denies what precedes it. Ustvolskaya fervently objects when her music is compared to anything else to find its roots or when it is referred to as chamber music.

When I was still in my first year at the College, I dared to inquire about her music. "Do you write mostly chamber music?" I asked. Without letting me finish, Ustvolskaya said calmly and firmly, "I do not write chamber music," which puzzled me. But I would like to emphasize that Ustvolskaya's non-chamber music is truly an innovation in music composition. It is a stunning mastery and demands acknowledgment. But it is only one method. It is not the only way to compose. And, in the end, it is not important, in and of itself.

What is important is music. It is interesting to compare Ustvolskaya's Symphonies and Compositions. Even though the number of players in her compositions is sometimes greater than in her symphonies (10 players in the Second Composition and only 4 in the Fourth Symphony), within Ustvolskaya's music, those are genres of differing density and significance. Undoubtedly, Symphonies and Compositions are two different genres. Her Compositions, which are less dense, I would classify as "relative chamber music." The composer's opinion should, of course, be respected, especially since her music does not, indeed, fit traditional schemes. But those wishing to understand her music look for the various traditions from which it sprouts. And they find them, but of course, within the limits of their own understanding, music education, and listening experience. Even the late Beethoven quartets are said not to completely fit the definition of *chamber music*. But this did not make the quartets symphonies. An age-old convention maintains that if there are fewer instruments it is chamber music; if a piece is written for symphony orchestra, then it is symphonic, and so forth. An artist often poses questions to listeners and researchers that are difficult to answer. It is not easy and sometimes impossible to change uprooted traditions. Music will speak for itself. There are methods, definitions, and techniques chosen by time, which are impossible and unnecessary to change. Prokofiev, for example, canceled clefs and transposition in his scores. He wrote everything as if for instruments *in C* and was surprised that nobody followed his example. Traditional, "wrong," or "difficult" score notation proved to be more practical because generations of musicians were accustomed to it; Prokofiev simply gave conductors more work.

How does Ustvolskaya achieve such a "non-chamber" effect? Her works are written for small groups of instruments, but what instruments are they? And how she uses them! Piano, trumpet, flute, oboe, trombone, tuba, and bass – all these instruments, even violin and cello, are used in extreme registers with extreme levels of tension and sound, sometimes reaching *ffff*. The piano in her music is mostly a percussion instrument, often playing *ffff* at extreme registers, using fists, elbows, the edges of palms. (The Fifth sonata has the dynamic *fffff*. It also has this characteristic remark: "The sound of knuckles hitting the keys must be heard." An American pianist Marian Lee, commenting on Ustvolskaya's remark, wrote: "It is an extremely painful act when repeated 144 times at fff. Some writers have equated the physical pain and discomfort of Ustvolskaya's works with the ecstatic pain of religious self-flagellation.* But these are not the most important things in her music. More important is the creative objective that is being achieved by these means. A composer, like any other artist, lives in a densely populated creative space, where crossings and collisions are absolutely inevitable. Using the same basic musical components, it is impossible to avoid repetitions (repeats) or micro-repetitions simply mathematically. Once they took one component - pitch - and substituted it with glissandi. Not all the instruments can be used to perform such music and a special system of notation is needed to write it down. Theoretically, it is new music. But is this music artistically convincing? (This is what will determine its future.) It will depend on the composer's creative capacity.

If this experiment proves successful, this discovery might have followers and this experience will have a continuation and development. And it will remain if this system has worthy representatives. In the development of any new system, authorship is important only if the system is artistically convincing. (This trend in the music of Polish composers in the 60s and 70s turned out to be unsustainable).

Dodecaphony, the invention of Arnold Schoenberg, was discovered independently by several authors, almost simultaneously. Josef Matthias Hauer discovered his system before Schoenberg, in 1911, and Schoenberg even discussed co-authorship with him. "With time, the danger of competition with Hauer – *a very weak composer* [emphasis by S.B.], who remained in the shadows, had disappeared. For the music world, Schoenberg remains the only creator of dodecaphony, the creator of the compositional school whose influence spread to many areas of the globe."[†]

An artistic invention is not a computer or an airplane. In art, one artist, figuratively speaking, digs the channels, while the other only uses

---

*　　Marian Lee, *Galina Ustvolskaya: The Spiritual Works of a Soviet Artist*. Ph. D. diss., (Peabody Conservatory of Music, 2002), 74-76

†　　G.Schneyerson, *Articles, 164*

them more fully. Whose input is greater? The somebody whose work is more interesting.

And how, sometimes, unexpectedly, and mysteriously an idea travels from one artist to another! And this does not detract from the worthiness of any of their works. For example, Rimsky-Korsakov's "Spanish Capriccio" would influence Ravel's "Bolero;" Ravel's "Bolero" affected the first movement of Shostakovich's "Seventh symphony"; and Rimsky-Korsakov was influenced by Glinka's Spanish miniatures "Aragon's Hota" and "Night in Madrid."

At the music college where I studied, there was a talented teacher Adam Stratievsky, who taught the course on Soviet music. Once, a student complained to him that Scriabin was too much under Chopin's influence and even wrote in the same genres: mazurkas, etudes, preludes. "Can you tell Scriabin from Chopin?" asked Stratievsky.

"I can," the student answered with confidence.

"Thank God," said Stratievsky.

Yes, Ustvolskaya is original. But what would her music be if there were no Stravinsky with his rhythmic keenness and the heavy rhythms of the "Rite of Spring," his percussive piano and his small instrumental groups, consisting of woodwind and brass instruments,[*] and if no atonal music or cluster technique had been invented by American composer Henry Cowell earlier.[†] Tradition and succession are the

---

[*] *"The Soldier (L'histoire du soldat – I.B.)* marks my final break with the Russian orchestral school." (*Memories and Commentaries*. Stravinsky and Craft, 132) Stravinsky was the first composer in history to write religious music for different religions, guided not by religious interest, but by the highest ideas which penetrate all religions – their spirituality. И. S. Bach used to do it before Stravinsky, but remained within the Christian denominations. Stravinsky, being Orthodox, composed the «Symphony of Psalms» on Latin texts and the sacred ballad «Abraham and Isaac» with the Hebrew text, for which he was criticized and condemned. The controversy on the Internet on this topic continues to the present day. Both works were written for concert performance. This is spiritual, non-religious music. Stravinsky anticipated Ustvolskaya's spiritual, by her definition non-religious, music.

[†] Marian Lee, in a phone interview with Ustvolskaya, had to ask whether the composer had "ever heard of American composer Henry Cowell whom we credit with the discovery of clusters." Ustvolskaya said she had not. (Marian Lee *"The Spiritual Works of Galina Ustvolskaya"*) This may be true, but it is unimportant. The method may have been discovered by Cowell, but the method is not music yet.

main principals of development. Innovation is unthinkable without them. The development of a creative space can only be done in stages. For example, when applying for a patent on an invention, one must refer to the prototype of this invention: something that was invented before. Only after comparing the two can a conclusion be drawn if the invention is valid. New is merely differently organized old.

I cannot help but share one observation. The systems of organization and formation of musical works copy the systems of organization and management of society in the evolutionary development. The tonal-harmonic system, in which the classical composers of the XVII-XVIII centuries were working is the analogue of the absolutist-monarchical system of social structure. The tonic is the king, the emperor. The notes which belong to the tonic triad symbolize the courtiers, nobles, grandees. Other tones symbolize servants, lower classes, serfs. The servants are strictly subordinate to the lords and the king's authority (notes of tonic triad and tonic itself). Dissonance is subordinate to consonance. The way of life is strict and unshakable. The forms are strict and verified. Emotions are sublimely restrained. Musical language is universal, which makes it accessible and understandable. Musical Romanticism, XIX century. The role of tonic and tonic harmonies has remained, but transitions from one tonality to another (modulations) are becoming more frequent, and because of it the role of the main tonality is not so clearly expressed. The role of dissonance in harmony is increasing gradually, and because of the complexity of harmony, functionality is weakening. Music becomes increasingly loose and colorful. Stylistics becomes more individualized. There is a growing interest in the national features of music: Grieg, Chopin, Glinka, for example. New emotions arise anger, struggle, sophisticated sensuality, pain, and fear. In the life of that time there were many socio-political movements to inculcate new views on religion, ways of life, and the state systems. The national consciousness grows. Rebellions and revolutions occur, because of which the monarchy is weakened or destroyed.

The system of total organization of the musical work, which appeared in the 20s of the twentieth century - dodecaphony, the brainchild of Arnold Schoenberg - is an analogue of the fascist-communist systems of society management. There is almost no freedom. Emotionally, this music is conditioned and limited by the system (in society - by party) closed on itself, isolated and constrained. Therefore, its imaginative sphere is limited. As in society, music of the 20th and 21st centuries are characterized by aspiration for democracy, equality, and liberalism, while in music there are equal rights of consonance and dissonance. The tonality is not always clearly heard to, and very often there it is not at all - atonalism. The composer considers how to organize his/her works by him/herself.

Only, for God's sake, it is not necessary to mix art with politics. This is wrong to think Schoenberg is fascist! With this sketch I just wanted to show how art can be sensitive to the phenomena of our being. Though it has its own way, but the life is unified and obeys not to someone's whim, but to the logic of evolutionary development, the meaning of which is rarely can be understood.

Thus, atonal music could only appear in the twentieth century, and not in the seventeenth or eighteenth. In those eras, human consciousness was not ready to understand and to accept this kind of discovery. Supposing someone dared such an experiment, he could not withstood the opposition of the esthetic consciousness of the public. Try to imagine yourself sitting in the stadium among many thousands of people. Inspired by a common impulse, everybody gets up tumultuously expressing ecstasy over the spectacle they see. They get up, but you, unable to share in their delight, keep sitting… Try. You will see – it is not simple, but rather, simply impossible to do. But the very idea of atonal music would not have been possible at an earlier time. In past eras, the thinking process was aimed in a completely different direction. The right time comes, and reforms happen because the need for them has become urgent. For example, fingering reforms for harpsichord and organ took place simultaneously by Bach in Germany and by François Couperin in France. It is known that before these reforms musicians used only three fingers to play those instruments.

---

* A wonderful exception is Mozart's symphony, where he portrays clumsy village musicians who play out of tune by using non-functional atonal harmony.

Galina Ustvolskaya resolutely refuses to admit to any relationship or succession between her music and the music of any other composer or of any other era or style. "I have my own music, only my own!" She speaks. (O. Gladkova, *Galina Ustvolskaya,* 4) But it does not work that way, Galina Ivanovna!

It is important to not only hear and see the innovations in an artistic occurrence, but also understand their roots. The music of Ustvolskaya with its esthetic (or anti-esthetic) principles is a logical result of the destruction of the classical harmony and with it – of its derivatives: symmetric structures and the classical orchestra.

I remember how we sat in Ustvolskaya's room in silence. Galya sat on the sofa, and I was on a chair across from her. Gradually, the twilight engrossed us, but Galya did not turn on the light. Suddenly, without any connection to anything that had been said she exclaimed: "Everything needs to be changed! Everything – the orchestra, the seating. Everything, everything is outdated!" She realized how strange her words sounded and added: "This sometimes happens when I work…" The creative tension never left her.

INTERLUDE

In her book "Galina Ustvolskaya", O. Gladkova writes about the "sunset of music" and says that Ustvolskaya's music is music for the end of music." She writes: "Ustvolskaya's music does not leave any hope; her Fifth symphony – this thought is frightening, but nagging – seems to be the last Russian symphony. Its style is eloquent dot. Music is suffocating, agonizing, but it will not breathe in the poisonous and narcotic air of befuddling mass-culture."

Regardless of whether this thought belongs to Ustvolskaya or the author of the book herself, there is a misconception. Nothing can be ended or stopped. The path of spiritual ascent is uninterrupted. Ustvolskaya's music, her road in art is complete. It cannot be traveled any further. Ustvolskaya's music convinces the listener that neither music nor life can continue along this path. Her art is the dead end to the aesthetic labyrinth. Life evolves in the opposite direction. And if, as

Stravinsky maintained, harmony had a brilliant, but short, history[*], the post-harmonic period happened to be even shorter. But who knows? Someone walking the new path will use her discoveries in a new way altogether.

Naturally, no one can do away with a symphony orchestra, string quartet, or any other classical ensemble that exists as a product of musical evolution. No one can forbid an artist from discovering new methods. Ustvolskaya is not the last composer, and her symphonies are not the last symphonies. But any serious musician – or simply a thoughtful person with an interest in art will recognize the importance of her discoveries. Her system of musical organization (in both sound and rhythm), her economical choice of technique and timbres, and her original meter – all those resources are exhausted by her music. It is amazing that despite many voluntary limits and prohibitions, she managed to find a new color.

It is difficult to find other examples of such a phenomenal use of instruments, which produce sound at the outer limits of their capacity, as in some of Ustvolskaya's works. Paradoxically, in this aspect she approaches to the extremes of rock-music with its super-dynamic polarity of registers and intentionally "unmusical" use of instruments.[†]

Most interestingly, she has no vocal music except for the First and the Fourth symphonies, where she has soloists. However, there is vocalism in the texture of her works. The Second piano sonata, for example, stands out for its vocal texture: the range (with few exceptions,) the voicing, moderate tempos, and the absence of big leaps in the voice leading. It is a special kind of singing – and it is very expressive – on a "non-singing" instrument. In the Second symphony, one can hear a choir of flutes and oboes impersonating female voices and brass - male singers. The homogeneity of timbres and the texture of the work with its minimal voice leading are akin to choral music.

Her compositions may seem monotonous to a superficial listener, but they are surprisingly diverse. She crosses a certain threshold of consciousness. Yes, consciousness. One of the characters in Gogol's

---

[*]   Igor Stravinsky, *Poetics of Music in the Form of Six Lessons,* transl. Arthur Knodel and Ingolf Dahl, (Cambridge, MA: Harvard University Press, 1970), 51 passim.

[†]   An album of a Petersburg singer-songwriter Yuri Shevchuk *"Black Dog Petersburg"*

play "The Gamblers" *admires a* piece of cheese which, "like a good quartermaster, says: 'Welcome in, gentlemen, there is still room…'" The artist is a "quartermaster" of consciousness. When it seems to be completely filled with prejudices and yesterday's truths, he finds a tiny spot, a small crack, through which, little by little, innovative ideas start to seep. They wake the consciousness and widen it. Its capacity grows. Our consciousness is not always equal to the information absorbed. It could be compared to a yet unknown language we cannot understand. The more thoroughly we study this language, the more of its intonations and nuances we would be able to perceive.

Life and its occurrences are full of multiple meanings. Many customary notions can be changed in our perception if we continue to change and perfect our consciousness. Prominent thinkers (a composer, as any other artist, is a thinker) help us perfect the apparatus of perception, of our consciousness.

SIXTEENTH VARIATION

♪

The Tsar. Sviridov and KGB.

Sometimes I would walk her to the Composers' Union after classes at the college. We would walk from Matveyev Pereulok along the Moika to the Krukov Canal, cross it, then stepping over the Moika, across the Potseluev's Bridge, we would follow Hertzen Street (now it is Bolshaya Morskaya, as before the Revolution) past the Yusupov Palace, which stood on the bank opposite the Composers' House. "Here, by the way, strolled Blok, and the Tsar used to walk here, and everybody would bow to him…" Galina Ivanovna would tell me…

A happy reminiscence.

Once, I remember, Galya and I were sitting and talking in her kitchen. She remembered how she had dined with Georgy Sviridov at the Astoria restaurant (they were young composers back then, or perhaps even students,) and he had told her intimately: "There, at the next table, sits a man who knows everything about you."

"I was very surprised," continued Ustvolskaya, "what is there to know about me?"

"But he knows!" said Sviridov.

Here I would like to tell you about one episode that happened to me in the eighties in Leningrad. My wife and I, and our little daughter were supposed to meet our penfriends, a young couple from England. They had come to Leningrad. We talked on the phone and decided to meet by the Academicheskaya metro station and have breakfast together. But our rendezvous was very rudely interrupted before it even began. Suddenly, just as we said hello to our friends, out of nowhere appeared a black "Volga"* and we were pushed inside by some hefty

---

*   A car model

fellows and taken to the nearest police department. Our friends were taken separately from us. I will not clutter my story with details. It was the notorious KGB. They confused our friends with some human rights activists and later, already in England, a Russian consul apologized for the incident. (No one apologized to us.) They behaved rudely. We were depressed. One of those KGB agents, dressed in all new foreign clothes ("perhaps confiscated from some unlucky fellows," I thought,) made me empty my pockets, he searched through my address book, and as he saw a phone-number of Vladislav Uspensky,[*] whom I had never met and never called, he said: "He's *our* man…" And for some reason he added with a disgusting grin: "and Petrov, Andrey Pavlovich,[†] is also our man… A good man…"

Once, after a concert in which Georgy Sviridov accompanied Alexander Vedernikov, who sang his vocal cycle on poetry by Robert Burns's among other vocal works, I hurried to share the "discovery" with Galina Ivanovna. I liked the music. It was my first year at the college and I was anxious for new impressions and absorbed everything with great interest.

"Galina Ivanovna, what do you think of Sviridov?" I asked naively.

"Well, what? He is a talented man, of course… He takes a C-major triad and holds it, and holds it… By the way, he is also excruciatingly hard composing music."[‡]

INTERLUDE

"If you create a great number of works, it is difficult to say something new in every one of them," said Ustvolskaya. It is also impossible, however, to say something in a new way when there are too few works as well. Only newness in the artist himself, along with a new perspective on life, can yield creative newness. Ustvolskaya determined her artistic credo early. Her philosophy did not change with time, but

---

[*]   A Leningrad composer, conservatory professor.

[†]   Famous Soviet composer, a head of the Leningrad branch of the Composers' Union at the time.

[‡]   This is a sarcastic reference to a popular Sviridov's song from his song cycle on the verses by Pushkin "Drawing Near to Izhory." The whole first page of the piano accompaniment consists of a C-major chord ostinato. (note by transl.)

only confirmed and became increasingly harsh and ascetic. This is my understanding of why her music is so stylistically stubborn, why the percussive piano became her leading timbre, why a dark ostinato of quarter notes, like some fatal power, moves offensively, passing from one work to another, crushing genre barriers. Her music is akin to religion. This religion, however, is not that majestic and organic belief, inherent in Bach, whose music was created with and for God. This is a religion of self-sufficiency.

SEVENTEENTH VARIATION

♪

Pushkin. Tchaikovsky… Pakhmutova.

I remember amazing evenings spent at Ustvolskaya's house. We would talk frankly about many things. Ustvolskaya believed in true and pure love and could talk about it with great inspiration and simplicity at the same time. We pitied Mussorgsky, who started drinking after an unsuccessful love affair he could never get over. He reached a point in his self-destructiveness when he took the letter "g" out of his last name and became Musorsky.* We talked about Goethe, who at the end of his life fell in love with a seventeen-year-old girl and she loved him too. He wanted to marry her, but his relatives were against it…

And Mayakovsky was, it turned out, incurably ill! He was amorous…

"So, this is why he shot himself?"

"Of course. You see, at that time they could not treat his condition…"

"And Pushkin, how he fell in love!"

"Oh, no! Pushkin did not love anyone!"

"So, what about all his love poetry? So passionate, ardent…"

"That is different, how do you not understand…"

"OK, but Tchaikovsky? How could he express love with such deep feelings if he could not love? Tatiana's letter, for example, or, let us say, "None, but the lonely heart…"

---

*   It is known that Mussorgsky's noble family is very old and that his last name is derived from the word "musorga," which is a kind of regal clothing given by the Tsar Aleksey Michailovich to one of the Mussorgsky's ancestors for a great service. The word "musor", on the other hand, in Russian means "garbage". (note by transl.)

"Why couldn't he? He loved, only differently. And how he loved it! There was such passion! I feel sorry for him... deeply sorry for Peder* Ilich," Ustvolskaya said without irony.

Once, she gave me read a poem by Emile Verhaeren†, which was, at that point, an inspiration for her.

> When you shall close these eyes of mine to light,
> Oh, kiss them long – for all that love afire
> May hope to give they shall have given you
> In that last look of ultimate desire.
>
> Beneath the moveless glow of candlelight,
> Oh, lean to them your face so fain and brave
> That on them be impressed this sight alone
> That they shall keep forever in the grave.
>
> And may I feel, before the tomb is mine,
> Upon the pure, white bed our hands that seek
> Each other once again, and near my head
> Feel for the last time repose your cheek;
>
> And know that I shall go away with heart
> Burning still for you so passionately
> That even through the mute and stony earth
> The dead themselves shall feel its ardency!‡

Her mood changes were shocking. She was enchanted by the singer Nanny Bregvadze§... A song by Pakhmutova¶ heard over the kitchen radio suddenly received her approval ("The world is empty without

---

*　Russian slang for "pederast". (note by transl.)

†　Emile Verhaeren (1855-1916), Belgian poet

‡　Emile Verhaeren, *The Evening Hours,* transl. Charles R. Murphy, (New York: John Lane Company, 1918), 72-73

§　Nanny Bregvadze was a very popular Soviet-Georgian performer.

¶　Alexandra Pahmutova is a very popular Soviet/Russian composer/songwriter.

you…") apparently, it echoed her mood. "Good words," she would say pensively. "… and the music seems to be alright…" It was the mood of the moment. Well, isn't that not happen? Especially as the song is really good. Serious people also listen to and admire frivolous things, laughing at stupid jokes and not always saying only wise and profound things. Konstantin Bagrenin told us about Galina Ustvolskaya's meeting with Alexandra Pakhmutova. "Khrushchev invited young creative talents to meet with him. It was in the Kremlin. A buffet table was set. Everybody gathered around the table and waited for him to show up, but he was not and had not come. Galina Ivanovna was tired of looking at a tasty table and she started to eat caviar, balyk,[*] sausages and everything she had never seen before. And one short Komsomol girl made a remark to her: "Everybody is waiting, and you should be waiting for Nikita Sergeyevich as well to be allowed by him to eat. Galina Ivanovna, who had intelligently continued to chew, "sent down" a short one mentally, and then asked someone if she was the administrator. And Ustvolskaya was told that she needed to know Pakhmutova, because you are also a composer, and Galina Ivanovna agreed that she and Pahmutova were composers, "only we have different specialties," she said.[†]

She admired Rachmaninoff. She would play his Third Piano Concerto performed by the composer himself on her old turntable. She would become ecstatic from the music. When a turbulent passage began, she would move the needle forward so harshly, that we could hear the poor disk grinding under it. "This is for horses! Further, further… here, this is a wonderful spot…"

Suddenly, Ustvolskaya would say: "I want to speak in German!" and so she did, fluently and clearly. We, her guests, could not, of course, keep up with this "conversation." I felt envious – just looking at her! But I did not give up and awkwardly, not always to the point, and with many mistakes, would try to answer. If I did not have enough German words (and I really did not have them enough,) I added some Russian to finish a sentence. For example: "such finsternis you have here, under the table." (Finsternis means "darkness.") Everybody laughed.

---

[*]   Balyk Russian: балык is the salted and dried soft parts of fish (or meat), usually coming from large valuable species: e.g., sturgeon or salmon, (pork). The word means "fish" in Turkic languages (written *balık* in Turkish).

[†]   "Ustvolskaya. Precision", Internet (translated from Russian).

Galya laughed heartily: "Such finsternis! Ha-ha-ha... finsternis! Such finsternis!" We admired "Solveig's Song" by Grieg... Who or what did not we admire! Rembrandt, Chekhov, Gogol...

Stop! We should stay here any longer.

As cited in O. Gladkova's book, Ustvolskaya says: "Of all the writers I always preferred and still prefer *only* Gogol. [emphasis by S.B]. I think that he was misunderstood in his time and that he is still misunderstood now."*

How can one understand Gogol if he is shrouded in mystery? Gogol is dark. (Dare I hope to be forgiven by his admirers?) During my friendship with Ustvolskaya, Gogol was among her favorite writers, but I never knew him to be the only one she liked best of all. Gogol was close to her as I understood it then due to his painfully challenging work process, his doubts, and his tormented heart. And it turns out now that she chose Gogol as her life teacher. I will quote some fragments from the books about Gogol. It is important for understanding Galina Ustvolskaya's inner creative impetus.

"Unquestionably, Gogol knew something about himself and the world that we do not know in the realm of *magical mystery* [emphasis by S.B.]. Awareness of the reality of that sphere comes into play [in his work] where other authors, as a rule, get along on folk tradition, the play of fantasy, or conjecture. Gogol has his own, personal approach and experience when it comes to superstition and ancient legends which were then discussed a lot, written about; about which Pushkin and Zhukovsky told wonderfully before Gogol as if it were something detached and far away, although amusing and worthy of the plot for a poem...

"On the same subject Gogol responded vitally; he realized folk demonology in *his biography* [emphasis by S.B.] of a repentant sorcerer and a poor madman; he became aware of its relevance, concerning current reality and himself, Gogol, personally...

"The dreams and hallucinations of Gogol are striking in their clarity and precision of images; incidentally, outer, and supernatural things appear brighter, fuller, and more real than this world. The

---

* Gladkova, *Galina Ustvolskaya, 30.*

next world is much more real than the visible reality: that is where true reality is hidden. Gogol recreated it as a natural experience and as a contemplation of a supernatural spectacle. Neither darkness, nor twilight, nor fog accompanies miracles and fear, but rather the brightest light, far brighter than anything you ordinarily see. The magical and fearsome things keep more towards darkness. Quite the contrary. The intrusion of the supernatural world in Gogol is marked by light, and often this light is of a natural origin, for fantastic light does not terrify as much as this complete unity of mysticism and reality…"

"It seems, in his poetic creations, Gogol is even more religious than in his bloodless and dissected Christianity. By a strict calculation of "soul" and "gain" he seems to have tried to temper some personal religious, albeit dark, powers, which became developed in his literature. Rationality in his Christianity was a sort of reaction to the pagan mysticism of his writer's view. This eternal Russian collision of the pagan vestiges and Christian consciousness in Gogol took form of an intense spiritual fight between his writer's genius, retreated into the dark past, and his late doctrinarism of a Christian-rationalist…" *

In S.T. Aksakov's *The story of my acquaintance with Gogol*† an amusing episode is described. Gogol and the Aksakov family were traveling from Moscow to Petersburg. Everybody was cheerful. One of the stops was in Torzhok.

"We arrived in Torzhok at three in the morning. Gogol was joking about our future morning meal in such an amusing way that we went up the stairs of the famous hotel laughing loudly, and Gogol immediately ordered us a dozen cutlets, so we would not ask for other dishes. In half an hour the cutlets were ready and just the sight of them, and the smell aroused a great appetite in the hungry travelers. The cutlets were, indeed, exceptionally delicious, but suddenly (it seems, Vera was first) we all stopped chewing and started to pull a long blond hair out of our mouths. The scene was very funny, and Gogol's jokes added so much comedy to this incident that for a few minutes we just

---

*   Abraham Terz *"In the Shadow of Gogol"*, (Overseas Publications Interchange in association with Collins, London, 1975), 544, 546, 547, 548, 549) Abraham Terz is a pen name of a prominent Russian author of the sixties Andrey Siniavsky, Russian.

†   *Aksakov, Complete works, v.3:160-161, Russian.*

laughed like mad. Once we had calmed down, we began studying our cutlets and what did we find? In each of them we found a few dozens of the same long blond hair! How they got in there I still have no idea. Gogol's suggestions were each funnier than the next. Incidentally, he was saying with his inimitable Little Russian humor[*] that the chef was probably, drunk and had not gotten much sleep; that he was woken up and pulled his hair out of annoyance while preparing the cutlets; or maybe he was not drunk and was a very good man, but was recently sick with fever, from which his hair was falling out and dropping on the food when he cooked it, shaking his blond curls. We sent for a footman to receive an explanation and Gogol predicted the answer would be received from the footman: 'Hairs? What hairs? Where would hair come from? This is, mmm, nothing really! Chicken feathers or fuzz, etc., etc.' At that very moment, the footman came in and to the given question he answered exactly as Gogol had said, much of it even with the same words. Laughter seized us so completely that both our man and the footman popped their eyes at us, and I was worried that Vera might get sick."

Gogol was tormented with questions of faith and, according to Vladimir Nabokov, he believed in the existence of the Devil "much more seriously than in the existence of God."[†]

…Yes, we were admiring then Gogol, Rembrandt, Chekhov, and Rachmaninoff. They comprised our, or rather, Ustvolskaya's, Academy of admiration. She did speak about starting an Academy. This was in the late seventies, when Ustvolskaya no longer taught at the college, and I was no longer a student there. At that time some of her works were published; her "Octet" was recorded. Concerts were performed featuring her music. She began to receive letters and phone calls. Some asked if she was teaching at the conservatory. Ustvolskaya would boast that if she agreed to work there, she could have a full studio right away. "We must start an Academy," she would say. This idea thrilled me. But she did not really consider anything of the sort.

---

[*]   Little Russia - that's what Ukraine was called then.

[†]   Vladimir Nabokov, *Lectures on Russian Literature,* (A Harvest book, Harcout, Inc. Bruccoli Clark Layman, San Diego, New York, London), 17

I remember I said that time absorbs all sorts of achievements. Time, they say, makes the real selection. But even time, it turns out, can make mistakes. So many majestic palaces and temples have been ruined; so much beauty is buried under those ruins. So many paintings and books have been burned and with them the names of their creators. All styles and methods eventually age. They age, are forgotten, and eventually vanish. And this is not unique to art. Animals and plants vanish, household items and fashion become obsolete. Everything is in the process of transformation, in its search for renewal, so necessary to evolution.

This is how the universe creates. An individual draws his ideas from the universal treasury, but the universe, needing new material for creation, incorporates the personal achievements of an individual into its work. The small creative work of an individual becomes a part of the cosmic creative process. Nothing vanishes entirely. All that is truly valuable is saved. The universe uses the best towards its creative work. The only things that vanish are names. Creation becomes nameless.

"So, will there be nothing left? And there will be no Beethoven, no Mozart?" asks Ustvolskaya.

"All the best will be transformed by the Cosmos into a more perfect, large-scale creation."

"I do not care about my music, but I feel sorry for the Moonlight Sonata."

INTERLUDE.

Thinking about all this, I authored a poem. I was thinking about the amazing and mysterious fate of Mozart, whose organic and light music hides tragedy. I wrote these verses on the book by Fromantin *"Old Masters"* which I gave to Ustvolskaya. She loved this book at the time. (It was in 1979.) However, I am not sure that she still has the poem[*].

Now I understand that it was insensitive of me to give Galya such poem. But what is done is done.

---

[*] The first edition of this book was written when Usnvolskaya did not leave this World.

Mozart

Time goes by,
Taking the burden of life,
Which
Is either difficult,
Or light and cheerful to bear,
Leaving photographs
On plaques and gravestones:
And these
Smiling faces
Peering into the Future
From their graves
Agitate us like
The images
Of Mozart's fairytale kingdom,
Whose name is a symbol,
Like the Sun, the Moon and the stars:
Whose glory is a mirage,
Like the light of stars,
Long extinct:
Time takes their light
Like the souls of saints
To the infinite space of the Universe.

And so, time takes memories of us
Only
Imprinting in dreams
That,
Which few will understand
Because twilight
Is turbid and dark
And the Sky is boundless...[*]

---

[*] Transl. S. Bokman and I. Behrendt, ed. A. Glaser. S. Bokman "Na Okraine Vselennoy", p.23. (" On the Outskirts of Universe")

152

As soon as Ustvolskaya reached the age of retirement, she left the college. It was 1975. I remember how she once said after a meeting at the Composers' Union: "After all, it's good to come in here," to the college, that is. (Maybe she said this because of coming from a meeting.) Later, when she had already retired, I reminded her about this phrase, surprised that she had left if she had liked it there so much.

"So, if you're saying this, you don't understand me at all!" she objected impulsively. "I never liked be there!"

However, I believe that her work at the college, her interactions with the youth, had a revitalizing effect on her. Of course, it was not always particularly interesting for her. Often, she had to instruct students who were not really interested in the subject. They were studying it for acquaintance and for "general development". This "ballast" was obviously necessary to have more hours; in other words, to earn money. Besides, the college program is not designed to prepare professional composers. This is the task of the conservatory. But Ustvolskaya did not want to work at the conservatory, though she was invited. I dare to think that her work at the college forced her to concentrate on something besides her own, not always cheerful, thoughts.

Her Life was not easy – her pension was small. There was almost no other income. Sometimes there simply was no food in the house and we, the few who were allowed to visit, tried not to come empty-handed. At first, we brought pastries, wine, candy, flowers. Then we realized we should bring more substantial food: bread, butter, cheese, and meat. Once we brought hazel-grouses, having plucked them beforehand. Galya had told us that in her childhood her family cooked incredible hazel-grouses. I had no clue as to how to cook them, but bravely went ahead. You cannot imagine what came out! I roasted them and roasted them again and they just would not get any softer. I finally gave up and we started eating. The birds were tough, skinny, and over-cooked. But we ate them and laughed. We were happy. Sometimes I would fry up meat.

"Galya," I once asked, "do you like fried meat?"

"I like everything but the Soviet power," she said.

I did not know how to cook, but I tried. Galya's presence had a euphoric effect on me, and she encouraged me, saying to her other guest (also a former student):

"Look what he is up to!"

I fried meat, ruthlessly overcooking, over-salting, and over-peppering it.

"And with hands, all with hands… Well done, Semyon! I wish I had a husband like you… Would you like to be my husband?

"Sure," I said, "I would cook and clean and you would compose music? No, I want to compose music too! -Suddenly for myself I "produced" such caustic remark while feeling uncomfortable and annoyed being understanding that I said wrong.

It could not be said to Ustvolskaya that. Even as a joke. And I am deeply sorry for my indelicacy for trying and defending my "self-importance" in this way. I felt my voice, but I lacked her approval. Once, kidding, I said that she already had masterpieces and I did not. "You Imagine how hard I have to work in order to compose a masterpiece," I said. Laughingly she said: "Well, why? You have that thing, based on Ehrenburg – it is not bad." (She meant "Pugach's Blood") Oh, this praise coming from Galya's mouth, was really great!*

SECCOND INTERLUDE

Everybody knows that health is better than sickness. A man aspires to happiness, and he is initially happy. Look at a child – how he rejoices at life's simple occurrences! If he is raised in relative comfort, and loved, a child is happy. He does not want to suffer. He loves life because for him it is the source of happiness.

I have always been surprised and bothered by the cult of suffering in art. It is as if, to compose good music or write real poetry and prose, one must suffer in one way or another. Otherwise, the work will be unworthy. And examples abound…A deeply spiritual person often

---

*   It was very naive to expect praise from Ustvolskaya, who once said smilingly, "I like Bach…" So, just "like." Did she really understand the greatness of Bach? So, you can be aware why her praise was so impressive for me.

happens to be physically weak. But does this imply that unhealthiness is a condition for spiritual growth? I doubt that strongly. Creative work is a comprehension of the world and of the self within it. It is a search for harmony. "I am not talking about those sad cases, when a genius misleads thousands, inculcating them all kinds of vices and darkening their way to harmony, passing it off as the new findings of truth, regardless of the field to which these misrepresentations belong."*

What harmony is in illness, in suffering from unsatisfied vanity or pride? It is disharmony. And the disharmony is not in the body, but in the person. Illness is an attempt to recover the lost balance. Creative work in its inherent resistance can make an artist suffer brutally and he is happy when he manages to overcome this resistance. An artist is happy when he creates, but the physical and moral sufferings do not help his creativity. But if he can elevate himself above his sorrows, then, of course, he will be looking at life differently. Only then can suffering enrich the spirit. An artist is an inhabitant of heaven. He must look down at the world from his high heavens without getting involved in its petty quarrels. He must carry light, harmony, and love into the world. If he cannot do it, he must learn.

> There are two worlds for every man:
> The first created us
> The second we, from day to day
> Create with deeds and thoughts.

(Nikolai Zabolotsky†)

Yes! The world is not a discovery, but a creation. Everyone living in this world is creating it with thoughts and deeds every minute. Here I am speaking of an average person. But what about an artist, a creature who is destined to create new forms? Is he aware that those forms

---

*   K. E. Antarova *Two Lives*, (Moscow: "Sirin", "Scorpion", "Satka",1994), part two, book one, p.303

†   Nikolay Alexeyevich Zabolotsky (Russian: Николáй Алексéевич Заболóцкий; May 7, 1903 — October 14, 1958) was a Russian poet, children's writer and translator.

and images created are a part of this life and world we live in? Artistic imagination is a game, of course, but a serious one.

Sergey Averintsev, a Russian philologist, and thinker, spoke about the September 11th attack on the Twin Towers. During his presentation at an international conference in Moscow in October 2003, he noted "…the choice of strategy, having little to do with the previous traditions of Holy War, was not completely determined by Western technological progress. That in itself would be understandable – an old maxim tells us to fight the enemy with his own weapon. Rather, this choice also, obviously, reflected the imagery of contemporary (global!) mass-culture, first, from American horror films. I am not an expert in horror films. However, we all remember that in the interviews, taken immediately after the events of 9/11, many noted the similarity of what was happening to the aesthetics of horror-films."[*]

This is how illusion becomes reality. From space into life come our personal demons. Life becomes a nightmare, and we cannot believe that we are the reason for this calamity.

The music of J.S. Bach is the best example of spiritual and emotional harmony. That is why it is so universal: there is no interpretation or edition that could spoil this music and it seems that Bach himself was not too concerned about it. The changes in tempos and dynamics, and even jazz and pop or rock arrangements do not spoil it. After listening to some of his music, a feeling remains of penetration so deep that time, however we understand it, ceases to exist. There is only an eternal, incomprehensible present. This music is always modern. But this is absolutely not applicable to Bach himself, to his personality. The psychology of people is changing rapidly. Therefore, it is difficult to imagine that Johann Sebastian, a man of the 17th century, would have a good relationship with our era. This paradox convinces us that great art is, in fact, anonymous. And the creator who creates it under his own name is a vessel of creation.

"Time was different," said Ustvolskaya. His time, undoubtedly, was different, but an artist never had it easy.

---

[*]   Russian language newspaper "Vzgliad", San Francisco, February 28, 2004. This newspaper does not exist anymore.

Where did Beethoven find the energy for such optimistic music as, for example, the Sixth or the Ninth symphonies, or his Missa Solemnis? He, who in life was so deeply unhappy with his ailments and loneliness; he, who was difficult and unkind to the people around him - he produced overly optimistic and convincing music. My guess is he was a strict believer in the Light which dispersing dark and Good which finally overcame evil.

"Joy is a special wisdom," wise people are saying. It truly is.

EIGHTEENTH VARIATION

The Museum-City. Nerves Again.

Culture is the core of our lives. Dependence is direct: Life is such as Culture is. Culture is not only beautiful works, smart books, and the filling of leisure time. Culture is thinking. And thinking needs to be nurtured. What can do it better than real and true Art?! The great Plato teaches us: "From beautiful images we will come to beautiful thoughts. From beautiful thoughts to beautiful life! The Thoughts (the Ideas) rule the world! Thinking is a material substance - science finds more evidence of it.

Ustvolskaya is a Petersburg composer. She and her music are very organic to St. Petersburg. She rarely left the city and only for a brief time. She was a part of this city. She used to like to fantasize about how it would be lovely to be in Paris suddenly or "in some Switzerland." Indeed, she really wanted to travel abroad and to see the world. But leave forever? God forbid.

St. Petersburg culture has a rich and difficult heritage. Besides elegance and aristocracy, there are sickliness, hypochondria, neurasthenia, insanity, mysticism, melancholy, fear. Pushkin was one of the few who was able to keep the spirit of his work healthy. Lermontoff is already quite different. Try to compare their *Prophets*. Lermontov's *Prophet* represents the future of Pushkin's *Prophet*; it is a disillusionment that would later penetrate Russian culture.

"Look, look," exclaims Ustvolskaya, pointing out of the studio window. "Don't you see?"

Above a typical Petersburg's well of yard, a huge black cloud hangs it over like an omen. "Of course, it will die, this city," she says. "It's a museum-city… how can one live in a museum?"

This apocalyptic, painful consciousness was characteristic to her.

She likes sickly, pale and nervous men. She likes it when a man smokes. "Are you concerned about your health?" asked me Galina Ivanovna sarcastically, having learned that I jogged in the mornings. "You are concerned with health…" she repeated somewhat reproachfully.

"Turgenev said that a male should be ferocious," I answered with a smile, uncertain whether this phrase really belonged to the great Russian novelist.

"Oh, yes. Only he, poor man, was sick all his life… oh, how sick he was!"

She often took valerian. She was afraid and disliked being alone at night. "God gave me health, but my nerves…" she was saying.

"What are you talking about, Semyon, how can I drink? With such my nerves?" asked Ustvolskaya when I showed up at her house with a bottle of wine. "But you go ahead and drink," she said, "don't mind me." We once did drink Champagne together, straight from the bottle on an open square on Sadovaya Street. We were celebrating the completion of my ill-fated "Variations." Ustvolskaya, I remember, said, "Well, Semyon, congratulations. Now you can walk proudly along Nevsky Prospect… Why don't we celebrate?" she suddenly said cheerfully, turning to Ira, another girl-student from her studio. So, we celebrated, drinking right from the bottle. Unfortunately, we did just for one gulp… When Ira started to drink, the bottle of champagne slipped down from her hands… We were extremely disappointed, but just for a while. There was enough joy! It was such a type of student prank, game. We did have a fun time, all three of us.

Being a quiet, even shy person in ordinary life, she expresses protest and disagreement with this world in her music. Fists are bared. The blows fall. Macro-fortissimo! These works need not only be heard but be seen in performance. The Sixth Piano Sonata, for example, leaves a frightening impression, not only from its music, which borders on insanity and where all compositional technique is as if absent, but also from a terrifying image created by the pianist playing heavy clusters with his fists and elbows. A fingerless cripple is playing, or a mute is attempting to sing, or some kind of octopus from a Hollywood thriller is at the piano. On September 11, 2001 ("Martober 11" - in Gogol's

"Diary of a madman") the twentieth century came to a terrible end, and the new, twenty-first, century began; I remembered this shocking Sonata of Ustvolskaya's and in my mind it is firmly associated with the frightening events of that day.

In my studentship life she played the role of a Guru. In spite of her and sometimes despite her I have come to understand some important truths. I let the reader guess which ones are in spite of her and which are despite of Ustvolskaya.

What is important is not the goal, but rather how one approaches it; nor is it success, but rather the work, the thinking that leads to it. ("And who are the judges?" Galina Ivanovna cited Griboedov's aphorism.˙) Kindness is important, as are thoughts about eternity; to accept more and not to limit your own world; to love oneself and one's art, but never put oneself and one's art above all else; not to ingratiate oneself with the "mighty" and "glorious"; to be oneself and let others go their way – everyone's path is different; grow; love and forgive; try to understand "foreign" and "incomprehensible" ideas... Know that all you give out will come back– good or bad; Find joy and share it; believe in immortality...

I wish that those who will read what I have written about Ustvolskaya will learn that there are heroic personalities in life, that it is not merely the invention of a dreamer or novelist, the concept that serving life can be above life itself.

INTERLUDE.

The absence of humor and cheer in her music, given that in life she can be brilliantly witty and cheerful, could be an exceptional quality of her gift. There are composers who write very deep lyrical music,[†] for example, Tchaikovsky. Rossini wrote mostly comic operas and Verdi – dramatic. Rimsky-Korsakov's music is coloristic and epic. Each of them

---

[*]   Alexander Sergeyevich Griboyedov (15 January 1795 – 11 February 1829), was a Russian diplomat, playwright, poet, and composer. His one notable work was the 1823 verse comedy Woe from Wit. He was Russia's ambassador to Qajar Persia, where he and all the embassy staff were massacred by an angry mob. "And who are the judges?" is the quotation from his play" Woe from Wit"

[†]   ...or only funeral marches. (see p. 19)

could be happy or sad in their everyday life, but the content of their lives did not necessarily become the content of their music. Talent and skill play, of course, a key role in how one creates, in his self-expression.

I am amazed and fascinated by Chopin. Perhaps he really did not feel the orchestra. However, as it is often the case with extraordinarily talented people, this shortcoming serves to his advantage. None of the well-known European composers, neither before nor after Chopin, understood the great qualities of the piano to such an extent! In the First, E minor concerto, for example, orchestra sounds clumsy in the exposition. And how beautiful those themes are when played on the piano! But I am positive that re-orchestration is impossible. We have already got along with this music. And, of course, it does not need any endorsements. I am only talking about this example because I marvel at how organically Chopin uses all the virtues of this instrument! He should have simply ignored the convention of the double exposition and skipped the orchestra altogether. Both themes, the first and the second one, are not orchestral. This is truly piano music. Only Chopin could compose like that!

Some composers like brightness and spark. Extravagance is not bad if one knows how to handle it. To perform one's own or someone else's music with brilliance, or to conduct it, to compose beautifully, with humor, and to be liked by the public for it – all this is great if, and only if, one knows how to do it. Versatility is a rare quality, but it does exist. Think of Leonard Bernstein, for instance, or Stravinsky.

Ustvolskaya's talent is totally different. It seems to me she is too proud for such public "servility." Once, I expressed my admiration for Anton Rubinstein – he gave a cycle of Historical Concerts where he performed the entire existing piano repertoire. "So what?" – said Galina Ivanovna. "Glenn Gould is, perhaps, more ingenious." It is known that Gould was not a particularly versatile performer.

Among the 20th century composers, Igor Stravinsky is the one who continues to astonish me. Indeed, he created plenty of wonderful music, but others did not sit idly by. There is no point in listing the masterpieces created by composers of this era. But here is what is surprising: except for the "Rite of Spring", in which Stravinsky foreshadowed brutal wars and revolutions, this composer did not respond in any way to the ominous realities of his epoch. And the time was terrible, and these horrible events significantly affected Stravinsky himself. He lost his estate, his homeland, his huge library, and had to support his relatives, who struggled as emigrants. Reading his biography, I saw how difficult it was for him, how painful it was! But his creative work was not affected by the social and personal turmoil and upheaval, although he was often reproached for his indifference. It is delightful that he did not participate in all these hectic activities by his thinking! His thinking was not influenced by the chaos around him! He said that music does not express anything, that music is "a thing in itself". No, it expresses, and it expresses strongly and a lot! But Igor Stravinsky, not always a pleasant aesthete, built his own reality, with no access for enmity, anger, hatred, or fear! This parallel reality continues to influence the world in its own way with its images. Stravinsky's music is diverse, but there is no aggression in it.

Peace be upon you, readers.

NINETEENTH VARIATION

We Have to Create!

In my book I try to express my feelings and attitude to the hero of the narration, as they were during my studies and our communications. You can see how they changed and developed in one direction or another. Having been the big distance - both vital, and spatial - from Galina Ivanovna - and she in this time became the acknowledged classic-composer of modern music - I had an uncommon opportunity, rare one, to understand value and a special place of the composer Galina Ustvolskaya in evolution of musical art. I also understood why and by what she is important for 20th century culture and why she should not and will not have the followers.

It was July of 1974. We graduated. Sashka and I were invited by Ustvolskaya to her apartment. We wanted to make something interesting and unusual to give her as a present. Sashka suggested beautifully binding the self-published, and otherwise unavailable, works of Mandelshtam[*] and Khlebnikov.[†] He organized the copying; I found the bookbinder. We completed two neat little books. We went to

---

[*] **Osip Emilyevich Mandelstam** (Russian: Осип Эмильевич Мандельштам, 14 January [O.S. 2 January] 1891 – 27 December 1938) was a Russian and Soviet poet. He was one of the foremost members of the Acmeist school. Osip Mandelstam was arrested during the repressions of the 1930s and sent into internal exile with his wife, Nadezhda Mandelstam. Given a reprieve of sorts, they moved to Voronezh in southwestern Russia. In 1938, Mandelstam was arrested again and sentenced to five years in a corrective-labour camp in the Soviet Far East. He died that year at a transit camp nearby Vladivostok.

[†] **Viktor Vladimirovich Khlebnikov**, better known by the pen name Velimir Khlebnikov (Russian: Велимир Хлебников, 9 November [O.S. 28 October] 1885 – 28 June 1922), was a Russian poet and playwright, a central part of the Russian Futurist movement, but his work and influence stretch far beyond it. Influential linguist Roman Jakobson hailed Khlebnikov as "the greatest world poet of our century".

her home and presented them to her along with a bouquet of flowers. Galina Ivanovna was sincerely happy with the presents.

"Thank you very much, boys…" In the kitchen which we could see from the hallway, someone was sitting at the table.

"Kostya," called Galina Ivanovna.

A skinny dark-haired man in a dark lightweight, long-sleeved shirt emerged. He was about thirty years old and had slanted eyes that seemed narrow behind his glasses.

"Comrades, let me introduce my husband." Ustvolskaya said, laughingly and a little bit stressing the word "husband." She was pleased to see our looks of surprise, which we attempted to hide, but could not.

"Kostya, these are my best students - Sasha and Semyon*."

"Well, if that's the case, I ought to run and get some vodka," he said, shaking our hands. "You hang out here, guys, I'll be quick." He vanished.

It was a hot day. It was muggy in Leningrad. Galina Ivanovna wore a light-weight sleeveless summer dress, and I was wearing a green nylon, then fashionable, shirt with sleeves rolled up to my elbows. Sasha wore a light short-sleeve plaid shirt. Ustvolskaya kept repeating: "It is so hot!" We readily agreed.

 Kostya quickly returned with two bottles of vodka and some snacks.

"Kostya, look what the boys gave me!"

"Wow, great! Well done."

"It is hard to buy a good book these days; even some kind of Akhmatova is hard to find," said Ustvolskaya.

"Let's go," said Kostya and off we "went." Ustvolskaya did not drink. She just took a sip from Kostya's shot glass and winced. We talked non-stop. We were excited and cheerful. Most of all, of course, we talked about the recent events: the college, the teachers, the exams.

---

*   Yea. That is what Ustvolskaya said. Undoubtedly, at that moment she was sincere, but her preferences changed, and often – on opposite ones, and I am not sure that I was among her" favorite" students. Probably not. Where are they, loved ones?

"You do not be offended on her, Semyon... She is a very ordinary and mediocre person."

"Why would I be offended?" I am trying to speak firmly. "Could I be upset with a horse for being a horse?" Everybody laughed.

"A horse? Do you hear what he said, Kostya? One cannot be upset with a horse for being a horse!" More laughter.

"He is right..." smiled Kostya. "So, let's go!" and again we were off.

"Kostya, what do we have for dessert?" she asked. "Ah, I have chocolates! I, say to truth, was supposed to give them to somebody, though...But why do I have to give them to God knows who if here are friends in my house right now!" and she put a box of chocolates on the table.

Sasha felt sick. He had to leave for the bathroom.

"It is ok, it is ok... It is, probably his first time..." said Ustvolskaya.

When he returned, embarrassed, she repeated, looking at him encouragingly: "It is ok, it is good that this is the first time here, with me. Once Sviridov was visiting me with his Finnish wife," she tells us, becoming animated. "She went to the bathroom right away; filled the tub and sat there. We were chatting here for maybe two hours, and she was sitting in the bathroom. I said to him: 'Does she always do this when she visits people?' 'Yes, she likes b-bath-th-thing,' he said laughingly."

Ustvolskaya laughs loudly. We enthusiastically match her...

I was twenty-four years old. I had been married for three months. Sashka was not yet twenty. Kostya – thirty-three. Ustvolskaya was fifty-five.

Our studies were finished. I did not go on to the conservatory. I was under the strong influence of Stravinsky's assertion that, for a talented composer, two years of study is enough to learn the basics of the craft. "I studied for four years at college under the real master," I thought. "Who would I go to now? I simply could not study with anyone else." I thought, "If only Ustvolskaya taught at the conservatory..." She said that the conservatory director Pavel Serebriakov had invited her to work at the conservatory. "And you did not accept?" I asked. "But it means constantly being under stress there. It is simply an unnatural state of being!" she replied almost insulted. Later she explained that she would have accepted the position as an associate professor, but Serebriakov did not find it possible to offer her that. Pavel Serebriakov was the first performer of Ustvolskaya's *Piano Concerto,* and the *Concerto* was dedicated to him. Later, I was surprised to find out that the dedication was "re-written" to Aleksey Lubimov.

I told Ustvolskaya about my decision. She took it enthusiastically. "You are like Jesus," she said, smiling tenderly. She probably thought that by refusing to go the normal way - the conservatory, the Union of Composers - I would give up my creative work. The refusal from creativity can be higher than creativity itself, Ustvolskaya considered. She often talked about it, and it seemed that if all the composers suddenly stopped composing, she would admire them. Of course, untalented composers. But who is talented?

I was brave, but it was the bravery of ignorance and the determination of despair: I feared all those tests and exams like the plague, all those countless problems with teachers with whom I would not get along; I was angry and upset.

I had a reputation as a "difficult" student. I was almost expelled, but Ustvolskaya stood up for me. She ran into the Dean's office and tried to convince the administration staff to let me stay and continue my education. The staff asked if she were so sure that I would become a great composer. Galina Ivanovna replied that she could not prophesy, but that I was, let us say, "no worse than others" and that otherwise she would not defend me. She said: "This is the second time in my life that I have stood up for a student." This argument of the teacher Galina Ustvolskaya, who even in the music college where she worked, only a few people knew and whose works were not in the school library, convinced the administration and I to remain in the school.

> *You were so talented that G.U. was fighting for you when you were to be expelled. I remember the story. And it was not just you she wanted to "save". She wanted to "save" herself in the first place. If the class is filled completely, she gets 170 roubles, and if even*

> **one is expelled – 135 roubles. And she, like other teachers, was fighting for her salary, and not just for your talent.** *
>
> From Konstantin Bagrenin's letter to me. Precision. Internet

On my final exam in composition, I received a "four" (a "B") Ustvolskaya told me how she had tried to persuade the head of the committee, some Kolovsky (whose first name I forgot,) "He is already

---

*   I do not think Galina Ivanovna was so mercantile. I remember she expelled a capable student from her class. His name is Yuri Krasavin (I do not know the reason). She told the class about it. She was upset. And what is more interesting regarding this expelled student Krasavin, that he finally finished conservatory, became a successful composer and as I discovered recently, his ballet was expected to be premiered in Bolshoi Theater, in Moscow. Truly, you never know where you will find it and where you will lose it indeed. Here one more recollection comes to mind connecting to this episode. When Ustvolskaya emerged from the Dean's office there a tall young man waited for her besides me. Seeing Ustvolskaya he said:

"Are you Galina Ivanovna?"

"Yes"

"I have come from Krasnodar to show you, my music."

"OK. Can you wait a little," and she pointed to me, by this gesture giving him know that we need to talk. The young man stepped aside to be waiting until we finish conversation in which Ustvolskaya expressed to me what I already told above. We were both happy: Ustvolskaya by saving her salary in170 rubles (if to trust Kostya) and me by rescuing myself from being expelled from the college.

"And now let us go and listen to this guy with me! This is your punishment!"

And after a while:

"Seemingly he is not talented."

"How do you know?"

"Very tall. You see, talented people are usually short. (Ustvolskaya herself was short). And Krasnodar again. (Hint to the Krasavin who also came from Krasnodar.) She continued:

"Pushkin, Tchaikovsky, Dostoevsky were short... Lot of examples."

"And what about Rimsky-Korsakov," I said pointing to a full-length statue of him which we had on the college campus.

"Not very much," she said with a laugh.

"And Mayakovsky, and Rachmaninov?"

"There are exceptions. But not so many..."

We were laughing happily while talking so deeply and thoughtfully.

a professional. He needs to be judged differently..." It did not help. It could not have helped because everything had been decided earlier.

There was another reason, of which I was not fully aware. I felt that by going to the conservatory I would "lose" Ustvolskaya. It had happened with her prior students. They left her forever. But for me during those years, Ustvolskaya was my only Teacher. Ustvolskaya's approval of my decision was as if she, like an ultimate Teacher believing in her disciple and, wishing to strengthen and to temper him, directed him towards a difficult, but voluntary path. And this path, chosen among all others, proved to be the most difficult indeed.

Ustvolskaya did not teach me how to build a career. She taught me to create. A career as such is neither good nor bad. But it is important how one uses success. Hypocrisy, profit, and lies are contrary to true creative work. Could it be that this is why Ustvolskaya so readily helped the weak and the untalented?[*]

Let us continue the story of friendship!

I made a visit to Ustvolskaya. Galya was happy and excited, and a little bit drunk. She told me:

"Mila came (*a composer, the wife of a famous Leningrad composer Weniamin Basner. Ustvolskaya was supposed to write her a recommendation to enter the Composer's Union – S.B.*), brought flowers and a bottle of

---

[*] Now, after many years, I understood that actually Ustvolskaya had never given any thought to my composition career. I could not understand it then. Observing my life from a big distance, I understand that my decision was hiddenly manipulated and organized by Galina Ivanovna by harsh criticizing of conservatory and Composer Union. While knowing well how I trust her she praised my decision but understood well that without these institutions my career is doomed! After composing "Poogach's Blood" and successfully recording it, what visibly did not make her happy, I was convinced that yes, I am composer! Galya with her experience and great scent understood it even better than me. Why did she stop me in such an inquisitor's way? I guess, but I will not tell my readers. You should guess too. Yes, it looks as if she did as a "wise guru" but keeping in mind something different. Everything worked out in the end. Composer Union has died as so Soviet Union does not exist anymore. I am residing in United States of America now, and I am member of National Association of Composers of United States of America- NACUSA. I am grateful to Galina Ustvolskaya because as a result I have an amazing fate which helped me to understand a lot! It opened to me a unique World! "To live Without Dying" - is my next book. Hope my publishers will be interested in it soon.

wine. She gave me a coffee-grinder… She played some cute songs for me. We laughed ourselves to exhaustion…"

"Do you like cute songs?"

"Uh-huh," she laughed and nodded.

"And about Gena, the crocodile?" (S.B. was referring to an incredibly famous birthday song – I.B.)

"Why not?" she said happily laughing and I could tell that she was still affected by the successful meeting.

I threw myself into an unknown and hazy future, which promised me nothing. My wife and I went to Kaliningrad, former Koenigsberg, where we were directed. (There was such a practice in the Soviet Union. Graduates of specialized secondary and higher education institutions were "distributed" on a national scale. This is how they "managed" to achieve universal employment). In 1974, Kaliningrad did not even have a decent concert hall; there was no orchestra, there were very few musicians, and concert life was inactive.

Gidon Kremer came to Kaliningrad on tour. The administration of the Kaliningrad concert agency did not know that he was a prominent violinist and sent him to perform in some sanatorium. Soon after, we learned that Kremer had emigrated. My wife and I decided that his experience in Kaliningrad was the last drop that helped him to make this decision.

It was a timeless exile. I thought to myself: "Joseph Brodsky was exiled; it was not right, of course, but he was officially accused of something, at least. He was on trial. His exile was his punishment. But why are we in exile?"

We used every opportunity to visit Leningrad so that I could see Ustvolskaya. It did not always work out. Sometimes, when I went expressly to see her, Ustvolskaya, though she knew this, did not want to meet. She was woman of changing mood. She categorically refused to meet my wife. There seemed to be something very womanly in this gesture. Our relationship, however, remained friendly. Later, we switched from the formal "vy" (you) to the informal "ty."(ye) . (This happened, of course, on her initiative.) My wife always treated kindly toward Ustvolskaya and never objected to helping her. After I got married, Ustvolskaya seemed to reassess something in me and assign a particular place for me in her soul. I seemed to begin "losing points." I remember telling her about my upcoming marriage. "Well, it is time for you to do. Everybody gets married," she said. And for a split second, it seemed as though I noticed a certain disappointment in the way she said this. Later, remembering her student years, she told the class how she expressed her attitude toward composers' marriages: "I was a hooligan at the conservatory. 'Ah, you are getting married? So, you are a talentless one!" I, to be honest, did not immediately understand that this related to me. I am a bit slow. But undoubtedly, she was saying this especially for myself.

I was thinking over and over the question of whether I had done the right thing in not continuing my studies, in not trying to build a career. I also wondered why Ustvolskaya while approved of my decision not to continue my education, when she herself had gone through all the steps, including postgraduate studies. She became a member of the Composers' Union and, although she was always unhappy with this organization, did not think of leaving it. ("WE are not you!" I had recollected the phrase she said to me when I was a student…)

Ustvolskaya, however, had studied with Shostakovich. Whatever their relationship became later, it was, undoubtedly, an especially important period in her life. When I graduated from the College, there was no one at the Conservatory I could study with. In any case, there was no personality equal to Ustvolskaya. I even dared to say to her that I already could do no less than "they" are.

"Of course!" she said firmly. "Because 'they' are nobody!"

And it was not clear whether this was a compliment for me or not.

Anyway, seeing clearly that my life as a composer was becoming hopeless, on one of my visits to Leningrad I decided to ask Ustvolskaya to help me. She looked pensive.

"Do you want to get into the Union, Senya?"

"It's not that I *want* to, but what else is there to do?"

"I understand… Andrey Pavlovich* is exceptionally good to me… I think he would help. But you must get into a conservatory. Study for at least three years and you will be in the Union," she said firmly.

I started to search for a school. It was not easy because the composition departments did not have a correspondence course† and I lived in a small town with no conservatory anywhere nearby. I had a family. And so, a strange conversation took place at the Ustvolskaya's apartment. I told her about all the tricks I would have to do to make it work. The conversation took an unexpected turn. It turned out that even talented people achieved success most often not because of their talent, but with the help of other outside influences. There were always extraordinary circumstances. ‡And suddenly, Ustvolskaya said angrily: "Everyone is trying to sneak in somewhere! Why not just sit and work!"

It was an emotional outburst. I do not think it had to do directly with me, but I became embarrassed: I was wasting my time and energy on nonsense instead of sitting and working; the thing I should do was just use up the music paper! There was never another conversation with Ustvolskaya about my going to the conservatory or getting into the Composers' Union.

Once, sitting in her kitchen, I said that composing was my religion. I write for myself because I believe in it.

"Yes, but you can't go on for long like that," said Ustvolskaya.

---

* Andrey Pavlovich Petrov, see also 16-th Variation.

† A correspondence course is a common form of study in Russia (and the former Soviet Union) for students with professional engagements or those with families. A student must come to school for a month-long session of lectures, lessons, and exams twice a year and for the rest of the time it is basically a self-study based on the instructions received.

‡ Ustvolskaya herself first became known abroad in regard to her widely advertised relationship with Shostakovich. "Things began to change in 1992-3 with the earliest foreign recordings and the simultaneous appearance of the first Western documentation of her controversial relationship with Shostakovich" writes Ian MacDonald. (http://www.siue.edu/~aho/musov/ust/ust.html)

This is how Shostakovich eventually helped Ustvolskaya. Of course, it would have been better if it had happened earlier.

She said that because she understood like no one else how difficult that was. I had no doubt, though, about her eventual victory and told her about this.

"When?"

"Soon. Soon!" I said confidently.

"Yes, but how long do I have left?" she asked sadly.

If a composer who has no access to publishers or listeners keeps on writing, what is pushing him to go? Is he a graphomaniac? Ustvolskaya wrote "for the drawer" for years, even though she had the highest degree and postgraduate in composition and was a respectable member of the Composers' Union*.

Such devotion to the chosen path, such faith, evokes respect. And how difficult it was for her!

But, after all this, I want to object. I want to tell Ustvolskaya that one cannot cease creative work, and no one must ever stop anyone, including oneself, from creating. It is better to be in the process of an imperfect creation than to be out of creation. Imperfect action is better than no action at all. Imperfect spirituality is better than no spirituality at all. A person will more easily find his place in life through active work rather than inactivity. He or she may need to turn to something else, but it is activity that will bring him this awareness. Creativity can vary. One must look at life with a wide-angle lens; life offers many opportunities.

---

*   Once, she" was sent" to the composers' convention in Moscow. It was the end of 1968. Knowing Ustvolskaya's character, the Union made her go, saying that if she did not, she would face some unpleasant consequences. There were composers who were upset that they were not asked to go, but Ustvolskaya, who did not want to go, was forced. Strangely enough, she came back in a particularly good mood. There were some meetings and receptions. She went to the Bolshoi Theater. "You, probably, have been to the Bolshoi Theater many times already, but for me, imagine, it was the first time," she said to us, her students. "…It turns out that Pakhmutova (see 17-th Variation) is shorter than I am by a whole head." She measured Pakhmutova's height by placing the side of her palm below her chin. Galina Ivanovna is not a giant and we were all surprised: how short Pakhmutova is!

I know of a man who was close to Ustvolskaya for many years (he was her former student), loved her as a teacher and as an extraordinary personality, being under her strong influence (so strong that even his handwriting started to change and became like Ustvolskaya's; her handwriting looks like a barbed wire). He managed to give up composition. Ustvolskaya, loving and valuing him in her own way, suggested this to him. He obeyed, of course, because he believed her without reservation and was absolutely devoted to her. Little by little, he started to lose himself as a person and, eventually, he stopped seeing Ustvolskaya as well. He, who shared with Galina Ustvolskaya her internal exile, gave up everything personal for her sake, became her alter ego for many years, tried, eventually, to change something in his life and was banished by Ustvolskaya from her "kingdom." What ever became of his life?

I composed and came to Leningrad to show what I had done. It was 1975. Ustvolskaya was during her last year of teaching at the College. We met there. After listening to the music, she, I remember, said something nice about some of the things, something not so nice about others, but what is more important, she uttered some very memorable words. The meaning was the following: if you are writing for yourself what does it means for the future, write in such way that it will be not erased with the time. Do everything thoroughly. You should work and suffer over every note. This became like a testament to me. I tried to stay connected with Ustvolskaya. I was writing to her, called her. She answered most often with telegrams. Once, I sent her a poem of mine dedicated to her. It was 1979.

> Friend of mine!
> It is difficult to express the feelings,
> These rare, simple feelings
> That touch my heart
> When I pronounce the words:
> Good friend of mine,
> My first troubled joy!
> Time grants encounters.
> And You disturb

And agitate me
Like a tragedy.
You inspire
As faith inspires
Those who tread the thorny path!
In the twilight of our century,
When reason is dozing

Your torch burns.
On the radiant day of rebirth
It inspires faith.
The future will not smother it.
This soulful energy
Will open to the World
The new possibilities
Of the Spirit's achievements.*

She wrote me a letter in which she said of poem: "… your poetry is excellent…" I was happy.

INTERLUDE

"(…) worse than war, and pestilence, and earthquake, worse than all disasters - the decay of consciousness. It sneaks up on us unnoticed, it commits such acts, by which will be horrified the future chronicles. People lose their dignity. Not only are they getting angrier, but they are also forgetting what the future generation should be about. And the writers will show the most disgusting images, and the judges will be nullities".

---

*   Simon Bokman, *Na Okraine Vselennoy,* (On the Edge of the Universe), (Baltimore: Seagull Press, 2006), 22 (transl. by I. Behrendt, ed. Amelia Glaser)

European Parliament, Strasbourg, France   *Tower of Babel*, by Breugel (c. 1563)

"Remember how it says in "Vishnu Purana". Among these instructions you can recognize the current days. It may seem that the monstrosity of the time which has been described was exaggerated but look at what is happening and agree that the ancient predictions were even diminished. Thus, the people, being in a state of horrible worrying, did not want to read the ancient warnings. But it is especially horrible that even now most people do not want to understand what is happening. They dance and trade, and even believe that it is now the heyday of their achievements. Compare the happening with some of the epochs of decline. Won't you find some common signs? People also dreamed of various enslavement and believed that they were legitimate conquerors of the world. And how suddenly these Babylonian towers collapsed! Many symbols have been left to humankind; but they have remained as smoldering remains".

Diaries of H. I. Roerich*, 18 April 1939.

---

*   **Helena Ivanovna Roerich** (born **Shaposhnikova**; Russian: Еле́на Ива́новна Ре́рих; 12 February 1879 – 5 October 1955) was a Russian theosophist, writer, and public figure. In the early 20th century, she created, in cooperation with the Teachers of the East, a philosophic teaching of Living Ethics ("Agni Yoga"). She was an organizer and participant of cultural activity in the U.S., conducted under the guidance of her husband, Nicholas Roerich. **Nikolai Konstantinovich Rerikh** (Russian: Николай Константинович Рерих), better known as **Nicholas Roerich** (/'rɛrɪk/; October 9, 1874 – December 13, 1947), was a Russian painter, writer, archaeologist, theosophist, philosopher, and public figure.

Helena Roerich, painting by her son Svetoslav Roerich

Nicolas Roerich, painting by his son Svetoslav Roerich

♪

Prophets. Conscience and Sainthood.

"…To me, Gogol is not a mere mortal. […] I consider Gogol to be a Saint," wrote Aksakov[*].

"Galina Ustvolskaya does not pretend to be a Grand Old Lady of St. Petersburg, although she could certainly be one. She lives a rather lonely life; musicians regard her almost like a Saint." *(T. Mayer)*[†]

This is what is being now written about Ustvolskaya.

The only composer on the planet (Viktor Suslin), who in addition to many letters has a piece of paper in front of his eyes, written by the hand of G.U which he has hung over his desk. -" I bless you. Galya".[‡]

From Konstantine Bagrenin's letter to me, the Internet. "Ustvolskaya. Precision".

What the artist believes in is, undoubtedly, incredibly significant. For what reason does the artist create? This question is equal to another: what does he live for? What kind of belief, what kind of power directs and moves him?

---

[*]   **Aksakov, Sergei Timofeyevich (1791 - 1859),** *The Complete Works,* (Moscow: "Pravda," 1966), vol. 3, *The story of My Acquaintance with Gogol,* 375,376

   Aksakov **became a writer under Gogol's influence. He introduced a new genre, a cross between memoir and novel, into the Russian literature.**

[†]   O. Gladkova *Galina Ustvolskaya – Music as an Obsession,* 25

[‡]   Probably Galina Ivanovna really felt herself "almost saintly", and maybe without "almost".

For Pushkin, for example, poetry determined God's presence in him. He was a joyous and solemn prophet.

He was a prophet, but he did not feel the need to convince anybody of it. For him, it was enough to create; to create joyously, cheerfully, sunnily!

Lermontov picked up on the motif of a God-chosen poet and the artist in general. But how differently he began to sound!

> "Look! Here was Pride -- be warned and dread it! --
> Would none of us to dwell among:
> This fool would have his neighbours credit
> That God gave utterance to his tongue."*

Awareness of the significance of the mission entrusted to the prophet gives rise to painful pride. His inability to self-denial in the name of truth and the insurmountable and unfulfilled need for ordinary human recognition, which he does not receive, makes him suffer painfully, leaving him lonely and misunderstood.

---

*   M. Lermontov "The Prophet" (fragment) transl. by John Swinnerton Phillimore; Bowra, C. M., ed. A book of Russian verse. Westport, Conn., Greenwood Press [1971], p. 43.

A. Pushkin, *The Prophet*	M. Lermontov, *The Prophet*
My spirit failed; lost and tormented,	The Eternal Justice made me seer,
I roamed the wilderness, wherein	All secret things to penetrate:
Facing a crossroads, I encountered	Since when, through eyes of men I
A glorious six-winged seraphim.	peer
He touched me, dreamlike, feather-	And read the page of Wrong and Fate.
fingered,	
Upon my very eyes he lingered;	Pure matters I began to preach
They shone, like a shocked eaglet's,	Of Righteousness and Love Atoning;
wide,	The neighbours ran to hear, and each
Prophetically revivified;	Was eager who'd begin ... the stoning.
He touched my ears, into them	
pouring	I scattered ashes on my head,
A ringing and a mighty roaring;	The beggars' road from town I trod:
I heard the shuddering heavens speak	In the wilderness I make my bed,
And angels soaring in the vault	And get my meat, like birds, from God.
And sea-beasts squirming in the salt	
And in the valleys vines that creaked.	Keeping the Eternal's covenant,
He touched my mouth and from it	All things of earth obey and love me;
wrung	Stars to my service ministrant
My sinfully backbiting tongue,	Sparkle with frolic lamps above me.
Full of deceit, and he inserted	
With fingers dripping yet with blood	But if with furtive hurrying feet
Into my palsied mouth for good	I slip through town amid the noise,
The sting and wisdom of a serpent,	I see the smile of self-conceit,
And with his sword he cloves my	And hear the old men tell the boys:
breast	
And tore out from the bleeding hole	"Look! Here was Pride -- be warned
My throbbing heart, and into it	and dread it! --
pressed	Would none of us to dwell among:
Another heart of burning coal.	This fool would have his neighbours
I lay like death where I had trod	credit
And hearkened to the voice of God:	That God gave utterance to his tongue.
Prophet, arise and follow me,	"Look well, you children. There he
Seeing and hearing, saith the Lord.	goes –
Go forth upon the land and sea	Haggard and sour and bad and grim!
And burn hearts with the living	Look, he's no money, he's no clothes!
*Word.**	And how they all think scorn of him!"[†]

---

*   *Alexander Pushkin Selected and edited by A. D. P. Briggs*, London: Everyman's Poetry, 1997, 22-23

†   transl. by John Swinnerton Phillimore; Bowra, C. M., ed. A book of Russian verse.

One who is spiritually devoted will inevitably experience a lack of appreciation and recognition, and even hatred and disdain. But the consciousness of himself superiority and exclusivity subtly replace the greatness of the service to the Truth with the service to the oneself.

Nikolay Gogol and Lev Tolstoy were tormented with the questions "Why?" and "What for?" The need to find answers to these tough questions changed their lives. Each of them re-examined his attitude toward Christianity, which led them to thoroughly reconsider what it meant to be a writer.

"By the verification of the mind I have accepted what others understand by clear faith, and what I believed until then somehow darkly and obscurely. The analysis of my own soul also led me to this: I saw also mathematically clear that it is impossible to speak and write about the highest human feelings by imagination: it is necessary to enclose in oneself a small grain of them, in other words – I must become better".*

O, God! How boring it is to read this! And why should one talk and write about higher feelings, if you do not have them in yourself and you do not possess them? A man who wants to "become the best" does not shout at the entire world: "Look, I am getting better! And now I am quite nice! And the God is certainly talking by my lips.

Both writers saw their mission in teaching moral ideals. Both felt themselves to be prophets. Did their works become better, higher, or freer because of this? Gogol was possessed by the maniacal idea of bettering humanity. This is how the strange book *Selected Passages from Correspondence with Friends* was conceived. Gogol was possessed by the maniacal idea of upbringing, betterment of humanity. (Why hasn't he started from himself?) So, the book "Selected Passages from correspondence with friends" appeared. And it is not surprising. The famous writer, who has become exceptionally good, wants to teach humanity how it is to be good also.

But it was actually a lot more serious than that. Jokes aside! It is highly likely that Gogol was afraid. Having knowledge of witchcraft

---

Westport, Conn., Greenwood Press [1971], 43

*   N. V. Gogol, *The Complete Works* in 7 volumes. (Moscow: Khudozhestvennaya Literatura, 1967), vol. 6, *An Author's Confession,* 446

and black magic, he used this experience in his creativity. He had a very tense and mysterious inner life. He could not share it. He was scared. He was very afraid of God's punishment! The paroxysm of fear bound his mind and soul, his whole nature. He could not create. He had to atone for the sin of his mysterious sorcery work in some way. He had to be changed! But how? By becoming a religious and godly man! And immediately! Otherwise... We do not know what, but something terrible could have happened to him. This book is one of his attempts at salvation, an attempt to avert the blow. And later - pilgrimage to Jerusalem, fasting and prayers...

Ustvolskaya was scared too. She was very afraid of death. She was secretive. A man or woman are secretive when they have something to hide. Her last four symphonies are penitential prayers and, far from being for humanity, for herself. Isn't that why she saw a soul mate in Gogol? Something depressed and tormented her very much. She was not so depressed in my studentship. It came gradually. I do not know the reasons, but th ey are certainly.

This is not the only case in the history of music when a composer tries to free his sick conscience with great passion. In 1930 Igor Stravinsky composed the Psalm Symphony. A beautiful work! Stephen Walsh in the first volume of his remarkably deep two-volume monograph about Stravinsky, examining his biography in detail at all times of his life - perfectly illuminating the Russian period - convincingly proves that the complex personal life of the composer, which increased his piety became the motive for the creation of this magnificent work. Being married, he fell in love with Vera Sudeykina, actress and artist, with whom he could not part. And he convinced his wife, Catherine Nosenko, to accept it. One day, in 1925, both women, at the insistence of Stravinsky, met in Nice. It is difficult even to imagine what painful suffering of resentment and jealousy experienced this woman, Catherine Nosenko, wife of the outstanding composer. She died of tuberculosis on March 2, 1939. Igor Fyodorovich met Vera in 1921. In 1920, he had an affair with Coco Chanel, according to Walsh. The composer confessed to his wife. And in the same year, Chanel sheltered the Stravinsky family in her villa. Stravinsky's wife was already sick at that time.

Louise Hay, an outstanding American psychotherapist, claims that almost all of our illnesses are of psychological origin. They come from mediocre quality thinking and emotions. Anger, resentment, irritability, and guilt cause profoundly serious diseases. Louise Hay has made a table of the cause-effect relationship of many diseases to psychological causes. Tuberculosis says, "Wasting away from selfishness. Possessive. Cruel thoughts. Revenge."*

For Tolstoy, his absorption in religion turned into his interpretation of religion. He said that writing is not important.

"You write, write if you want it so badly, but remember that it should never become the goal of your life." [...]

Thus, Lev Tolstoy instructed a young writer Ivan Bunin,†and continued to write.

"The theological explanations that the precepts of the Sermon on the Mount are indications of the perfection, towards which a man should strive, but that fallen man, immersed in sin cannot by his own strength attain this perfection, and that his safety lies in faith, prayer, and the sacraments, - such explanations did not satisfy me.

[...] In reading these rules it always seemed to me that they related directly to me and demanded my personal fulfillment. Reading them, I always experienced a joyous confidence that I could immediately, from that very hour, fulfill them all and I wished and endeavored to do this. But as soon as I had trouble in doing this, I involuntarily remembered the Church's teaching that man is weak and cannot do these things by his own strength, and I weakened. They told me we must believe and pray. [...] But both reason and experience showed me that only my efforts to fulfill Christ's teaching could be effective.‡

And this moralizing is also very boring and unconvincing - forgive me!

I want to speak of J.S. Bach again. Johann Sebastian Bach, who used a then unfashionable composition technique and was not concerned

---

*   Louise L. Hay. "YOU CAN HEAL YOUR LIFE", Hay House, Santa Monica, 1984, p. 187

†   Ivan Bunin *"Okaiannie Dni"* (Cursed Days), Moscow: EKCMO, 2004, 528

‡   L. N. Tolstoy What is my faith? trans. Aylmer Mande, (London: Oxford University Press), 315-316

with discovery or innovation, was a prophet. He predetermined an era of harmony and drew it nearer by means of his music. But he was not a "proud prophet", and he did not need to convince anybody believe "that God gave utterance to his tongue." It is very unlikely that he thought this way about himself.

Trying to understand Bach, analyzing his works, musicologists admire his excellent technique and compositional mastery. But even the tiniest aria by Bach is an example of harmony and beauty.

Professionally, Bach was affiliated with the church, but he was not a religious composer. Bach was not religious. He was spiritual. Religion alone cannot give a man faith. Either you have it, or you have it not. Faith is a very intimate and mysterious feeling that cannot be taught. Religion is an institution of faith. There are rules and rituals for a believer to follow. Bach was free and spiritual; he was a deeply spiritual composer and human. With his music he sometimes contradicted church principles. He could not say that he had discovered something new – he had not. On the contrary, he was responsible for closing the era of polyphony. This is widely known.

Many significant directions and trends of the music development of the subsequent epochs were outlined by Johann Sebastian Bach. Even the prototype of the twelve-tone system can be found in his music. Monumentality, romanticism, orchestral and harmonic inventiveness are all present in Bach's work. But unlike anyone else, Bach was extremely organic. He was organic to such a degree that Bach's innovation went unaware for a long time and his music was forgotten for many years. There is no other composer in the history of music so balanced and organic, for at the core of his creative work is true spirituality, which penetrates all his compositions, religious or secular. He sacrificed his ego for the sake of higher ideals. He served these ideals with his art and understood the meaning of this service. He did not sacrifice himself or those close to him for the sake of his art. He had a large family and took care of them. Here, too, he was devoted to God because God is in everything; God is love. His letters are full of petty concerns with everyday life, food, and income. So, did Bach not understand his creative power? (He would say that he achieved everything simply through diligence). No, he understood, but he correlated his power with the power of That and Whom he served; the power of That and in Whom he selflessly believed. This selflessness and self-denial are what make his work so organic.

Ustvolskaya said many times that composing itself is not the most important thing. She said of her music:

"If my music is fated to stay around for some time, then *a not standard (emphasis by S.B.)* musician will understand that my music is new in its meaning and content; it is uncomfortable for me to speak like this about myself, but I have decided to do it. I included in my 'Catalogue' my truly spiritual, non- religious works."[*]

But can there be non-spiritual creativity? Yes, of course, as there can be non-spiritual and immoral acts or immoral and non-spiritual life. But any action, any thought or deed carried out with the High Ideals in mind cannot be spiritless or immoral. True art is always spiritual.

Incidentally, the era of "great discoveries" in art is the twentieth century. The peak of the artistic discoveries of the twentieth century is Malevich's "Black Square" in which, according to some witty critic, "collapsed all our art."[†]

It is the apotheosis of spiritless creativity, selfishness, disconnection from higher ideals. There are many such achievements and discoveries in twentieth century art.

We know of innovations of the composers of the past but cannot feel them as sharply as their contemporaries. There were collisions and fights. There were Gluckists and Piccinnists , those in favor of Verdi or Wagner. There were arguments about the new harmonies where a particular chord used in a new way could provoke admiration in some and outrage in others. Yes, all of this happened; happened and vanished, as everything vanishes and now it has no decisive meaning for anyone. Music simply lives. The same is true for contemporary art. Some works

---

[*]   O. Gladkova, *Galina Ustvolskaya – Music as an Obsession,* 3

[†]   But it turns out there were black squares before Malevich, and the earliest of them was "invented" by physician, philosopher, and alchemist Robert Fludd in 1617. (Robert Fludd, 1574 -1637). This painting was called "The Great Darkness." According to the author's idea, it symbolized Infinity. But it is not a work of art. It is an illustration of his idea of the origin of the physical world where blackness symbolizes the beginning of Creation.

will remain for a while but will vanish in the space of life. Other works may pass over this border and will be alive longer. How will they be received by future generations? The piquancy and sharpness of many opuses will not seem as poignant as they once were. Style will not be a challenged and the music that will remain in the future will enchant audiences with its deep understanding of the fundamentals of life.

What if we subtract from Ustvolskaya's music the adjectives: "spiritual," "non-chamber," "new"? There will be, simply, music, the outstanding (really?) music of the twentieth century!

INTERLUDE

I had been passing the test of foreign music to Adam Stratievsky. He asked me about Beethoven's Sixth, Pastoral Symphony in F major. An easy question. I loved this symphony, and I still do. It seemed as if there was nothing to talk about it. Bright, slightly ironic music, only single programmed Symphony of Beethoven. It has not four movements, as in the usual symphonic cycle, but five. Nature's paintings are beautifully written in music. The second movement, "The Scene at the Creek," is charming! A herder and a herdswoman, who are in love with each other, of course, cannot part in any way. A murmuring creek. Birds singing, conveyed by exquisite, witty orchestration. And it was heard by the deaf composer!

" Is it all?" - Stratievsky asks?

"Well, it was composing in 1808 and had composing almost simultaneously with the Fifth, and it is surprising how such different things were composing at the same time..."

"Very good. But still, take the piano-score and look and study the development of the first movement."

I took the piano-score obediently and I started to browse without realizing what a surprise Adam Solomonovich was preparing for me. And he was a master of surprises. Unfortunately, I did not learn harmony from him. He had his own system of teaching harmony. There were sensations in the class every now and then. He gave to composers and theorists to harmonize classical examples: Glinka's romances... Or Gurilyov's ones. A student brings a task. Everything

is in the place. It sounds quite classical and there are no mistakes. Red-bearded, artistically ironical, a bit like the creator of the VChK *
Felix Dzerzhinsky, - but only outwardly, of course - Stratievsky, having listening, smoking a cigarette with a filter, having released smoke is saying:

"Not bad..." (puffs)... Releasing the smoke:

"Only it's not Glinka... You have a sequence of the triads of the first and sixth steps, but it was first used by Wagner in the Introduction to "Lohengrin...""

And now it is my turn. I flipped through the score, not knowing what I had to find.

"So, Senya, you got it?"

"Not very, Adam Solomonovich."

" Well, let us look together. Pay attention to the tonal plan in development. I sat down at his table, and we started to look together. I was naming the tonalities aloud.

"Well, haven't you figured it out yet?" - asks.

" Well, you have not guessed yet?" - asks.

"There are no one minor tonality among the tonalities you've mentioned..."

Yes, that is so! Absolute major tonality! Joy and Light. Amazing. The deaf composer, lonely, not healthy, not very sociable, sharp, and not very cheerful, composes such joyful music! Where did Beethoven draw joy from? Where did he find its source? It was undoubtedly the Faith. An indestructible, great, inexhaustible Faith in Good and Light. There was also Knowledge. But Faith and Knowledge are identical. F major - the tonality of the symphony is green. And the note "F" is green too. Did Beethoven know about it, or did he hear it out? In both cases it is astounding!

---

* The All-Russian Extraordinary Commission (Russian: Всероссийская Чрезвычайная Комиссия), abbreviated as VChK (Russian: ВЧК, *Ve-Che-Ka*) and commonly known as Cheka (from the initialism ChK - Russian:ЧК), was the first of a succession of Soviet secret police organizations. Established on December 5 (Old Style) 1917 it came under the leadership of Felix Dzerzhinsky, a Polish aristocrat-turned-communist.

And at the same time, in Spain, a noticeably big artist named Francisco Goya was creating his paintings. And he was deaf. Just like Beethoven. And while Beethoven was composing the Pastoral Symphony, Goya created a series of etchings "Disasters of War". These painting pictures are terribly like modern online news photos of the horrors of our world. The last, dark paintings of Goya or murals of the House of the Deaf Man, as they are called, are not an exposure of evil. It is an ecstasy of evil and a triumph of evil. It is the world of a man dying of lonely despair... I wrote it, and I thought... No, why the dying one? He creates! He does evil and violence. He creates them with his imagination and conviction. And this conviction, transferred into the images of his terrible paintings, gives him pleasure. The offender receives the same pleasure from his atrocities. This is a special state of mind. In his consciousness, evil overcomes the world and creates its own: a world of overpowering darkness, fear, pain, torment, and despair. The world of Light and Good is unknown to him. But evil cannot defeat the world. It can destroy a man who lives in evil. The ill one is not the one who is in pain, but the one who does not feel the pain of others. And the worst disease is to cure one's own pain by hurting others.

St. Petersburg, Volkovskoye Lutheran Cemetery, June 17, 2009, unveiling of the monument in the 90th anniversary of the birthday. The author of the picture is Victor Suslin.

TWENTY FIRST VARIATION

♩

Conclusion

I was sitting at the piano and looking through Ustvolskaya's Preludes. Somehow, I fell asleep… Suddenly I woke up, sensing someone's presence. It was she, Galia… She was standing before me holding an open score of the Preludes.

"You have the opportunity to take my inscription with you," she said, looking around for something to write with…

"Why take with me?" I thought. "Are we leaving indeed?"*

Then she unexpectedly put her hands around my head and kissed me tenderly on the lips…Suddenly she shouted: "Look me in the eye! Why did you shut your eyes?"

"But you shut yours too," I objected.

"No, I did not close them tightly."

Galia sat down on a chair looking fatigued. She was sitting and staring blankly… I wanted to talk to her, but I was gasping for breath. I needed more air. I talked, avidly gasping in the air with my mouth open.

"Galya, you know… Boris Tishenko… wrote a book… about you?"

"So what?"

"I am, you know, also trying… to write about you…"

"It's OK… it's OK" she kept repeating almost soundless, sad, and tired.

I woke my wife.

---

*   It happened that after this dream we moved soon.

"What happened?" she asked.

"Galya… Ustvolskaya… was here…"

It was the night of April 23, 2003.

A human being is a process aimed at the future. This is why we cannot know everything about a person. A true creator is bigger than his creation. Internal work, work with oneself – this is what is impossible to observe and to analyze. Ustvolskaya is unique, first, in her inner spiritual knowledge and, therefore, in her belief that the spiritual world is a key to everything else. She is indifferent to material benefits, although very often she has had to suffer for lack of means. She is indifferent to fame, although the public's lack of understanding has hurt her. She is like a visitor from another planet. A fragile and delicate being, God knows how she ended up here. She is not amazed, but terrified by our world. Her music is a frightening world in its incomprehensibility. There is no harmony in that world, but there is no harmony within her either. She feels the loss of meaning in those lofty words: truth, serenity, and eternity. She longs to cross the threshold of mystery, beyond which is hidden their true meaning. She yearns for a high spiritual ideal that is incompatible with the real world. She lives in this contradiction and internal conflict and so does her creative work. Here even no conflict anymore. The darkness is thickening. And the dramatic effect is not in the opposing poles, but in this thickening darkness. Does it mean that darkness has triumphed over light? Is evil stronger than Good? Does death defeat Life? And is there no Hope? And what is the meaning of life? Ustvolskaya answers this question with her life: "Creativity!"

There are two images or two substances of her being. One is earthy; the other hovers above the earth. Her unearthly spiritual image sees in earthly, material life its businesslike and vain emptiness. Fame requires a lot of time and energy. Why bother? But the unearthly world is also complex. There has been much discussion around whether the gift of creativity is from God; the eternal battle of Good and Evil reveals itself here with particular strength. This battle can either strengthen the spirit or kill it. Insanity may become the result of this frightening battle. Ustvolskaya's creative work does not give her peace. It devours her. Artistry and virtuosity of craftsmanship - these qualities are not inherent to the music of Ustvolskaya. Special bright artistically mastery presupposes the interest and special warm attitude of the public to the composer, the artist. While composing, the composer feels what the public will like, what it will understand; what will be picked up by it and grasped. Ustvolskaya has learned to look above the heads of the crowd. Her goal is immeasurably higher, but the attention of people is also important to her. Therefore, understanding and respect of her music, not of the part of the crowd, but of a few thinking connoisseurs, is dear to her.

The creativity of arts man this is his biography. His work is his world, his story, his thoughts, and his particular opinion on the matter of the most important ideas and problems. He wants to be, and can be, sincere. Thinking by images affords an opportunity to reflect without reservation on the most intimate topics and to open the secrets of one's soul. This creative magnet attracts images from space that are in tune with the ideas he ponders. Creative work is sometimes the encoding of the most unexpected qualities, thoughts, or tendencies. The most reserved person is completely opened in his art. Gogol, in revealing the secret of the creation of his antiheroes in Dead Souls, confessed:

"This is how it was done: having taken a bad quality of mine, I chased it under a different name and into a different field of endeavor; I tried to portray it as a deadly enemy, who inflicted upon me the most sensitive insult, and chased it with anger, with taunts, and anything that came along. [...] This is where I saw what it means to take a matter from the soul, and the soul's truth itself, and that what can be the most terrifying for a person is darkness and the frightening absence of light."

*"To concoct nightmares – I also did not concoct them, those nightmares suppressed my own soul: whatever was in the soul emerged from it."**

Fear is the prevailing emotion in Ustvolskaya's music. She is afraid of death, afraid of non-existence. In this regard, the last four symphonies of Ustvolskaya come close in their idea to the *Fourteenth Symphony* of Shostakovich. The composers' attitudes towards death are similar. Shostakovich is more open and outspoken than Ustvolskaya. It is important for him to be understood. Ustvolskaya, on the contrary, avoids all the comments on and interpretations of her music.

---

*   N.V. Gogol, *The Complete works,* (Moscow, 1967), vol. 6, *Selected Passages from Correspondence with Friends,* 287.

Shostakovich explains the idea of his *Fourteenth Symphony* as follows:

"I, partially, try to engage in polemics with the Great Classics who touched upon the theme of death in their music… Let us remember the death of Boris Godunov: when Godunov dies, there follows a sort of enlightenment. Let us remember Verdi's *Othello*; at the end of the tragedy, when Desdemona and Othello die, you will also hear a wonderful tranquility. Remember *Aida*. When the heroes tragically die, it is alleviated with light music. All that, it seems to me, comes from a different kind of religious teaching that maintains that life, so to speak, could be bad, but once you die all will be well and complete tranquility awaits you."[*]

Does God, or the Cosmos, needs a human?? In this regard, Ustvolskaya's work reflects the consciousness of twentieth century humanity, which lost the most important guidelines of life: faith in a Higher Spirit, kindness, and justice; faith in beauty, fearlessness, and love. (Absolute love defeats fear!)

"Human intolerance toward everything high has converted people into degenerates. Upon all concepts and principles man has imposed his stigma. In each higher affirmation man has displayed his blasphemy. Not the World is cruel, but man. Not the World affirms injustice, but man; for man's choice of the path of isolation and selfhood has brought on a most threatening destiny. Intolerance toward everything high and enlightened has become the disgrace of humanity[†]

I could not say this about Ustvolskaya as an individual because she believes in a spirit, in some higher being, but not without some contradiction. This contradiction is well expressed in this Russian Orthodox prayer: "I believe, Father, I believe! Father, cure my lack of faith!" Ustvolskaya contradicts herself merely by the fact of her creative work. If darkness rules the world and death equalizes everything, then high aspirations are meaningless. But if an artist creates, it means his inner faith is alive. Music about evil is still music. Poetry about the end of the world is still poetry and a continuation of the "end."

---

[*]   Sophia Khentova "*Shostakovich in Moscow*" Moskovskii Rabochii, 1986, 191

[†]   "*Agni Yoga*", *Fiery World*" III, &337

She is a prophet. She foresees a catastrophe, the downfall of this terrible world, which is cut off from higher ideals and is being ruined as a result. Stephan Zweig, who likewise saw the world in a catastrophic light, committed suicide during World War II. In Hitler's invasion he saw not just a catastrophe, but the beginning of the destruction of the world's culture and the civilization.

Ustvolskaya's music demonstrates the exhaustion of a means of expression. It is the last attempt, the last opportunity for artistic expression, as though the music itself were agonizing and dying. Hers is the last music of the Twentieth Century. It seems to be the last music of all time.

But in reality, darkness is followed by light just as a dark night is followed by dawn, as destruction is followed by creation. Everything has its own terms. Everything ages and then there appears something – Huns, some frightening cataclysm, disease, epidemics that devour the old, clearing the way for the future. An artist who has faith in a truly bright future can draw it closer. Then, creative work can and must become different. In its harmony, it may influence the world and humankind to return to our spiritual (not religious!) base, which is so vital to us. The prodigal son should be returned to his Father. This is the true Prophecy!

Where are you, nearing Huns? Over earth, like a cloud you smear. I hear your strong iron stomps Over yet undiscovered Pamirs. Drop on us your drunken hordes From your dark and ugly field-camps To revive our feeble bodies In the blazing pool of blood waves. You, the slaves of the will, Set your huts by the palace's door. Grow a joyful field In place of the throne-room floor. Burn the books in bonfires and dance In their light that's so bright and so cheerful. In the temples perform nasty antics – You'll be innocent always, like children!	And we, wise men, and poets, Keepers of secrets and faith, Will carry our burning lights To the catacombs, desert, and caves. And what in this violent tempest, In the thunderstorm of devastations, Will playful chance preserve Of our cherished creations? It is possible, all will perish That was known to us alone, But I greet you, my slayer, with relish And a salutary hymn I intone. *

Ustvolskaya is a prominent Soviet composer. Only in Russia, with its merciless tyrannical system, the consequences of which have yet to be outlived, could such powerful and spiritual opposition appear. Ustvolskaya is its most outstanding representative. She is not rational and controversial. She, one might say, contradicts her own contradictions by denying her previous preferences and opinions and then denying and refusing the disclaimer itself with new contradictory statements. But how consistent and principled she is in her music! It leaves no doubt that in it she is sincere. And here is another contradiction: just as Stalin and his successors rewrote the facts of Russian and Soviet history to keep their images pure and sterile, Ustvolskaya, in an impulse to keep her musical legacy wholesome and pure, destroyed her "politically correct" compositions, borrowing a method from the regime with which she was in opposition. The same could be said regarding her relationship with Shostakovich. She wants to belittle his influence on her, and the reasons for this could well be very personal.

---

*   Valery Brusov "Nearing Hunns", 1905. Translated by Irina Behrendt, edited by Oni Buchanan.

Consciousness can be ruled and directed by time. Tendencies and fashions pass, but the art of an epoch lives on. And yet, only real art survives.

Time must pass… Not time, but eternity is the highest judge. But time also has its own criterion by which it dictatorially determines what artistic achievements belong to it and to what extent. Time determines the price it should be worth.

May 2004. Daly City.

*Thomas Mann and... Galina Ustvolskaya

Instead of the Epilogue

"And there's no devil either?" the sick man suddenly asked Ivan Nikolayevich gaily.

"No devil either...."

"Oh, but this is really interesting," the professor cried, shaking with laughter.

"It seems, no matter what you name here, it does not exist!"

(Michael Bulgakov "The Master and Margarita")

After the book about Ustvolskaya was written, I happened to read a letter by Thomas Mann.

---

*   **Paul Thomas Mann** (6 June 1875 – 12 August 1955) was a German novelist, short story writer, social critic, philanthropist, essayist, and the 1929 Nobel Prize in Literature laureate. His highly symbolic and ironic epic novels and novellas are noted for their insight into the psychology of the artist and the intellectual. His analysis and critique of the European and German soul used modernized versions of German and Biblical stories, as well as the ideas of Johann Wolfgang von Goethe, Friedrich Nietzsche, and Arthur Schopenhauer.

> *"…I have a notion of something satanically religious, demonically devout, at once stringently disciplined and criminally loose, often mocking art, also something reaching back to the primitive and elemental, abandoning bar divisions, even the order of tonalities (trombone glissandi*); furthermore, something scarcely performable: ancient church modes, a cappella choruses which must be sung in non-tempered tuning, so that scarcely a tone or interval on the piano occurs."†*

He was writing about a composition of Adrian Leverkühn, the hero of his novel "Doctor Faustus", which is based on fifteen prints of Dürer's "Apocalypse." Thomas Mann is trying to imagine the music of a composer who made a deal with the devil in order to overcome a creative crisis. I was stunned by the similarity of this description of the music of an invented composer with the existing music of Ustvolskaya! Much of what is said in the letter is present in Ustvolskaya's music

Interestingly, the description of the music after Dürer's prints in the novel slightly differs from the one in the letter cited. Perhaps, Thomas Mann found it to be too radical, or maybe Theodor Adorno, who was consulting him, suggested a correction. In any case, the novelist's imagination, the way it was expressed in the letter, undoubtedly turned out to be a prophetic one.

Ustvolskaya's symphonies, starting from the Second, also make up a sort of "Apocalypse in pictures." These pictures are painted with her music, yielding something akin to musical icon-painting. Her music is "stringently disciplined" and calculated to the smallest detail, and this strictness borders on chaos, on something "primitive and elemental." There are no bar divisions. There are ancient modes. They are not cited but have been recreated and are reminiscent of something akin to a Znamenny chant. This is why there is no "order of tonalities." Trombone glissandi can be heard in the Third symphony, although

---

*   Apparently, there is a mistake in the translation -"trumpet glissandi ". In the German edition of the "Letters" (*S. Fisher, Frankfurt am Main, 1961-65*), Thomas Mann is mentioning trombone glissandi (Posaunenglissandi), not trumpet glissandi. I have dared to correct it by myself.

†   Letters of Thomas Mann (1889-1955) Selected and transl. Richard and Clara Winston, (Alfred A. Knopf, New York, 1971), 496.

this is not characteristic detail that makes her music most resemble the imaginary music of Adrian Leverkühn.

The use of the cluster technique, which is so characteristic of Ustvolskaya's music, creates an illusion of non-tempered tuning because the intonation becomes blurred. (Contrary to Mann's idea, this happens most in the piano part.) A cappella choirs can be heard in the texture of Ustvolskaya's symphonies; not warm human voices, but their masterful instrumental imitation. ("Has the sun better fire than the kitchen?" asks the devil sarcastically in the twenty fifth chapter of "Doctor Faustus"*.)

Ustvolskaya spoke of Thomas Mann with admiration, but the novel could not have influenced her because in the sixties, when it was published in Russian, Ustvolskaya's original style was already determined. And, naturally, Thomas Mann could not have known anything about Ustvolskaya and her work in the forties, when he was working on the novel.[†] Rather, he seems to have predicted the appearance of Ustvolskaya, whose music marks the peak of the twentieth century's musical and cultural crisis and, as a result, concludes it. Any further development in this direction would be impossible. (In her Catalogue, Ustvolskaya's Fifth Symphony, her last work, is dated 1989-90.)

In the novel, Thomas Mann warns that striving to be ever more exquisite, the artist risks exhaustion, "for with every finished work he made life harder for himself, and in the end impossible. Spoilt by the extraordinary, his taste ruined for anything else, he must at last deteriorate through despair of executing the impossible. The problem for the highly gifted artist was how, despite his always increasing fastidiousness, his spreading disgust, he could keep within the limits of the possible."[‡]

---

*   Thomas Mann, *Doctor Faustus. The life of a German composer Adrian Leverkühn as told by a friend.* Transl. from German by H.T. Lowe-Porter, (New York: Alfred A. Knopf, 1948), 236

†   There is also another interesting coincidence: *Doctor Faustus* was published in 1947. In the same year Ustvolskaya's First Piano Sonata was written. It is the first work where her style was beginning to form and it is #2 in the Ustvolskaya's *Catalogue*.

‡   Mann, *Doctor Faustus,* 259

Doctor Faustus is a novel which functions as a parable; the fictional composer's crisis represents the crisis of 20th century art. In his letter to the conductor Bruno Walter, *Thomas Mann wrote: "Music, as well as the other arts – and not only the arts – is in a crisis which sometimes seems to threaten its very life."[†]

The writer did not deny the fact that his own work comes from the period of decadence. Not without sarcasm, he wrote to Jonas Lesser: "I must say that the denial of my work in such a wide spectrum, in a spectrum of the general decadence that has been going on since the end of the Middle Age, does not cause me any pain. Here, at the same time, so many great people are being affected that I may be calm."[‡]

The cultural crisis of the 20th century is the result of a general crisis of spirituality, because of which the crisis of art sprang up. The meaning of the word "Culture" is forgotten. Originating from the Sanskrit the word was originally formed from "Cult" – service, and "Ure"- light; "Service to Light." Therefore, it is a terrible misconception that only the Devil, a servant of Darkness, can help to overcome the crisis. Such ignorance, or forgetfulness, is typical for 20th century art, although the method is not new. Even Goethe was not the first to use it. But the spiritual crisis did not begin yesterday. This is why the problem of newness in music is not important. There is, however, a problem of sincerity, warmth, and emotional emancipation. "Where work and sincerity no longer agree, how is one to work?"[§]

There cannot, and there should not, be any outer criteria that restricts an artist. Regarding the "newest" and the "modern," Ustvolskaya often said: "Do not think about it. If you have talent it will stay with you." I am repeating myself, of course, but it is striking what simple and wise advice this is!

---

[*] Bruno Walter (1876-1962), a prominent conductor, became a close friend of Mann's during the period 1912-1922, when Walter served as general director of musical activities in Munich. In later life he was a neighbor of the Manns in Beverly Hills.

[†] Letters Of Thomas Mann 1889-1955 selected and transl. Richard and Clara Winston, (New York: Alfred A. Knopf, 1971), March 1, 1945

[‡] Ibid., March 21, 1946

[§] Mann, *Doctor Faustus*, 254

The music of the future, as well as other arts, will be romantic, of course (if we view romanticism not as a trend, but as a spiritual quality). It contains the source of its own life. Therefore, a sensitive artist will find a way, without ignoring the achievements of the 20th century composers, to return to ever new origins, to everything that evokes joy and the soaring of the spirit; to return to that which is as unwavering as consonance. No one can "cancel" consonance because it is in the nature of sound: the overtone series represents a complete set of consonant intervals; the most complex opus is hiding a triad.

Schildknapp had given expression to his disbelief in the deromanticizing of music. Music was after all too deeply and essentially bound up with the romantic ever to reject it without serious natural damage to itself. To which Adrian replied: 'I will gladly agree with you if you mean by the romantic a warmth of feeling which music in the service of technical intellectuality today rejects. It is probably self-denial. But what we call the purification of the complicated into the simple is at bottom the same as the winning back of the vital and the power of feeling. If it were possible – whoever succeeded in – how would you say it?' he turned to me and then answered himself: - 'the break-through, you would say: whoever succeeded in the break-through from intellectual coldness into a touch-and-go world of new feeling, him one should call the saviour of art.' *

There is an obvious controversy. If one understands the necessity of a breakthrough, why not attempt one? It seems too abstruse, and the author could be accused of inconsistency.† However, it is even more surprising to find, here, a parallel with a similar inconsistency in Ustvolskaya. She gave wonderful advice: listen to your talent, follow it without beating around the bush, and be your natural self. ("If you

---

*   Ibid., 321

†   The "conspiracy of mediocrities" (see note on page 55) probably existed already for long, and T. Mann knew or guessed about it, but he did not dare to speak out openly. And the whole intrigue around the pact with the devil is about this, but in an allegorical way. "Conspiracy of the mediocrities" is a conditional name, as it often involves very talented creators. The meaning of this phenomenon is the destruction of true Culture as a service to the Highest ideals, service to the Light.

have talent, it will stay with you.") Why, then, did she not follow her own advice? It seems intentional.*

Here is a fragment of another of Thomas Mann's letters:

*Now I am imagining and composing for my musician the Symphonic Cantata, with which he bids farewell to the life of the mind –*The Lamentation of Doctor Faustus *(after the chapbook), and ode to sorrow, since Adrian's destiny obviously does not include the Ninth Symphony's 'Joy,' whose heralding must therefore be canceled.*†

The composer-hero of the novel and Galina Ustvolskaya, coincide in their opinions about the Ninth Symphony and its "Ode to Joy." The concept of the universal brotherhood, so wonderfully and inspirationally extolled by Beethoven, found no compassion in Ustvolskaya.

"But is it good: 'be embraced, millions,' she said once and puzzled me with her question.‡ (12 Variation).

Adrian Leverkühne is even more categorical:

'I have discovered that it ought not be.'

'What ought not be, Adrian?'

'The good and the noble," he replied, *"what people call human, even though it is good and noble. What people have fought for, have stormed citadels for, and what people filled to overflowing have announced with jubilation – it ought not be. It will be taken back. I shall take it back.'*

'I do not quite understand, my dear fellow. What do you want to take back?'

---

* There's no doubt there is a intentional! G.U. Wrote music of the Apocalypse. Her style is conditioned by it.

† To Emil Pretorius, December 30, 1946

‡ The idea and the optimism of the Ninth Symphony are sound with those, proclaimed, but never fulfilled in real life by the Soviet ideological doctrine. It is very likely to be at least one of the reasons of Ustvolskaya's rejection. Obviously, Beethoven meant something quite different. Stravinsky, very bravely, shockingly boldly criticizing Ninth, then apologizing for his criticism, says: "I am undoubtedly wrong to talk this a way about "the Ninth". It was already sacred when I first listened to it in 1897. (I am impressed by this: "It was sacred when I listened" - S.B.). I have often wondered why? Can it actually have something to do with a "message" or with a proletarian appeal? (Memories and Commentaries. Igor Stravinsky and Robert Craft, Farber and Farber. This edition Robert Craft, 2002, last edition, pp. 284, 285).

'The Ninth Symphony,' he replied. And then came nothing more, even though I waited.*

In rereading the novel, I never cease to be amazed at the coinciding esthetic principles of Leverkühne and Ustvolskaya. *Thus* Kretschmar *[teacher of Leverkühne] lived in the natural, taken-for-granted conviction that music had found its definitely highest manifestation and effect in orchestral composition; and this* Adrian no longer believed. *To the boy of twenty, more than to his elders, the close link of the most highly developed instrumental technique with a harmonic conception was more than a historical view. With him it had grown to be something like a state of mind, in which* past and future merged together; *the cool gaze he directed upon the hypertrophy of the post-romantic monster orchestra,* the need he felt for its reduction *and return to the ancillary role that it had played at the time of the preharmonic, the polyphonic vocal music;*[†]

"[...] *Adrian had repeatedly expressed to me the view that the old distinctions between chamber music and orchestral music are not tenable, and that since the emancipation of colour they merge into one another. The tendency to the hybrid, to mixing and exchanging [...] was growing on him.*"[‡]

Ustvolskaya basically "cancelled" orchestra in her music. This un-chamber-like quality of her music equates works of different length and instrumentation. The subdivision of genres is very subtle in her music. Neither chamber, nor orchestral, her works are that very "hybrid, mixing and exchanging," about which Thomas Mann speaks regarding the music of Adrian Leverkühne. The astuteness of the author is stunning.

In chapter 20 he writes:

"*It was, at that musical time of day and at the young adept's age, almost inevitable that here and there the influence of Gustav Mahler should be perceptible.*"

---

*   Mann, *Doctor Faustus, 501*. This is not the end of Ustvolskaya's resemblance to the hero of the novel "Dr. Faustus". She, as well as Adrian Leverkühn, became the cause of misfortunes among the people in her orbit. Read Bagrenin's comment on the page 220.

†   Ibid., 150

‡   Ibid., 457

Gustav Mahler's music influenced the music of Shostakovich, Ustvolskaya's teacher, and through him it influenced her as well.

Sickliness and nervousness appeal to Ustvolskaya and have her particular compassion. Her favorite writers Chekhov and Gogol were nervous and sick. Incidentally, Shostakovich had fragile health and was always overly sensitive. This strangely peculiar preference for the unhealthy is hard for me to understand. She had this attitude toward optimism as well. An optimist is most likely a fool or, at least, an insensitive and a narrow-minded person, according to her. Ustvolskaya herself does not seem to be physically unhealthy, but she is emotionally fragile and easily perturbed.

In Mann's monologue of the Devil, one reads:

"And I mean too that creative, genius-giving disease, (disease as genius-engendering is very Ustvolskayan! – S.B.) with drunken daring from peak to peak, is a thousand times dearer to life than plodding healthiness. I have never heard anything stupider than that from disease only disease can come. Life is not scrupulous – by morals it sets not a fart. It takes the reckless product of disease, feeds on and digests it, and as soon as it takes it to itself it is healthy. Before the fact of fitness for life, my good man, all distinction of disease and health falls away. A whole host and generation of youth, receptive, sound to the core, flings itself on the work of the morbid genius, made genius by disease: admires it, praises it, exalts it, carries it away, assimilates it unto itself and makes it over to culture." [...]

Art in the Soviet Union was in a special situation. It was developing (if I may use such word) according to the directions from the government, the Party, art unions, and any number of conferences and conventions. In other words, Soviet art was "developing" under instructions. Obviously, in a situation of total control of culture there could not be a normal and free creative process and exchange. The common ideological precepts were: comprehensiveness for the broad masses, encouragement and optimism, and ideology, which meant the glorifying of the system and its leaders. Thus, popular songs became the most common genre in Soviet music. Nowhere else in the world has this genre enjoyed such popularity.

---

*   Ibid., 242

"Art that 'joins the folk,' that makes the needs of the crowd, of the average man, of small minds, its own, will end in misery, and such needs will become a duty, for the sake of the state perhaps; to allow only the kind of art that the average man understands is the worst small-mindedness and the murder of mind and spirit."

That, again, was the quote from the "Doctor Faustus," chapter 31.[*]

This is exactly what was happening – "the murder of mind and spirit." Big talents either adjusted or became the artistic "underground." Few were able to save their artistic personality and often paid a big toll for it. A deal with the devil became a condition for survival for the population of the whole country, let alone the representatives of the creative professions. It was a diabolical system. Ustvolskaya is an extremely strict and serious exception. She was not a member of the Party. She did not work for the KGB to build a career. She paid the system her dues with some of her works; she later destroyed them, however. It is impossible to condemn her for it. There are few examples of such compromise in her music. And how different those works are from the Octet, Twelve Preludes, the Fifth and the Sixth Sonatas for Piano! It is as if they were written by a different composer.

In Mikhail Bulgakov's[†] novel *Master and Margarita*, Satan and his retinue visit Moscow to help an ingenious writer – Master.[‡] They punish literary scoundrels who tormented Master, leading him into madness. They recover the manuscript burnt by Master and take Master and his beloved Margarita away from the abhorrent city. The devil in the novel is kinder than the diabolic system, which kills vital creativity. He helps Master to regain his freedom and independence… Satan helps the artist and his beloved to leave the evil world for the world of dreams and illusions, for immortality.

At that tough time for Russian (Soviet) culture, there was a burning interest in what was happening with art in the West. It was considered great luck to hear the works of Stravinsky, even the early ones. However,

---

[*]   Ibid., 339

[†]   Bulgakov, Mikhail (1891-1940), a prominent Russian writer and playwright.

[‡]   This novel is an example of the "artistic underground." It was not published during the author's lifetime. "Master and Margarita" was first published in the sixties, during the Khrushev "thaw," over twenty years after Bulgakov's death.

some things seeped through with the touring artists; records and scores were brought from abroad. Few things, very few, were performed and published in the country. Given such a deficit, the interest in the "decadent" art of the West only grew stronger. But the life of Western art was also not completely safe. The free market and competition demand of an artist a particular kind of creativity, flexibility, and refinement. A need for sensation determines cultural demand. It is ridiculous, but it is true. This is why Adrian Leverkühne is unable to have a breakthrough to romanticism, to the warmth of feeling. It would not be in demand. Refined novelty is necessary. Without it a modern artist cannot count on success. But the possibilities for such innovation without the presence of true spirituality are limited. This was an artistic crisis about which Thomas Mann wrote to Bruno Walter. To overcome this crisis is possible only through the return to spiritual ideals. Who has enough courage to do this?

Despite all the innovativeness of her music, Ustvolskaya drew a lot from the progressive composers of the West. Atonality, cluster technique, and experimentation with small instrumental groups, - all of these were used previously by Western composers. Ustvolskaya found a way to use these techniques in her own, new way. Her music is very original. It is as original and unusual (shockingly unusual) as her philosophy. Under conditions of the Soviet system with its "iron curtain," when the doctrine of general festivity and optimism determined the methods, such work could imply a challenge to the system and unwillingness to "march in sync" with everyone else; even an attempt to go against tradition, to swim against the current, takes a lot of courage. Unfortunately, she did not break through into a "touch-and-go" world of new feeling. It is difficult to expect this from an artist surrounded by a curtain of fear and darkness. She believes in the righteousness of her ideas, believes in herself and her talent, and her mission. But, unlike Bach, she does not forgo herself in the name of the Superior. She forgoes the world in the name of herself… Her work concludes a whole epoch of music evolution. But the music has not stopped.

The music of Galina Ustvolskaya is an angry protest against the lack of liberty, tyranny, and the system of dictatorship.

"But if it was very bold music he wrote, was it after all "free" music, world music? That was not. It was the music of one who never escaped […] " [*]

August 15, 2005, South San Francisco.

---

[*]   Mann, *Doctor Faustus,* 83

APPENDIX

1. Letters and Telegrams.

With a thrill, I am opening a dear little box in which I keep all the telegrams and letters from Galina Ustvolskaya. Yes, letters. There are few of them. They are laconic. They remind me of a hugely different life, the life from which these letters came. Ustvolskaya requested that I mail letters to a P.O. box because her mailbox was broken, and the mail would disappear. To my letters she first responded with telegrams. It was difficult for her to write, as you could see from her handwriting. How ecstatic I was once, when I received a letter from her, written "with her own hand!"

To a scholar of Ustvolskaya, her letters written during the 1977-79 period might be of particular interest. In 1979 she wrote the Second Symphony.

Some of the letters were written together with Alexander Fridman (Sasha), her former student, with whom at the time she had a very warm and close friendship. He was also my friend then.

You write that the G.U. sent you letters and telegrams. But it is a small lie, since all this was written at the request and under the pressure of "Fridman." I was witness to this repeatedly. G.U. only reluctantly signed up. One letter was written by a "stranger's" hand. Right. This I wrote at the request of G.U., who promised to Sasha that she would write to you and at the same time said: "How do I tire of this Bokman. And Sasha asks me to sign all the time." That is all, end of "co-authoring."

From Konstantin Bagrenin's letter to me. Internet. "Ustvolskaya. Precision".

1. Telegram

30 October 1974

SEMYON THANK YOU FOR YOUR LETTER WISH YOU ALL THE BEST

LET US KNOW ABOUT YOURSELF IT IS RAINING AND DARK HERE SINCERE REGARDS = GALINA USTVOLSKAYA –

2. Telegram

30 April 1974

THANK YOU FOR YOUR LETTER WISH YOU AND YOUR WIFE ALL THE BEST YOUR OPINION ABOUT ART IS AMAZING SINCERE REGARDS = GALINA USTVOLSKAYA –

3. Telegram

13 November 1976

= DEAR SEMYON THANK YOU FOR PARCEL DON'T KNOW HOW TO THANK YOU SINCERE REGARDS = GALINA USTVOLSKAYA

4. Telegram

18 April 1977

= DEAR SEMYON THANK YOU FOR YOUR LETTER WISH YOU ALL KINDS OF SUCCESS KEEP IN TOUCH SINCERE REGARDS = GALINA USTVOLSKAYA

5.Letter

An air-mail envelope with no address. On the envelope Sasha's handwriting in large letters reads: "FOR SENYA." Perhaps, this letter was inside E. Fromantin "Old Masters," a book which was returned to me in a parcel. The letter is written on plain letter paper. Most of it is from Sasha with a little note from Ustvolskaya at the end:

Dear Senya!

My new address: Per. Kahovskogo, d. 4 (crossed out)
kv. 44. Tel 230 – 63 – 93 (maybe it will change)
Did you receive the parcel with the book and shoes?
I am sorry that I did not reach you in Kyiv, but
2 times you were not there, and the third time (August 2) –
I could not get through. (Every phone call there is really a problem).

Wanted to thank you again for the Fromantin,
under the impression from this book, we lived this whole
period of our lives in Lithuania.
Continued – in Ustvolskaya's hand:
Your shirt (black) is sitting in my apartment.
If it (the shirt) needs to be sent
to you, I will send it. Let us know,
please, either me or Sasha.
I embrace you, Senya, and
your whole family.
Galya (then Sasha's hand) and Sasha. 26 VIII 77 y.

Original layout

That summer Sasha went on vacation with Ustvolskaya to Lithuania. Before that, "on the way" he visited us in Kaliningrad. I handed him a shirt and a pair of shoes in case of cold and wet weather, as well as the book by Fromantin "The Old Masters" in which he was interested but did not have enough time to finish it. This book became a favorite of Ustvolskaya that summer as well. The shirt ("black") was then worn by Kostia (Ustvolskaya's husband), which is why it was "sitting" in her apartment.

---

6. Letter

This letter is written on a plain note card. The address on the envelope is written in Sasha's hand.

(seems like 2 – hard to read) VII – 1978

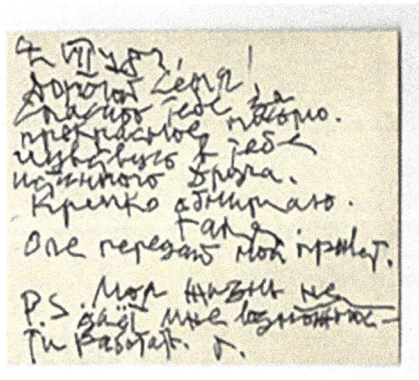

Dear Senya!

Thank you for the beautiful letter. I feel the true Friend in you. I hug you tightly.

Galya.
Say hello to Olya.

P. S. My life does not allow me to work.

    G.

(original layout)

7.Letter

This letter is written on a glossy piece of paper, a little bigger than a postcard's size. The address is written by Sasha's hand. The letter stuck to the inside of the envelope and the text is a little damaged.

20. IX. 78

Dear Senya!

I did not ... (the text is ruined here) to reply to your letter. I hug you tightly and I wish you to have maximum in your life according to your "inner quality" in this terrible time.

We are – here to be dying.... (in Russian harsh - *"подыхать"*...)

I kiss you and value you for your Soul and understanding (to me).

God grant you . . . . . .

Galya.

On the back, in Sasha's hand:

Just now with Galia (next word is crossed out a lot) talked about you. We really want everything we discussed to remain with you always!

Hugs. Your Sasha. (cont'd by Ustvolskaya) And

Your Galya. (cont'd by Sasha) The strongest that is written about Rembrandt we read in Lithuania – it is a book by E. Verhaeren. Nature, Chekhov, and Verhaeren's "Rembrandt" – these are the things that for us will forever be tied with the past summer.

(original layout)

I do not remember what I wrote in my letter to Ustvolskaya then, but most likely I notified her about my already formed decision to immigrate (which at the time did not materialize.)

G.U. did not write to D.D., but to Bokman she would. Amazing!

From Konstantin Bagrenin's letter to me. Internet. "Ustvolskaya. Precision". (D. D. - this is Dmitry Shostakovich!)

---

8. Letter

The whole letter is written in Sasha's hand on glossy paper. The envelope is signed by him as well.

Dear Senya!
I received your two letters and Poem!
Your poetry is great and for that I thank you again!
I do not know where I will be living this summer and what and how I will eat. For that reason, I cannot rent a villa for you in Lithuania…
It is nice that you have a good daughter Irochka. It is again very stuffy in here; therefore, it is difficult to live, work and think…
Therefore here I will end.
Sasha Fridman misses you a lot; apparently, the old friendship does not get old.
I conveyed (cont'd on the other side) your regards to him. He is very grateful.
Kisses to you from both of us.

Galya, Sasha.
13.06.79

(Original Layout)

As far as I remember, I did not ask (and I would hardly dare to ask) Ustvolskaya "find out and to rent me an estate". Sasha told me with admiration how well they rested with Ustvolskaya in the summer in Lithuania, where they rented a low-cost house with food. I only asked whether other villagers were also renting out their cottages, addressing the question more to Sasha, for they were reading my letters, and sometimes were answering them together. In response to their letter of 13.06.79 I sent 120 rubles to Galya. I want to assure the reader that I am not bragging. But without this confession it is impossible to explain another event. There is my comment about it after the next letter from Ustvolskaya.

9. Letter

This letter is written by Sasha F.'s hand on glossy paper. The address on the air-mail envelope is also written by Sasha's hand.

29.06.79
Dear Senia!
Very unexpectedly you made me
happy because, firstly,
you are such is and you've sent me such
a kind present, and, secondly,
because I received this present.
I accepted it. There is in yourself
that, which is called feeling and
friendship. Somehow I sense that
not too many people in the world are getting
such attitude from you.
I hug you and kiss you.
Pass my warm regards
to Olya and Irochka
I would like to write stronger
and more. I cannot. (Then, by Ustvolskaya's hand):
Senichka, it is difficult for me
to write with my own hand.
I kiss you. Galya.

Original layout

G.U. sometimes recalled Shibanov, Novikov, Lomizov, others. But
you – never[*].

From Konstantin Bagrenin's letter to me. Internet. "Ustvolskaya. Precision".

---

[*]   I am not surprised, and do not suppose she has remembering me forever. If it happened anyhow that she would not be Galya Ustvolskaya who is not just composer of the passing Era, but also its typical representative.

"Gift" being the money. 120 rubles. These were from me. But once, when my relationship with Galina Ustvolskaya had already stopped, and I could neither call nor write to her, in 1982 (I do not remember the exact date), I received a transfer of 100 rubles from Sasha, with request to send them to Galya, allegedly from me. He asked me very earnestly and warned me not to name him and not to ask him about anything. Something happened between them - I still do not know what. I knew he was asking me, because I had already done it and he would be out of suspicions, and for some reason it was important for him not to be recognized. I followed the instructions. I simply sent the money. I was not wonderfully comfortable with that, and I waited for an opportunity to explain myself. I was waiting for an answer from Galya, of course. I expected gratitude from her eventually. (Worst case scenario, a refund of that money). And in that case, I thought I would find a way to open the truth. Strangely enough, there was no answer in any form. I could not inquire.

10. Letter

This letter is written on a piece of paper ripped out of a school notebook across the lines. The date at the beginning is unclear. The envelope is addressed by a strange hand. The Leningrad postmark has a date: 07.01.82

(Date unclear) Dear Senya!

Thank you for your constant memory and understanding. Hug you. I wish you, Olya and Irinka a Happy New Year. I wish you joy and happiness.

Galya.

This letter is striking for the disparity of its context and the way it is written.

2. Pages from the Diary

My rather regular association with Ustvolskaya took place over the course of a few months in 1977-78, while I was trying to apply to the conservatory and relocate to Leningrad. I wanted to keep a diary then but could not really do it. I only recorded one episode. I think it is appropriate to reproduce it here. It was the end of February of 1978 (there is no exact date).

I called Ustvolskaya. She recognized me. Her voice sounded suppressed and hoarse.

"Senechka, how are you, what is happening?

"I am all right, Galya. How are you? How are you feeling?"

"Senia, I cannot talk right now. Something terrible happened to me…

"What happened?" (I am yelling)

Something vague in reply-

"I will come over to you tonight!"

"OK, ok… Good. Come. It will be difficult for me to be alone…

(The conversation was going at a fast tempo.)

In the evening I came to Galya. Sasha opened the door – he was already there. He whispered: "Galya's feeling is very bad. She is resting…"

I heard Galya's voice from another room: "Is this Senya? I will get up in a moment."

It felt awkward. I went into the kitchen tormented by the unknown. I did not know how to behave. I asked S. quietly what happened. He replied, also quietly:

"Salmanov died."

Once more, there was an awkward silence. I felt discomfort and bewilderment. I did not realize that Salmanov was close to Ustvolskaya. I did not know Salmanov. I only knew that Galya did not have a high regard for him as a composer.

Galya came in. Her face was puffy from crying. She asked us not to look at her. She went to the cupboard, opened a small door, chose a small bottle, took a few pills, and swallowed. She asked us again not to look at her. She apologized for her appearance and said:

"What a f***ing life – I haven't got the nerves to handle it!"

She gently rebuked me for not coming for a long time, and that I didn't recollect about her. I answered as gently as she was that it was quite the opposite – she was the one who did not asked me to meet… Galya waved her hand: "Ah…"

Little by little, the atmosphere became less tense. I felt encouraged.

On the table there were oranges and bags with tea cakes. Galya said:

"And now we will drink tea."

I asked cautiously, "Would it bother you if I smoked?"

Galya waved her hand. "Go ahead, smoke." She pointed to the oranges: "These are from Sasha. I have nothing, as usual… I would like a smoke…What do you have? No filter? Ugh, how disgusting! Why didn't you bring regular cigarettes? (Ustvolskaya did not smoke, and I never brought cigarettes for her. Her words were provoked by the emotional turmoil.) You did not come for so long and came empty-handed?

I feel terribly embarrassed.

"What, you have no money?"

"No," I mumbled.

"I have no money either. Neither I, nor Kostia earn anything."

"Why is that?"

Galya turns to Sasha,

"He does not believe me…"

To me she says, "You see… Kostia receives a hundred rubles a month and borrows more money than he can return.

"Happiness is not about money", I said.

In reply there is hysterical laughter. Galya apologizes,

"This is hysteria… Although, we do always laugh when you come…"

From that point on, things were more relaxed. We talked about everything. Galya can speak freely and sometimes crudely about the most intimate things; even angrily, but it does not evoke any negative feelings in me. This is her way of showing intimacy and trust -- she jokes.

It turned out she did not have dinner. I suggested the simplest dish, potatoes in their skins – luckily, there were potatoes in the house. For the first time ever, I saw a person intolerant of any kind of housework. I showed initiative. Very quickly I washed the potatoes and began cooking them. Galya constantly interfered. She kept saying, "It is probably ready." I asked her to wait, gave her one to try. Finally, the potatoes were cooked. Everybody ate and praised me. Sasha kept burning his fingers; he did not know how to peel them and swore. I said that this is the first time I managed to complete this operation. But even this time around it was difficult because she was fidgety and kept interfering.

"Yes, I'm not a housewife at all! Could you marry me?"

I hesitated. "I have my own, very specific…"

"Criteria," suggested Galya, saying stressfully.

I said resolutely and fast: "Yes. No, you would not fit me!"

(What an idiot! Well, why didn't I lie or joke about something? – this is what I am saying from nowadays, what was of those times Future. Well, how could I be acting so?)

"That is right. You would not fit me either!"

"Did I offend you?"

"Not at all. But incidentally, if that was your criteria for marriage, it does not say much for you."

"Why did I marry?" (We were smiling and laughing throughout this squabble. Sasha laughed with us.)

"I am not asking you why you married. We are talking about housekeeping. You got married because everybody does! And hippopotamuses get married too…

"I got married because I fell in love. But if you got married according to this criterion it does not say much for you either!

--loud laughter—

Our "Academy" at times resembles a company of "Rabelaisian Pantagruelian."

I cited from memory frivolous excerpts from Pushkin's "Gavrilliada (A sexually explicit work, a satiric description of the beginning of the New Testament, making fun of the Immaculate Conception – I.B.) We laughed.

S. cited from the book <u>Tolstoy in the Memories of his Contemporaries</u> Tolstoy's statement about Gorky: "He has a soul of a sleuthhound." This is enough to understand how Tolstoy felt about Gorky.

We listened to some music. I did not listen well. I was distracted and confused. Galya constantly changed vinyl disks. She listens to whatever she likes with delight. We listened to "Woman's life and love," performed by L. Marshall, excerpts from the Second and Third Rachmaninoff concertos… Rachmaninoff's lyricism is close to her. She said that when Rachmaninoff was trying to perfect or modernize his technique (in later works) he did not do the best thing.

"One should never go against his nature," she taught us.

When we listened to the Third concerto, she skipped all the "watery" places; Galya moved the needle with a scraping noise. About the finale of the Second she said: "This music is for horses!" She said this in a lot of similar situations: "This is for horses…", and scratched the records, mercilessly moving the needle… We laughed a lot, joked around.

Suddenly I uttered: "Render unto Caesar a caesarian section" and it cheered everybody up incredibly.

The next day Kostya was supposed to leave for Moscow. Galya was scared to be alone. I offered to come.

"This is when it will become the real Academy!" she said expressively. Naturally, she did not invite me. The next day I called and learned that Lida would be with her.

Now, as I re-read these notes made more than 25 years ago, most of all I am surprised by how Ustvolskaya dealt with the death of the composer Vadim Salmanov. Undoubtedly, it was a shock. She cried hysterically. Having said that, not even once during that evening did, I hear her mention Salmanov's name. I have learned about his death not from her. It was whispered to me secretly. There was no reminiscing, no regrets about the deceased, which usually accompanies such events. The way her mood switched, becoming almost cheerful during the evening, also made a mysterious impression. Was there really any regret about the deceased? More than anything, it looks like fear, even terror. The terror and shock were provoked by death in general and especially by the death of a familiar person whom she saw alive not too long ago.

A joky exchange of caustic remarks about my hypothetical "marriage" to Ustvolskaya, the second case described in this book - it was a kind of test, a test of me. And I could not stand the test. I had to laugh about this "proposition", turn it into a joke, to lie, and that would have been enough to confirm my loyalty, but I could not. I loved Galya very much, but I wanted to keep my independence. I did not want to give in to her and thoughtlessly agreed with her. I admired her, but I aspired to keep my own way in art and life. My behavior became too demonstrative, too provocative! I started writing her daring letters. Once in one of them I copied an alchemical article about gems from the book "The Patterns of Symmetry". This is a collection of interesting articles about symmetry: in nature, in mathematics, in music. I still have this book. In the article I have copied, I have underlined the following phrase: (...) "only in rare cases / two substances, no matter how small / the difference between them / will grow together." (A mineral is a living substance, and it grows. That phrase delighted me. It solved the question of why creative people often argued and did not get along with each other). I also stressed the lines: "So I chose a place for the lab away from earthly vessels and stoves, / I leave it here / for Heraclitus / if he'll come back / when the Time of the Giants will come again." I am still surprised how was I dare it! It was a challenge! And, of course, it was one (but not the only one) of the sum of the reasons why our relationship ended. I do not regret that - it just could not be otherwise. Even my marriage meant some kind of apostasy for the Ustvolskaya-woman. According to her royal self-esteem, the person whom she, Galina Ustvolskaya, allowed to approach her, should belong to her. She could only be surrounded by people who fully shared her views, her beliefs, sympathies, and dislikes. She, a woman-creator, tormented by contradictions and doubts, was in dire need of approval, harken them! She had to hear the praise of herself, feel love and worship even.

Especially since she had no strength for arguing and struggling with her opponents. That is how I explain her frequent frustrations with people who until recently were fervently loved and appreciated by her, were her "favorites". Once she said: "I only have two close people in my life right now - you and Sasha. Sasha is a friend. And you, I do not know..." That is such an intricate definition of me: close, but not a friend*. Then, I remember, besides bitterness, I was confused: why not a friend? There was nothing I could not seem to do for Galya. (Except for the crime, of course. But she could not demand it from me). It took many years before I was able to solve this mystery. Now I really understood how it turned out to be good that Galina Ivanovna and I broke up in time. I managed to get the best from her; the best she could give then to me.

---

*You live in that naive antiquity and probably do not quite understand that it was a GREAT person, who had the right to **neglect** Vasya, Sasha, Mitya, Syoma, as she pleases. (It made by me in bold font - S.B. In original Russian it has written "**РАЗМЕНИВАТЬСЯ**" [**RAZMENIVATSYA**], and this word has not English equivalent to express such insulting attitude!)*
(From Konstantin Bagrenin's letter to me, the Internet. "Ustvolskaya. Precision".

Vasya was a student of G.I. Ustvolskaya. I did not know him. He entered the school when I was not in it anymore. He was in love with Ustvolskaya. He committed suicide. Sasha – this is Alexander Fridman. He was a student of Valery Gavrilin, but Gavrilin left the school, while Sasha in his fourth and final year became a student of Galina Ivanovna. Sasha was incredibly devoted to her and, in fact, shared in her inner "exile". His parents and sister with family emigrated. He decided to stay near Ustvolskaya. But afterwards something broke down, and their communication ceased. For him it was a shock. Syoma is me. I was not damaged, but just won!
Mitya, no doubt, is Dmitry Shostakovich!

---

*   And with "friend" Sasha Ustvolskaya also parted.

Adrian Leverkun's phantom inspired the formula of greatness. Reread this!

In my last letter to Galina Ustvolskaya, I quoted a poem by M. Lermontov:

> We parted ways, but I would keep
> your portrait close, upon my breast,
> a pallid ghost of years that leap
> into my soul, remembered best.
>
> In love with others, did I feel
> that I forgot you? I could not.
> Forsaken shrines are worshipped still,
> an idol fallen - still a god!

21 июня 2016, Belmont, California

3. OLEG MALOV

Pianist Oleg Malov is an outstanding promoter of music by Galina Ustvolskaya. He is the first performer as well as the organizer of most of her compositions. It was impossible while thinking about Galina Ustvolskaya, about her creative work, not to ask him.

Monday, January 11, 2010
Dear Semyon!
I am sending you answers to your questions and, as an appendix, the content of my report in the Composer's Union spoken several years ago. You may need it.
Your O.M. (I do not reproduce the report - S.B.)

S.B. How did you start your cooperation with G.Ustvolskaya: did you buy the music, or did she address you?

O.M. G.I. called me (obviously on someone else's recommendation) and offered to play (for the first time) "Sonata № 3". I had already bought the music of 12 Preludes which did not arouse much interest at that time. I did not understand the style.

S.B. How did you work on the music: were there discussions, could you suggest something, or should you have followed the author's instructions exactly, did you have any performing discoveries in your reading that were approved or not approved by the author?

O.M. There were no discussions. The most general recommendations. Basically, my positions in interpretation were accepted. I think I have guessed the main thing in the direction of the style of performance. The Znamenny chant as the main reference point was clear to me, but other performers before me (for example, T.A. Voronina in Sonata No. 2) tried to "sing" on the piano, but I wanted to achieve an instrumental pronunciation (as it would have been played by Glenn Gould). The work on ensembles and symphonies included the preparation of material. All the parts in the duets and symphonies <u>were rewritten by me by hand</u>, (emphasized by me - S.B.) *At that time there were no computers.*

S.B. I remember the concert in the Small Hall, where you performed Beethoven's "Diabelli Variations" and after them "12 Preludes of Ustvolskaya". It was remarkably interesting, and I shared my impression with Ustvolskaya, congratulated her on the concert and on the fact that she has such a wonderful performer. She confirmed that you are a thinking creative person. There was Ustvolskaya's Sonatina performed in this concert as well. I have never heard of this work again. Maybe it dreamed to me about it?

O.M. Sonatina was played in another concert together with "Sonata № 1". After "12 Preludes" I played "Sonata № 3". Hindemith. In the following editions this work* (Sonatina - S. B.) *was called "Sonata № 4".*

S.B. Have you ever played Ustvolskaya's music, including other authors in your programs of recitals, and how did Ustvolskaya feel about it?

---

*   "Diabelli Variations" were performed in the first division of concert, and "12 Preludes" in the second one.

O.M. *It has been repeated many times. I think that G.I. was dissatisfied. I do not exclude that this was the main reason for breaking off relations. My independent artistic position did not coincide with the dictatorial principles of the composer. I did not wish to serve one, even an outstanding author.*

S.B. Have you discussed the repertoire of the works to be performed?

O.M. *In author's concerts the programs were established by her, in my own concerts - by me.*

S.B. Why did your relationship with G.I. deteriorate?

O.M. *I cannot say for sure. Maybe she said it to Lyubimov.*

When she started being played in the West after 1989, she decided that she did not need me anymore. (Thus, her compositions have been rarely performed in St. Petersburg for almost 20 years. Even rarer - good. Such an attitude to performers was typical for her. When I appeared she used to make improper statements about M.V.Karandashova, who made colossal efforts to promote the music of G.I. I think that contemptuous attitude to other composers and arrogant attitude to her pupils is not a secret for you. "I don't have any teachers or students".

S. B. You have been in touch for over 20 years. Was G.I. telling you anything about herself, how she began to compose music and so on?

O.M. *Strange as it may seem, there was almost no personal, human communication. Only professional ones. I know truly little about her life, her bio. I never had a desire to get close to a dictatorial personality. Nevertheless, I consider G.I. one of my teachers in music.*

S.B. How are Ustvolskaya's music accepted in Russia and in the West?

O.M. *How it happens now - I will look in Spain. In the beginning of the 90s it was a sensation from Russia. They accepted it with great interest.*

S.B. Which works of Galina Ustvolskaya were played by you for the first time?

Premieres (world premieres):
Sonatas ## 1, 3, 4, 5, 6
Big Duo for Cello and F-no
Symphonies 2, 3, 5.
Composition No. 2 (8 double basses, drum, grand piano)
Composition #3 (4 flutes, 4 bassoons, piano)

Solomon Volkov and Alexander Genis (right)

4. RADIO LIBERTY

"A Music Shelf" by Solomon Volkov[*]
(excerpt)

Alexander Genis[†]: Today's issue will be completed by Solomon Volkov's traditional column "Music Shelf". Today all its segments

---

[*]   **Solomon Moiseyevich Volkov** (Russian: Соломон Моисеевич Волков; born 17 April 1944) is a Russian journalist and musicologist. He is best known for *Testimony*, which was published in 1979 following his emigration from the Soviet Union in 1976. According to him, the book was the memoir of Dmitri Shostakovich, as related to him by the composer.

[†]   Genis was born in Ryazan, USSR, born February 11, 1953. After graduating from the Latvian State University in Riga, Genis immigrated to the USA in 1977 at the age of

will be dedicated to one character - the outstanding composer Galina Ustvolskaya, who passed away at the very end of 2006. Solomon, I suggest you start with the musicology part of our "Music Shelf".

Solomon Volkov: I do not like the word "musicologist" very much, we will just talk about what kind of composer Galina Ivanovna was. Her death is a great loss for Russian music in general and for St. Petersburg music culture in particular. I must say that 2006 was a very unhappy year for St. Petersburg in this sense. Andrei Petrov and Galina Ustvolskaya passed away in one year. These are two opposite poles of St. Petersburg music, both of which are significant in their own way and, of course, without them, the musical map of modern St. Petersburg has become much pale. This, as I said, is a huge damage to St. Petersburg.

The paradox of Galina Ustvolskaya is that in recent 10-15 years, she has been much more popular among connoisseurs of modern music in the West than in Russia. In Russia, in St. Petersburg she lived in solitude for quite a long time not participating in mainstream public music life and even not so often showing up at her own music performances. When she was there, I just knew it from the performers, it was always an incredible event for them. The attitude towards her was extremely trembling among professionals in St. Petersburg and here in the West. In particular, her death become the subject of an extensive obituary in the New York Times. For comparison, I will point out that the New York Times did not even mention Petrov's death. But Ustvolskaya is an authoritative and large figure for musical critics of the New York Times.

A.G.: Because she is a classic of modernism.

S.V.: Of course. And in this sense, it is possible to say that with Ustvolskaya's death the last modernist left the St. Petersburg musical life. I would like to present today a very curious book called "Variations

---

24.

Genis is an anchorman of the weekly radio-show *American Hour with Alexander Genis* broadcast in Russian by Radio Liberty since the 1990s. Genis is a columnist and a contributing writer for the main liberal Russian newspaper *Novaya Gazeta, and used to be the host of the TV show Alexander Genis. Letters from America,* shown on Russian TV channel "Culture".

on the theme of 'Galina Ustvolskaya''', which was published just a few days ago. I have in my hands one of the first copies of it in the USA. It was published in Germany in English, and its author is Semyon Bokman, a Russian musician, composer, and poet who now lives in San Francisco. He was a student of Ustvolskaya. She taught at the music college in Leningrad, and there was a circle of close students around her who worshipped her, of course. He conceived this book quite a long time ago. We talked with him on the phone from time to time, so I knew how his work was going. And finally, there are such coincidences in life, just a few weeks after Ustvolskaya's death, a book that was considered by and wrote, and even went to print before it became known about her death, this book is now in my hands. It became a memorial book. I would say that even though there is already one book about Ustvolskaya published in St. Petersburg, I would call it the first real book about her, because the first one was a hagiographic work yet, there was not serious discussion of the figure of Ustvolskaya, which is presents in Bokman's book*. I would like to quote what Bokman says about Ustvolskaya.

"Ustvolskaya had formed her style already in the fifties. At that time in the Soviet Union, not only was her style unacceptable on an aesthetic level, but it could also have been seen as criminal and treasonous by the state. That predetermined her spiritual isolation and financial troubles. In boldness, she surpasses many of the innovative works of Western composers. Her music differs from the music of the Avant-garde. Avant-garde music is a sensation, not because of *what* it is, but because of *how* it is made. Ustvolskaya's music is a sensation of another kind. Her music is over saturated with emotion. She breaks aesthetic taboos no one has yet dared to break and allows emotion into her music that no one before her has dared to reveal. This is her philosophy, and it is clear by her compositions - from the first piano sonata to the fifth symphony. But her music is not only that of frightful emotions. It is an attempt to understand the world more fully, a world that includes apparent forms and habitual feelings, but also something invisible, intangible, and unexplainable, which is equally important to life."

---

*   First Edition. VERLAG ERNST KUHN. Berlin. This Publishing-house not exists anymore. But more than 60 libraries around the World have this book in English and in German.

I think it is an excellent introduction. I would not call it musicology. It is just a good prose about Ustvolskaya's music, which I will illustrate with the example of "Piano Sonata Number 3". This is her 1952nd year's work, which was possible to be played only 20 years later according to the conditions of Soviet life what Bokman wrote about. The sonata is performed by pianist Oleg Malov.

A.G.: The next section of our column is "Personal note". Solomon, what was especially close to you personally in Ustvolskaya, especially significant?

S.V.: When I think about Ustvolskaya, I always recollect one concert which took place at the end of the 60s in Leningrad, at which I was lucky to be present. This music immediately fascinated and captivated me. Because of this motive, which the listeners will hear, it was something magical, it was a music spell, causing exceedingly difficult emotions. Ustvolskaya's music does not cause positive emotions, and Semyon Bokman writes about it in his book. It causes some extreme, radical emotions. It is difficult to listen to this music. Composer Barber after listening to Ustvolskaya's work, something like "Struggles for Peace", said that if it is a struggle for peace, he prefers war. And about this violin sonata also the American composer (strangely enough, that there was such a negative reaction from the Americans about Ustvolskaya) Roy Harris once said that it was ugly music. And I understand Harris' reaction. But I will also never forget the impression this sonata made on me then, in Leningrad.

(Published on the Internet on 13.02.2007)

5. RADIO LIBERTY
"MUSIC ALMANAC" WITH SOLOMON VOLKOV
(excerpt)

Alexander Genis: The next section, familiar to our regular listeners, is "Musical Almanac" with Solomon Volkov.

Solomon Volkov: Today I will tell you about an unusual and significant concert held in New York. The youth ensemble "Continuum", consisting of students at the famous Juilliard school, showed a monographic evening of the composer Galina Ivanovna Ustvolskaya, who died in December 2006 at the age of 87. In general, the performance of Ustvolskaya's music now is not very frequent in Russia and the West, so the evening dedicated to her work - it is certainly an event. The event is also because Ustvolskaya's music attracted the attention of connoisseurs during her lifetime. And in this quality, it has spread in the West and has received such a circle of devoted admirers. Ustvolskaya is a cult modern composer. Of course, after her death, her reputation in this narrow circle is high. And I was extremely glad to see the full hall at the concert.

A.G.: Solomon, I think we should talk about Ustvolskaya's music here. Who are its connoisseurs and in what context should it be perceived?

S.V.: I talked a lot about Ustvolskaya with Semyon Bokman. This is a composer, poet and journalist living in San Francisco, one of the closest students of Galina Ustvolskaya. He published in English the first considerable research book about Ustvolskaya, where he analyzes her position, her work, her personality, which is also especially important because she was an unusual person. In connection with this book, which, in fact, received helpful reviews, we talked about the similarities and differences between Ustvolskaya and Akhmatova. Two outstanding, extraordinarily strong women, both were leaders in the underground world. One in the world of literature, the other in the world of music. Of course, Russia is a literary-centric country, Akhmatova became famous even before the revolution, and it is impossible to compare Akhmatova's influence with that of Ustvolskaya. But in her circle, Ustvolskaya's influence was comparable. I remember how we went to every exceedingly rare performance of Ustvolskaya's music. Ustvolskaya herself was formed largely under the influence of the work of Stravinsky. It is just as harsh, very archaic in language and, at the same time, purely modernist, but it is Stravinsky, from which all the oxygen has already been pumped out, it is cubed Stravinsky, so to be spoken

A.G.: Or a cube root from Stravinsky.

S.V.: And Semyon Bokman insists that Ustvolskaya has discovered a certain artistic secret, and this secret, this terrible discovery lies in the fact that we will all perish, everything will perish - and art, and the world will perish, no one and nothing can save us[*]. That is, it is the creative work of absolute despair. He is very right in this remark. It is not easy to bear Ustvolskaya's music evening.

A.G.: Nevertheless, she has her own admirers in America. How do you explain the penetration of such strange music into America?

S.V.: There will always be a small number of people who want to contact the creativity of the highest emotional tension. And such tension, almost ecstatic, Ustvolskaya demonstrates in her work, including the late compositions. Her symphony number five, which is titled "Amen", was performed. This is a work from 1990, which shows us this ecstasy of Ustvolskaya's music.

(Published on the Internet on 08.04.2008 02:01)

6. LETTER FROM MARKUS HINTERHAUSER

SALZBURGER FESTSPIELE
Markus Hinterhauser
Intendant

Dear Simon Bokman,

Thank you very much for the Ustvolskaya's book!!![†]
Patricia[‡] told me so much about the book and now I can read it!
I am very happy!
All my best and thank you again.

(The signature is illegible)

---

[*]   What a great discovery!

[†]   The First Edition. "Vsriations om the Theme *Galina Ustvolskaya*". Verlag Ernst Kuhn. Berlin. 2007

[‡]   Patricia Kopatchinskaja, violinist

BIBLIOGRAPHY

Abert, Germann. "Mozart". Musica, Moscow. 1987 (Russian)

A Book of Russian Verse. Translated into English by various hands.

Westport, Conn., Greenwood Press, 1971

Agni Yoga. Fiery World. New York, 1935. III: &337 (Russian).

Aksakov, Sergey Timofeyevich. The *story of My Acquaintance with Gogol,* Complete Works. Moscow, 1966 (Russian). Moscow

Antarova, Konkordiya Yevgenievna. *Two Lives.* Moscow: "Sirin", "Scorpion", "Satka",1994 (Russian).

Beethoven. *Letters (1817-1822.)* Trans. L. S. Tovaleva and N.L. Fishman. Moscow, 1986 (Russian).

Blok, Alexander. *Lyric Poetry. Theater.* Russian Moscow: Pravda, 1982 (Russian).

Bokman, Simon. *"Na Okraine Vselennoy"* (*On the Edge of the Universe.*) A book of poetry. Seagull Press, 2006 (Russian).

Bulgakov, Mikhail Afanasievich. The Master and Margarita. Moscow, 1984 (Russian).

Bunin, Ivan. *Okaiannie Dni* (Cursed Days). Moscow, 2004 (Russian).

Einstein, Alfred. *Music in the Romantic Era.* New York, 1947

Gladkova, Olga. *Galina Ustvolskaya: Music as an Obsession.* S. Petersburg, 1999 (Russian).

Glikman, Isaak. *Letters to a Friend.* S.-Petersburg, 1993 (Russian).

Glikman, Isaak. *Story of Friendship*. Trans. Anthony Phillips. Cornell University Press, 2001

Gogol, Nikolay Vasilyevich. *The Complete Works*. Collection in 7 volumes. Moscow, 1967, vol. 6 (Russian).

L. Hay, Louise. "YOU CAN HEAL YOUR LIFE", Hay House, Santa Monica, 1984

Khentova, Sophia. *Amazing Shostakovich*. St.-Petersburg, 1993 (Russian).

Khentova, Sophia. *Shostakovich in Moscow*. Moscow, 1986 (Russian).

Lee, Marian. *Galina Ustvolskaya: The Spiritual Works of a Soviet Artist*. Ph. D.diss., Peabody Conservatory of Music, 2002

Lee, Marian. IREX research report http://www.irex.org/programs/iaro/research/lee.pdf

Lenin, Vladimir Ilich. *Complete works*. Moscow, 1958. 52:179-180

MacDonald, Ian. *Music under Soviet rule: Ustvolskaya, "The Lady with the Hummer"* http://www.siue.eku/~aho/musov/ust/ust.html

Mandelshtam, Nadezhda. *My Will*. New York, 1982 (Russian).

Mann, Thomas. *Doctor Faustus*. Trans. H.T. Lowe-Porter, New York, 1948

Mann, Thomas. Doctor Faustus. Trans. S. Apt and Natalia Mann. Moscow, 1993 (Russian).

Mann, Thomas. *Letters*. (1889-1955) Selected and trans. Richard and Clara Winston. New York, 1971

Mann, Thomas. *Letters*. Selected and trans. S. Apt. Moscow, 1975 (Russian).

Nabokov, Vladimir. *Lectures on Russian Literature*. San Diego, New York, London, 1981

New Beethoven Letters. Trans. Donald W. MacArdle and Ludwig Misch. University of Oklahoma Press: Norman 1957

"Pattern of Symmetry". "Mir" ("World"). Moscow. 1980. (Russian)

Pushkin, Alexander Sergeyevich. *Letters* ed. B.L. Modzalevsky. Moscow, Leningrad, 1928 (Russian).

Shostakovich in memories of son Maxim, daughter Galina, and protoierey Michail Ardov. Zakharov. Moscow, 2003 (Russian).

Schumann, Robert. *Letters.* ed. Dr. Karl Storck, trans. Hannah Bryant. London, 1907:70

Schneyerson, G. *Articles on Contemporary Foreign Music. Essays. Memoirs. "Arnold Schoenberg – Musician and a Man."* Moscow, 1974 (Russian).

Schweizer Albert, J. S. Bach, Dover Publications, Inc, New York

Stravinsky, Igor. *The Dialogues.* Leningrad, 1971(Russian).

Stravinsky, Igor and Craft, Robert. *Memories and Commentaries. London, 2002*

Stravinsky, Igor *Poetics of Music in the Form of Six Lessons transl.* Arthur Knodel and Ingolf Dahl. Harvard University Press, 1970

Tchaikovsky, Peter Ilich. Complete works. Moscow: Musika, 1977. vol. 15b *Literary Works and Correspondence.* (Russian).

The Holy Bible. Revised Standard Version published by Holman Bible Publishers for Cokesbury, 1982. *Revelations*

Terz, Abraham. *In the Shadow of Gogol.* London, 1975 (Russian).

Tolstoy, Lev Nikolaevich. *What is my faith?* trans. Aylmer Mande. Oxford University Press. p. 315-316

Tsiolkovsky, Konstantin Eduardovich. *Monism of the Universe. The Cause of Cosmos.* Novosibirsk, 1993 (Russian).

Uspensky, Nikolay. *Early Russian Art of Singing.* Leningrad, 1968 (Russian).

Verhaeren, Emile. *The Evening Hours.* trans. Charles R. Murphy. New York, 1918

Volkov, Solomon. *Testimony. Memoirs of Dmitriy Shostakovich.* New York, 1999 York

Walsh, Stephen. STRAVINSKY, *A Creative Spring: Russia and France, 1882-1934*

Woolf, Peter Graham. *Galina Ustvolskaya and the Piano.* http//www. musicweb.uk.net/classrev/dec99/Ustvolskaya.htm

INDEX OF NAMES